UGANDA

The Bloodstained Pearl
of Africa

And its Struggle for Peace

From the pages of DRUM

With the assistance of:
Charles Binayisa
Garth Bundeh
Emmanuel Dduta
Don Kabeba
John Nagenda
Joseph Nnambale
PG Okoth
Alan Rake
Renny Ssentongo

Compiled and Edited by Adam Seftel

A Bailey's African Photo Archives Production

Uganda: The Bloodstained Pearl of Africa: And its Struggle for Peace

A **Bailey's African Photo Archives** Production
PO Box 37
Lanseria
1748
South Africa

© JRA Bailey 1994

ISBN: 0-95838546-6-5

Executive Editor: JRA Bailey
Compiled and edited by Adam Seftel
Printed and bound by Colourprint Ltd., P.O.Box 44466, Nairobi, Kenya.

CONTENTS

FOREWORD

Ronald Mutebi
Kabaka of Buganda

DRESSED IN LEOPARD SKINS and tree bark, Ronnie Muwenda Mutebi was crowned King of Buganda on July 31, 1993, 27 years after his father was deposed. Tens of thousands of Baganda thronged the enclosure at Buddo Hill, outside Kampala, to cheer Mutebi, 37, as he emerged in his royal finery as their Kabaka.

For the Kabaka, his coronation was the culmination of a dream he has harboured since he saw his father, King Freddy, deposed in 1966 by Milton Obote. Current Ugandan president, Yoweri Museveni watched as the Kabaka promised to serve his people well, to love them and to always listen to them.

Thirty years after Uganda's independence, it is difficult for some people to remember that the new nation was born with very great optimism and that it was endowed with so much human and material potential. The years of darkness have cast such a long and persuasive shadow that, for a long time to come, the popular image of Uganda will be that of a nation eternally in the grip of tyrants and locked in an endless cycle of bloodshed, poverty and misery.

DRUM has been a sharp and persistent observer throughout those 30 years. From the hopeful birth in 1962, through the period of turmoil, right up to the dawn on the new times and the new hope. In the darkest days DRUM correspondents doggedly pursued the stories of oppression and injustice, and informed the world. Long after most of the world's media had closed their eyes and ears to Uganda's plight. It was com-

mendable and exemplary journalism. And this book is a record of those achievements.

Some of these pages will also remain as a testament to the work of Don Kabeba, the Ugandan journalist who worked so courageously and determinedly to expose injustice in Uganda. He longed to see a prosperous, free and stable Uganda but died before he could see the first signs of his dream taking shape. Had he lived, he would have made his own mark on the new society.

We all hope that DRUM will continue to watch and record as Uganda picks itself up from the ashes.

Ronald Muwenda Mutebi
Ssabataka of Buganda
Kampala, October 1991

PREFACE

John Nagenda

I first met DRUM in the early 1950s, probably not long after its birth. I was a young schoolboy at Kings College, Budo (where else?), ten miles from the capital Kampala. It was stunned love at first sight. What an exotic creature!

Girls! Mobsters! Wideboys! Please Dolly I love her but she loves another, what shall I do? Leave! The language! The pics! The exposés! I couldn't believe it. We had a *matalisi* (messenger), a venerable old gentleman who cycled to town and back every day to bring the mail. To him you entrusted what money you had and he would bring you a loaf or orange squash or jam. Henceforth, at the month's beginning, I would hand over, was it fifty cents, or a shilling, and in a day or two DRUM would be in my hands. So bright and enticing. Read it as slowly as possible so that you don't finish.

Later on, in another country, I was to meet those who wrote it and who were to write for it: Zik, Lewis, Bloke, Arthur, Cameron (Duodon't), poor Nat who killed himself in New York when I lived there first in 1965 – and some of the girls who appeared in it, not least Dorothy Masuka who sang *My Yiddishe Mamma* better than any few. (She would sing it as soon as she saw me in a concert or nightclub in Nairobi. Once in Moshi, she glimpsed me at some Non-Aligned conference and belted it out, and was mystified when all the Arab brothers staged a walk-out!)

DRUM! The fifties, with all DRUM's lurid clothes and wonderful flashy talk, were at the the same time, incredibly, its crusading years. Thereafter it became better behaved. Your mum could read it. The wicked boys and girls became, almost overnight, middle-aged. You walked past DRUM on street corners without a backward glance.

Which is what makes this book amazing. Because the articles in it were written when ostensibly DRUM was at the opposite to its peak. I had forgotten that even then so much of what was happening in Uganda was covered by DRUM. This is Uganda as it was happening. If the bluff old field marshal (each of these last four words a lie!) said he was a reluctant and temporary leader, that is how it was reported. Time has added to the irony. Here are the bodies of our dead and dying. Rivers of blood. Obote. Mutesa II. A poignant tear-stained Princess Toro (her best pic?). Towards the end: Museveni. How, aided by Bailey's book, the memories flood back.

I cannot end without a word on Jim Bailey. The very rich guard their pennies like rottweilers and I derive endless pleasure in pointing this out to rich Bailey, although in his extreme middle-age he appears to be weakening a bit. No matter. Your DRUM trod paths anew in our continent, and was part of opening new ones yet. This book is proof. Let's inject new adrenaline into the old body and blast away again. Strike home James, and don't spare the horses!

John Nagenda
Kampala, October 1991

PREFACE

Jim Bailey

As DRUM magazine began to gain momentum in South Africa during 1951, letters from different parts of English-speaking Africa arrived on our desks in the Johannesburg office asking: "Why don't you start publishing in our country too?" – readers in South Africa were sending copies to their friends, who were sending copies to their friends, and from such chance missives our cosmopolitan correspondence sprang. We even had an occasional letter from the West Indies.

In those days you could take Swissair from Johannesburg to Dar es Salaam – Haven of Peace – and then voyage on by East African Airways to Mombassa, Nairobi and Kampala. So, early in 1952, I arranged with Alan Nihill, then distribution manager of the *East African Standard* in Nairobi, to distribute our magazine. As polo-playing Lord Cowdray's newspaper group published – in its own peculiar white-settler way – very competently across Uganda, Kenya, Tanganyika and Zanzibar, we benefited from an excellent distribution service and one that paid us punctually.

At this time I made my first acquaintance with Katwe, Kampala, and its happy citizens. In those days, Uganda was known as the Pearl of Africa, while the University of Makerere was known as the Athens of East Africa: the wonderful climate and countryside contributing to the first attribution and the many dedicated teachers and pupils of the community contributing to the second.

The British colonial government of Uganda largely functioned through the monarchs, so the colonial political structure was, in essence, more of a federation than that of a unitary state. For Uganda was formed out of four separate treaties with Queen Victoria signed by four separate monarchs. In this peaceful ambience the country flourished. And before too long, DRUM in Uganda was outselling Uganda's daily newspaper, with many times more readers per copy sold for a monthly magazine than for a daily newspaper.

I brought up my Durban journalist, GR Naidoo, and he did a magnificent job, developing our sales and encouraging our freelance writers and photographers. At that time many of East Africa's businesses were Indian-controlled and GR developed a happy circle of Indian business friends, some of whom became advertisers. In the course of time, I required the late GR's skills back in his home territory of Natal, so I replaced him with an Oxford graduate, Alan Rake, who still runs African magazines from London.

But death was slowly advancing on us in Uganda – with its lovely people and its history more ancient than anyone knows, arising from being one of the sources of the Egyptian Nile: Egypt, an African lighthouse of civilisation to the entire world.

For several years before independence, on occasions I used to discuss with Julius Nyerere or with Tom Mboya the future of Africa, far into the tropical night. We slowly came to think that a federation of the three East African countries would provide a certain market of 50 million people and thus we could develop an economically powerful grouping on the Indian Ocean.

Julius Nyerere said that Milton Obote was of the same opinion as himself, so, at their request, I went to Whitehall to discuss this concept with the colonial secretary. Sir Alec Douglas Holme was in Scotland shooting grouse, so I talked to his number two, Lord Alport, nicknamed Cub Alport, who gave to me – I was then speaking on behalf of Milton Obote – a most dusty answer. Our plan was that the federal cabinet of East Africa should at the start retain several British members to provide continuity with the past. Thus Uganda went into independence alone: no exciting federation.

Governor Cohen had fallen out with the Kabaka of the Baganda, King Freddie, and had exiled him. He was staying with a mutual friend, Major Carr-Gomm, – they had been in the Grenadier Guards together – in what was virtually an old-age home in London run by the major. It must be remembered, to King Freddie's eternal credit, that unlike so many rulers in Africa, King Freddie had no stolen money stashed away in Switzerland.

When Milton Obote took over Uganda he followed the socialist policy of the period, centralised the government under himself and abolished the monarchies, including the Baganda Lukiko (parliament). Thus he stirred up tribal tensions, each group trying to command the centre. As political tensions rose, people in Uganda began to be murdered. Alan Rake demanded that we should publish who lay behind these murders: I told him that we would be banned if we did so and, on balance, it would be better to hang in and continue our service to our public, worse might follow. Around that difference, Alan and I regrettably parted company.

Then Idi Amin, who had once been a corporal in the King's African Rifles, led a military coup and took over government after Milton Obote had flown away to a Commonwealth country. My information at the time being that the secret services of two foreign governments had prompted him to this. Little, I suppose, did they understand what they were doing.

Idi Amin's knock-about humour and his guying of the British colonial governors in Uganda made him an all-African favourite at first. But DRUM slowly discovered the course of hideous murder he was pursuing. The London Sunday newspaper, the *Observer*, came first to these conclusions, but DRUM was the first paper in Africa to report the start of Amin's career of mass murder. So DRUM was banned in Uganda and it was not safe for me to travel there. Consequently, many stories we carry here of this period come from freelance journalists of whom the Ugandan, Dan Kabeba, was the most notable and all honour to his shade!

During this time, the vice-chancellor of Makerere university was picked up by the army and interrogated. When he got back to his office he contacted his friend, Sir Ian Macadam, who had devoted his life to building up the teaching hospital at Makerere. He told Ian what had happened and said that he felt, nevertheless, that he would be alright. The following day the army came for the vice-chancellor and murdered him. One method they were using at the time was to sit their victims in a line upon the floor, give the one at the back a hammer and compel him to smash the skull of the man in front, and so on down the line. Ian put his immediate effects into his car, abandoned his lifelong collection of medical books, and drove for the border.

King Freddie died in London on a Saturday morning. The London coroner, after the autopsy, concluded that he had died of drink. I asked our mutual friend about it, Richard Carr-Gomm. He told me that he had telephoned the king the previous evening and he was perfectly sober. He had telephoned him again about something else that Saturday morning and he was perfectly sober. So he said it was quite unlikely that he would thereafter drink himself to death that afternoon. But this is what had happened, Richard told me. King Freddie was lonely. Three days before, a Ugandan lady had turned up and stayed with the king. Before she quit, she left him a box of groceries. Richard was of the opinion that they contained poison. After all, London coroners are inexperienced about African poisons. But Richard's explanation would seem to tie in with our story concerning the Athi River murders and the use of police women under Milton Obote.

One day, much after this, there walked into our Nairobi office a certain Ugandan refugee, Captain Patrick Kimumwe, who told us the story of how Idi Amin had murdered Archbishop Luwum and the extraordinary narration of his own escape from goal. Subsequently, I was told that he and his fellow escapees later joined the Ugandan liberation movement, and while crossing Lake Victoria were machine-gunned to death by certain supporters of Milton Obote in a passing boat.

As the Tanzanian army, in response to Amin's invasion of Tanzania, advanced upon Kampala to throw the mass-murderer with his Libyan allies out of the country, the Organisation of African Unity held a meeting in Nairobi. Certain forces were trying to protect Amin at the conference. I wrote the DRUM editorial for that month, saying that you do not perpetuate the rule of a murderous lunatic, you lock him up. I was not present at the meeting but I was told by a friend that Ben Makapa, the Tanzanian foreign minister, stood up at the meeting, waiving DRUM magazine in the air, saying: "This is it! This is it!" and it helped sway the meeting.

After Amin fled, one of his cabinet came to Nairobi – I forget his name now – and I spent a good part of a morning with him. He explained to me that Idi Amin's government, from first to last, with all its massacres, had been financed by Saudi Arabia. They secured their arms from Libya, for which they had to pay, and Saudi provided them with the money. I suppose it was to convert Uganda from a predominantly Christian country into a predominantly Muslim one. The murderer of a quarter of a million of his fellow-countrymen now lives in comfort with his paymasters in Riyadh. We dwell in a world where, if you murder one person they hang you, if you murder a quarter of a million, you live in comfort evermore.

Long afterwards, I was chatting with a Ugandan lady in a bar. I asked: "How many brothers and sisters do you have?" She replied: "One hundred and three." She continued: "My father was one of Amin's cabinet." It became clear that while they murdered the men, the murderers also appropriated wives and daughters.

When, after a suspect election, Milton Obote took over Uganda for a second period, an era known as Obote Two, Ugandan friends told me that even more Ugandans were murdered under Milton Obote than under Idi Amin. And Milton Obote also now lives in extreme comfort.

So, when I returned to Uganda two years ago, now under Yoweri Museveni, and found it transformed – where as a lone white man you could safely wander across Kampala in the middle of the night – back to its old loving self, for me it was like a religious experience. Our former journalist, John Nagenda, was my most courteous host. What tribute must we not pay to Yoweri Museveni and his colleagues!

One evening, a totally unknown young man crossed the bar and stood beside me. "The reason," he explained "that Europeans spent so much time in the last century looking for the sources of the Nile is that the Baganda women are the most beautiful in East Africa."

Jim Bailey
March 1994

PREAMBLE

The original inhabitants of the territory which had become known as Uganda are not definitively known. They were probably Stone Age communities which were gradually absorbed or replaced by iron-using cultivators and pastoralists from the neighbouring regions during the first millennium of the Christian era. At the beginning of the colonial era there were over 30 ethnic groups with diverse political institutions in Uganda. These ethnic communities can be divided into four broad linguistic categories: Bantu, Sudanic, and Luo-speaking peoples, and the "Paranilotic" people.

The Bantu-speaking peoples live in the southern half of the country and make up over half Uganda's present population. Included in this group are the Baganda, the Basoga, the Banyankore, the Bakiga, the Banyoro and the Bagisu. The Sudanic-speaking peoples, such as the Lugbara, the Madi and the Kakwa presently live in the West Nile District in north-west Uganda. The Luo-speaking peoples are found throughout northern and eastern Uganda: the Acholi and Langi live in northern Uganda, the Alur and Jonam live in West Nile among the Sudanic communities, and the Jopadhola live in eastern Uganda among the Bantu-speaking peoples. The "Paranilotic" peoples, who include the Karamojong, the Jie and the Iteso, inhabit the eastern and north-eastern part of the country. Despite this categorisation, considerable inter-ethnic integration has taken place in Uganda over the centuries.

The main economic activities of pre-colonial Ugandan societies were pastoralism and agriculture. These activities were supplemented by hunting, carpentry, fishing and iron-smelting. Ancestor worship was an important aspect of religious life. The extended family was the basic social unit in every community and above the family were the patrilineal clans. In almost every pre-colonial Ugandan society most of the social and communal activities were carried out either at family or clan level.

Before the advent of British colonialism the various Ugandan peoples had developed a variety of different political systems. In southern and western Uganda sophisticated centralised kingdoms developed. In other parts of the

1

country small chiefdoms and principalities emerged alongside relatively simple egalitarian societies which did not extend past the clan or village level.

The best known political entities of pre-colonial Uganda were the inter-lacustrine kingdoms such as Buganda, Bunyoro-Kitara and Nkore. The precise origins of these states are still obscure. Kinyankore and Kinyoro traditions trace their origins back to the legendary period of the Batembuzi or The Pioneers. According to tradition, the Batembuzi period was followed by the establishment of the Bachwezi Empire during the fourteenth century. Although the exact extent of this empire is not known, it is generally accepted that it did not last more than two centuries. The Bachwezi Empire broke up under the strain of rebellions, successive human and animal epidemics and a Luo invasion. In its place, Kinyoro tradition has it, successor states such as Bunyoro-Kitara, Nkore and Buganda, emerged. The Baganda, however, dispute this account, arguing that their ancestors came from the Mount Elgon area and settled in Buganda around 1,200 AD.

Most of the post-Bachwezi states in southern Uganda were established during the late fifteenth and early sixteenth centuries. Until the eighteenth century Bunyoro-Kitara was the most powerful and most ambitious of all the states in Uganda. During the sixteenth century the Bunyoro armies attacked and defeated both Buganda and Nkore, but never occupied their lands. In the eighteenth century the Banyoro launched an ambitious and far-reaching expedition against Nkore and Rwanda. Although sweeping victoriously through Nkore, the Bunyoro forces ran out of luck in their attempted invasion of Rwanda. Their king was killed, and as the demoralised troops retreated through Nkore they were intercepted by the Banyankore and routed. Thus began a gradual decline in the Bunyoro-Kitara kingdom and by the late eighteenth century Buganda had replaced it as the most powerful state in the region.

Buganda had started as a small kingdom on the northern shore of Lake Victoria in the shadow of Bunyoro-Kitara. Unlike Bunyoro and Nkore, Buganda was a forest zone kingdom and it had a predominantly agricultural economy. Buganda was the most centralised kingdom in the region. Although it nearly lost its independence during the reign of Kabaka Nakibinge, it began to expand gradually from the seventeenth century, mainly at the expense of Bunyoro. Buganda was able to evolve an elaborate administrative system and established a complex and efficient system of communications. However, like all the inter-lacustrine kingdoms, Buganda had no smooth and established mechanism of succession. The death of a reigning king was usually followed by succession wars and a period of chaos and instability. Nevertheless, with the exception of the short-lived eighteenth century kingdom of Mpororo, all the kingdoms in southern Uganda were able to survive these succession disputes.

In eastern Uganda chiefdoms or principalities of varying sizes developed. In Busoga, for example, there were numerous petty principalities founded by Bunyoro princes. None of these principalities ever managed to control the whole of Busoga. In other parts of eastern Uganda such as Bukedi, Bugisu and Teso, the people developed small polities which hardly extended beyond the village. In Teso and Karamoja political and military activity revolved around the age-set system and political decisions were made by an ad-hoc council of elders. In the event of war all able-bodied men were called upon to fight and the military commanders were chosen on the basis of experience and ability. Once the war was over the military units would be disbanded.

The people of northern Uganda were also organised in small chiefdoms. In modern Acholi there were over 180 chiefdoms. During the nineteenth century the Langi established a powerful military confederacy and many Langi soldiers were employed by the Bunyoro king Kabarega to revive his power and later to resist the British.

The "Discovery" of Uganda
The first foreigners to arrive in Uganda were traders from the East African coast. By the end of the eighteenth century trading links between Buganda and Zanzibar had become well established. The activities of these pioneers were closely controlled by the Kabaka of Buganda. The Zanzibaris introduced guns which considerably improved the military strength of Buganda. They also introduced Islam and by the 1860s Islamic culture had taken root in the country. In the meantime Egyptian and Sudanese Arabs had begun to penetrate northern Uganda on slave-trading expeditions. During the second half of the eighteenth century the Egyptians attempted to establish an equatorial empire. This was the first real threat to the independence of the peoples who constitute modern Uganda.

In the second half of the nineteenth century European travellers and adventurers began to penetrate Uganda. The first Europeans to set foot in Uganda were the Englishmen, John Speke and James Grant, who were in search of the source of the Nile. In February 1862 they were granted an audience at the Kabaka of Buganda's court. Speke and Grant were well received by Kabaka Mutesa I and they were led to Jinja to see the Nile's source. Meanwhile, Sir Samuel Baker and his wife had started another expedition from Egypt and in 1864 they reached Bunyoro. The Bakers were not well received by Kabarega because he suspected that his uninvited guests might be Egyptian spies.

In 1874 Henry Stanley, the famed Welsh American correspondent, arrived in Buganda. Great changes had taken place in Buganda since Speke and

Grant's day. Its population had risen to almost a million and the kingdom stretched for over 200 kilometres along the north-west shores of Lake Victoria. Guns had become commonplace in Buganda and Kabaka Mutesa could now deploy a force of 150,000 soldiers in addition to his fleet of war canoes. Mutesa expressed to Stanley an interest in Christianity and the explorer accordingly promised to send missionaries to Buganda on his return home. Mutesa, like Kabarega, had been worried by the danger of Egyptian expansionism. He hoped that he could establish a mutual alliance with the British against the Egyptians. He did not realise at the time that the British, who were behind the Egyptian adventure, were a greater threat to the independence of his country.

The first batch of missionaries to arrive in Buganda were Protestants of the British Church Missionary Society. They arrived in 1877 and two years later they were followed by Roman Catholic missionaries. All the missionaries resided near the palace of the Kabaka and their activities were closely watched. Although Mutesa had initially welcomed the missionaries, he was soon disillusioned by their fierce rivalry to win converts. Mutesa was also worried by the enthusiasm of the young Baganda courtiers for Christianity. He came to see the missionary activities as a potential threat to the political stability of his kingdom, but was not bold enough to expel them. He continued to tolerate them until his death in 1884.

Kabaka Mwanga, who succeeded Mutesa I, was more hostile to the Christian missionaries. Although Mwanga had initially sided with the younger men at court, irrespective of their faith, against the older chiefs, he soon started persecuting the Christian converts. The tension which had been building up since the arrival of the missionaries flared up into open conflict in June 1886. In one incident alone, 32 Christian converts, including the Catholic martyrs, were burned to death at Namugongo. The White missionaries were not harmed, nor were they expelled from the country. The only exception was Bishop Hannington who was killed on his way to Buganda, apparently on the orders of Mwanga. The Kabaka's ruthless persecution of the Christians marked the beginning of a period of political-religious strife which culminated in the Catholic-Protestant war of 1892.

Kabaka Mwanga's attempts to reverse the growing influence of alien religions in his country were counter-productive. In 1882 an alliance between the two Christian factions and the Muslims forced the Kabaka out of power and had a new Kabaka installed. In a bizarre turn of events, the new Kabaka turned on the Christians, who in response rallied behind their former enemy, Mwanga. In 1889 they overthrew the Muslim-backed regime and reinstated Mwanga as the Kabaka. Mwanga, was from then on, a pawn in the hands of the two Christian factions, which were still competing fiercely against each other.

The Uganda Protectorate

For the first time the future of Uganda was now being determined by the European powers. In 1885 Carl Peters seized Tanzanian territory on behalf of Germany, and this provoked Britain to seize what is now Kenya. In 1886 East Africa was divided between British and German "spheres of influence" – but the western frontiers were not determined. In 1889 Peters went to Buganda and, with the support of the Roman Catholics, persuaded Mwanga to sign a "treaty of friendship". This treaty was opposed by the Anglican faction which invited the Imperial British East Africa Company (IBEAC) to come to Uganda at once and sign an agreement with Mwanga on behalf of the British. The potential clash between Germany and Britain over Uganda was averted by the Heligoland Treaty of 1890 in which Germany recognised Uganda as a British sphere of influence. The IBEAC was entrusted with the administration of Uganda and in 1890 Captain Lugard arrived in Kampala to act as the company's agent.

Captain Lugard was soon involved in the war between the Roman Catholics and the Protestants. While the Protestants favoured British colonialism, the Catholics preferred French or even German control. In 1892 war between the two factions broke out. Lugard naturally sided with the Protestants and the Catholics were defeated. This victory marked the beginning of Protestant political ascendancy in Buganda and, later on, in the rest of the country.

In 1892 the IBEAC, finding itself in serious financial trouble, threatened to withdraw from Uganda. In response the British government took direct control of the territory, and in 1894 the Uganda Protectorate was declared. However it took decades to establish an effective colonial administration over the whole country, and indeed the western borders of Uganda were not delimited until 1919. Between 1894 and 1919 the British were preoccupied with the conquest and pacification of the country. Through the Protestant influence on Buganda, Britain was able to take control of that kingdom without the use of force.

The conquest of much of Uganda was made easier for the British by the collaboration of notable chiefs. The collaborators actively participated in the conquest of the rest of the country and were rewarded with influence and power. The most prominent were Apolo Kagwa and Semei Kakunguru of Buganda and Nuwa Mbaguta of Nkore. Semei Kakunguru, for example, played a crucial role in the conquest of eastern Uganda in the hope that he might be installed as the king of that region. Because of Kagwa and Mbaguta's collaboration both Buganda and Nkore expanded at the expense of their neighbours. Nkore even became known as Ankole Kingdom.

There were, however, peoples who actively resisted the British, and this resistance was met with devastating force. The most famous resistor was the Omukama Kabarega of Bunyoro who fought the British for nine years. He was eventually captured in 1899 and exiled to the Indian Ocean islands of Seychelles. As a result of his resistance Bunyoro was severely punished and her territories ceded to Buganda. These territories later became the controversial "Lost Counties" of the 1960s. The Banyoro continued to resist the British and the Baganda agents and in 1906 there was the famous Kenyangire passive resistance which forced the British to phase out Baganda agents from Bunyoro. Unlike Buganda, Toro, and Ankole which signed agreements with Britain in 1900 and 1901, Bunyoro was treated as a conquered territory until 1933 when a treaty similar to those of the other kingdoms was signed.

There was also notable resistance to colonialism in other parts of Uganda. In 1897 Kabaka Mwanga, disenchanted with his puppet status, fled Buganda and joined forces with Kabarega. He was captured and deported to the Seychelles. His supporters resorted to guerrilla warfare but were defeated. The Bagisu also strongly resisted conquest but their defiance was ruthlessly crushed by the British and their agents in a number of punitive expeditions in the 1910s. In Ankole the king of Igara committed suicide rather than submit to the British and their Nkore collaborators. In Buhweju, King Ndagara was killed in battle while resisting absorption of his kingdom into Ankole.

After the conquest of Uganda the British set out to establish an administrative system in the protectorate. In an attempt to implement "indirect rule" the British transplanted the Kiganda pre-colonial administrative structure to all districts in Uganda. Baganda chiefs and clerks were posted to all parts of the country to staff the colonial administration. The deployment of Baganda agents was deeply resented by the peoples of other parts of Uganda and from the 1920s the British began to replace them with local people. During the colonial period, education was left to the missionaries. They established schools such as King's College, Budo, Busoga College, Mwiri, Mbarara High School, Gulu High School and Mvara School. It was not until the 1950s that the government set up its own schools.

The Ugandan colonial economy was dominated by British and Asian commercial traders. The Asians, mainly from the Indian subcontinent, originally came to East Africa to build the Uganda railway. During the 1920s they were encouraged to set up businesses and to buy land. Generous commercial loans, export licences and other credit facilities were made available to Asian and European businessmen.

While the Asians were given assistance to establish businesses, African traders were deliberately prohibited by law from commercial trading. It was impossible for Africans to obtain loans from British banks in Uganda, nor could they obtain import and export licences from the colonial government. As a result, the Asian community was able to dominate commercial life.

In contrast to the European and Asian dominance of the marketplace, African peasants dominated the production of Uganda's cash crops. In 1904 cotton was introduced in Buganda and it was later extended to other parts of the country, especially eastern Uganda which became the leading cotton producing area. By 1910 cotton had become the country's leading export. Coffee was another important crop which was produced at peasant level. Buganda became the most important coffee producer. Tea and sugarcane were grown in plantations by the British and Asians, but they were of lesser economic importance.

From the 1920s the official colonial policy was to develop Uganda as a primarily African country, however this was not reflected on the ground. In 1921 Britain established the Uganda Legislative Council (Legco) to represent European and Asian interests. Africans had no representation on the Legco. Between the World Wars there was no serious political activity on the part of the Africans. The Africans, and especially the Baganda, were not interested in the Legco, and the British policy of divide and rule encouraged parochial aspirations. All political activity during this period was strictly provincial. Attempts to break out of this mould, such as proposals from Ankole, Toro, Bunyoro, Buganda and Busoga to hold regular meetings to discuss common interests, were vetoed by the colonial administration.

In the 1920s a number of provincial organisations which had some political objectives did emerge. In Buganda there was the Young Buganda Association, the Bamalaki and the Bataka movements. The main aim of these associations was to fight the milo-land system which the British had established under the 1900 Buganda Agreement. Under this system, land was given to chiefs who had supported the imposition of colonial rule. The new land-owners had used their powerful positions to exploit peasants by imposing unbearable land rents. The Bataka movement in particular demanded the revision of the Buganda Agreement of 1900 to provide for a more equitable distribution of land. Another important political activity during this time was the African opposition to the establishment of a settler dominated East African Federation comprising Uganda, Kenya and Tanganyika.

DRUM

africa's leading magazine

OCTOBER, 1957. 6d.

SPLIT IN UGANDA CONGRESS

Also Aga Khan Pictures

Registered at G.P.O. as a Newspaper.

Strange beauty
of East Africa

A NEW NATION IS BORN

Uganda's passage to independence was hampered by lack of national unity. Provincialism, threats of separatism and the absence of a countrywide nationalist movement inhibited Britain's attempts to forge a united independent Uganda. The first nominally national party was the Uganda National Congress (UNC) formed in 1952 and led by Ignatius Musazi. It was the first party to demand self-government from the colonial administration. However, the leadership of the UNC was of Buganda and although the party attempted to open branches in other parts of the country, it never became a mass nationalist movement. In 1959 the UNC was split into two factions, one of which was led by Apollo Milton Obote.

In 1954 the Democratic Party (DP) was formed. The main objective of the DP was to promote the political interests of the Roman Catholic community in Uganda. The DP did manage to become a national party, and at independence it was one of Uganda's most important parties. In 1960 Obote's faction of the UNC merged with a non-Baganda movement, the Uganda Peoples' Union, to form the Uganda People's Congress (UPC) under Obote's leadership. The UPC aspired to be a genuine national party, but in practice it drew its support from the Protestant and Muslim communities.

Despite the lack of a mass nationalist movement, the main stumbling block to independence was the political status of Buganda within a united Uganda. During the colonial period Buganda had developed as a state within a state and when, in 1953, Governor Cohen began preparing Uganda for independence as a united country, the entire process was thrown into crisis. The Kabaka of Buganda, Edward Mutesa II, rejected any attempt to integrate Buganda into Uganda and demanded independence for his kingdom. Governor Cohen had him deported and for the two years that the Kabaka was in exile in Britain very little constitutional progress was made. In 1955 the Kabaka was allowed to return to Uganda in terms of a compromise agreement. However the Buganda government continued to obstruct political changes which treated Buganda as an integral part of Uganda, much to the annoyance of non-Baganda Ugandans.

In 1961 at the London Constitutional Conference the British put forward, and had accepted, a constitution which granted Buganda federal status within Uganda, while the three western kingdoms were to have semi-federal status. In May 1962, after a series of elections and much party politicking, the UPC and the Kabaka Yekka, a monarchist Baganda party, formed a coalition government under the leadership of Milton Obote. On October 9, 1962, Uganda became independent.

A KING AND NO KING

THE KABAKA, MUTESA II, with the assistant governor of Uganda in polite attendance, on the king's birthday in 1954.

THE FOUR KINGS OF UGANDA pose with the British governor. From the left: Bunyoro's Tito Winyi II, Buganda's Edward Mutesa II, Sir Andrew Cohen, Ankole's Edward Gasyonga II, Toro's George Rukidi III.

DRUM: January 1955

In November 1942, a young, cheerful, Black prince called Edward Mutesa received the 500-year-old throne of his ancestors as a birthday present. For on his birthday he was crowned the thirty-seventh Kabaka of Buganda: he was proclaimed His Highness Mutesa II, by the Anglican bishop of the Protectorate of Uganda.

Eleven years later, a few days after his 29th birthday and the anniversary of his coronation, he was deposed from his throne and banished from his kingdom by the British government. He was flown to London, where he had talks with Colonial Secretary Mr Oliver Lyttelton.

In a White Paper, the British government accused the Kabaka of failing to co-operate with the governor, and of seeking independence for the province of Buganda. The Buganda delegation to London said in a reply that they had never sought an independent Buganda, and that they sincerely desired their "beloved Kabaka" to be restored, and that they "are deeply troubled for the future".

It is nearly a year since the Kabaka of Buganda was sent into exile. The sudden removal of the Kabaka from Buganda caused a storm which has not yet died down. The Kabaka and his future

THE KABAKA AND HIS WIFE, the Nabagereka.

IN EXILE: The Kabaka celebrating his brother Henry's graduation from Oxford.

11

THE ROYAL PALACE or **Lubiri** *of Baganda. The Kabaka lived in this 20-roomed mansion with his wife and staff of over 50.*

THE NABAGAREKA and her son, Prince Ronald Mutebi.

watching his country from 4,000 miles away.

His Highness Mutesa II, Kabaka of Buganda, "Freddie" to his many friends, is one of Africa's most interesting figures. He is aristocratic, cheerful, intelligent, with wide interests and a restless spirit: his small, slim body can be at once alert and dignified. He combines the traditional dignity of an African monarch with the polished ease of an educated English gentleman. More completely than any other African in the continent, he spans the two worlds of Africa and Europe.

He was destined to be king from his birth, and everything was done to fit him for his great task. At the age of five he was sent to King's College, Budo, near the royal seat at Kampala, to live with a White missionary family, where he stayed till the age of 18. Then, at 18, came the great moment of his life, when he was crowned king of Buganda by the bishop of Uganda. The ceremony was a strange mixture of Christian and African custom. The young king sat on the ancient throne of Buganda, made three centuries ago for King Mulondo, the 9th king.

Later in his coronation year, Mutesa went to Makerere College, the great university college of East Africa. From there he went to Cambridge University in England to study history and colonial administration. "Freddie" enjoyed his time at Cambridge. He was popular, easygoing and lived life to the full. He played tennis, cricket and soccer. When he left Cambridge he served for a short time with the Grenadier Guards, one of Great Britain's most famous fighting regiments, who guard Buckingham Palace. He was the

are now more than ever the object of earnest speculation and discussion. Will he come back? Can Buganda carry on for long without a Kabaka? Can another Kabaka be appointed? While all these vital questions are being discussed, the Kabaka himself remains an enigmatic figure; he lives in a small, select London flat away from the public eye intently

THE KABAKA BITES A CHERRY off a cocktail stick held out by a friend at a London party. "He likes to enjoy a cocktail here, a celebration there, music and dance often" wrote DRUM of the Kabaka's time in exile.

first African to become a captain in the Grenadiers.

In 1948 he came back to his kingdom: and later that year he married Damali Kisosonkole, in one of Africa's most fabulous weddings. The Kabaka's income is said to be around £36,000 a year, derived from the 350 square miles of Royal Estates, where cotton, coffee, ground-nuts and corn are grown. But this inheritance carries with it many responsibilities, and the Kabaka is expected to entertain lavishly and maintain a high standard of living. He owns a fleet of ten cars, including the latest Rolls Royce.

In Buganda, the Kabaka is still looked up to as a symbol of manhood and fatherhood, for traditionally the Kabaka is known as *Ssabassaja* or "our husband". ❏

IN FULL REGAL ATTIRE: The Kabaka at an official function.

CALLED HIMSELF GOD AND FOOLED THOUSANDS

KIGANIRA IS ARRESTED, AGAIN. In 1961 Kiganira escaped "by magic" from Luzira Prison where he was serving time for his

DRUM: April 1965

He climbed a tree on Mutundwe hill and declared he had been sent to deliver the Kabaka from exile. He said he could blow messages to London through a hollow stick. He said he was Kibuka, Baganda god of war. Strangely enough, many believed him.

Eleven years ago there was a bitter political crisis in the kingdom of Buganda. The Kabaka, symbol of

Baganda unity, had been sent into exile by the British. The Baganda had united to a man to fight for the Kabaka's return, but their hopes looked dim. It was at this time that the voice of a self-styled prophet by the name of Kibuka Kiganira Omumbale was first heard.

He preached a clear and definite message which he shouted from the housetops and the treetops. He said he had come to prepare the way for the Kabaka's return.

His ideas were amazing (some said mad) but his sincerity burned and people listened, first in hundreds and then in thousands. The name of Kiganira became a byword, and people started to believe some of the extraordinary things he told them. He even said he could send letters to the British government and the Kabaka in London by putting them in a hollow stick and blowing them through the atmosphere.

exploits during the Kabaka's exile.

Kiganira finally decided to preach his message from the heights of Mutundwe hill near Kampala. The hill then had few trees and its outline was clear against the sky. He climbed the hill and began pouring forth the most extraordinary stream of inspired oratory and absolute gibberish that the Baganda have ever been treated to. Some believed he was the messiah, some thought him mad – anyway he was certainly a great showman!

He ended up by sitting in a tree and declaiming from the lofty branches, playing the while with a snake which he coiled round and round his body. Thousands of people brought food, money and offerings to the god of the tree. They squatted on the hilltop and stayed there for several days and nights.

Kiganira said he was god of war. He said he could cure women of barrenness by giving them medicine, but more important he said that he had been sent by Kibuka as a prophet to lead the Baganda's beloved Kabaka back from exile. The crowd was so excited and the atmosphere so charged with its political and religious overtones that the people actually began to worship him. He kept up their spirits by chanting according to the Baganda religion and they, in return, chanted back.

Meanwhile the more sober Kampala citizens were becoming increasingly afraid, for hundreds of people were daily leaving their homes and joining the thousands already sitting on the top of the hill. From the distance, astounded European civil servants could see the long column of Baganda like a column of ants as they swarmed up the slope and collected into a crowd.

No European dared to go to the top of the hill and even the Kabaka's own police were afraid of the violence. And all the time the people gathered and things looked more and more dangerous. Finally the authorities decided to act and sent in the Kabaka's police. In the scuffle that followed, the head of the Kabaka's police lost his life.

The prosecution in Uganda's High Court failed to find the real murderer of the Kabaka's police chief and Kiganira was found guilty of organising an unlawful assembly where a murder was committed. He was given a 20-year sentence in 1955, after a year-long trial.

Kiganira, whose original name is Mathias Sewanyana, comes from an ardent Christian home. His father, Mr Joseph Baliddukamu, is a first class Catholic and a catechist at a village church. When his family was so strongly Christian, how is it that Kiganira took a different line? DRUM asked his brother: "Well, the ghosts were originally possessed by his great-grandfather and, as you are well aware, in Buganda when the old people die the spirits pick up one of the young grandsons," his brother replied. "In the case of our family they chose Mathias Sewanyana to be their priest and gave him the name, Kibuka Kiganira Omumbale. They forced him to abandon his schooling at a primary school at Kyamaganda village at an early age."

The Kiganira family is quite extraordinary because two diametrically opposed religions have gained ground. Kiganira's uncle became a Catholic priest and his father a catechist at a village church. The ghosts or spirits or gods, whatever one prefers, also penetrated the family and Kiganira became a self-styled prophet.

The same thing really happened to the Baganda people. During the 1953–55 crisis the people had a double mind over what powerful god would help speed up the Kabaka's return. Some went to pray to the real God, but others said He was letting them down and they should pray to their ancient gods instead. ❏

RETURN OF THE KABAKA

TRIUMPHAL ARCHWAYS AND CHEERING CROWDS welcomed the Kabaka back to Kampala on October 18, 1955.

INSPECTING A GUARD OF HONOUR upon his return from exile.

DRUM: December 1955

Half-a-million people thronged the airport to wave and cheer the triumphant return of the Kabaka. When King Freddie got off the specially-chartered plane, the governor, Sir Andrew Cohen, was forced back into second place, when the Nabagereka rushed first to greet and exchange kisses with her husband. The Kabaka was cold and unsmiling when he turned to acknowledge the greetings of the governor.

Seventy-two hours before the landing of the plane which was returning the Kabaka to Buganda af-

AT THE AIRPORT: His family waits.

BAGANDA PERFORM A WAR DANCE at the newly-returned Kabaka's palace.

ter a two-year exile, about 3,000 bearded men camped in a special enclosure at Entebbe airport. For two nights they sang, danced and cheered speeches from their leaders of the two-year struggle to get His Highness, the Kabaka, back. These bearded Baganda had grown their beards as a protest against the deposition of the Kabaka.

During the Kabaka's exile, the government had increased pressure on the Lukiko to elect another Kabaka, and although the name of one of the Kabaka's half-brothers was openly suggested, bitter opposition came from the other members of the royal family, and the Lukiko vigorously resisted all attempts. The Great Lukiko advised the British government that in the present mood it would not be possible for them to give a warm welcome to the queen's forthcoming tour of the country. In the face of this hostile opposition the colonial government was forced to review the position of the Kabaka.

So now he has returned to his people. The Kabaka turned round to wave at the frantic multitudes. A

ROYAL DRUMMERS POUND OUT a thunderous welcome as the Kabaka nears.

MR KAMAYA BET HIS fattest cow on the Kabaka not returning, and lost!

SCHOOL CHILDREN WELCOME the Kabaka on his arrival at Nakivuba Stadium.

BAGANDA DIGNITARIES PAY their respects to the returned monarch.

warm feeling surged through his heart in the face of the love of the people. In his speech he spoke of the struggle for independence by 1960 and said: "My work for the future is for tranquillity and peaceful progress..."

The celebrations were highlighted by the signing of the agreement which made the Kabaka a "constitutional monarch", loosely along the lines of the British system. With the new deal signed by the governor and the representatives of the Kabaka, Mutesa II will no longer be absolute but will be responsible to the Lukiko and the governor.

It is widely believed that under the new deal Buganda is well on her way to independence "within the

18

ON THE DAIS of the reed pavilion where the Buganda Agreement is to be signed by Governor Cohen and the Kabaka.

framework of self-governing Uganda". But there can be no practical future for the self-government of Buganda, while the kingdom's neighbouring provinces remain under the yolk of the Union Jack. Before Buganda or the whole of Uganda can reach a favourable settlement with the colonial government, it will first have to settle the disputes that have torn the country apart. ❐

THE GOVERNOR AND THE KING.

THE TWO LEADERS SIGN – and the Kabaka becomes "constitutional".

UGANDA CRIES FOR SELF-RULE

AUGUSTINE KAMYA ADDRESSES a Uganda National Congress meeting.

DRUM: July 1956

"We want self-government!" was the deafening cry which highlighted the Uganda National Congress Week. In the cheering and yelling other slogans rose above the thunder... "Forward with Congress," "High Commission stinks", and "Away with Quislings".

THE UNC LEADERSHIP soon after the organisation's formation in 1952.

A procession of motor vehicles and a swarm of about 30,000 people trotted on foot through the streets of Kampala. A resolution demanding the opening of "immediate negotiations for Uganda's self-government", was cabled to the colonial secretary. After the Congress Week membership swelled extravagantly. "I fear the Congress as much as I fear lightning," said Sir Andrew Cohen, Governor of Uganda.

The Uganda National Congress (UNC) was formed in 1952, by Mr Ignatius K Musazi, a man who sought the salvation of his country. He had four objectives in mind: to unite all the people of Uganda, to get independence for Uganda, to raise the standard of living of Africans, and to fight for human rights for all the people of Africa. The

UGANDA CONGRESS SPLITS

RINGING OUT THE OLD ORDER? Joseph Kiwanuka at a UNC meeting.

DRUM: September 1957

Seven years to build up, then smash, the Uganda National Congress goes down the drain. That's what many members of the Congress are saying now since a group of the younger leaders raised a rumpus in the Central Executive Council of the Congress and then stomped out, telling everyone they were going to form a new party. And they did too. It's name: the United Congress Party.

There were many small rehearsals for that final row, and a big blow up in August 1956. But these seemed to have been patched up before the annual delegates' meeting in June, 1957, at which a new president general, chairman and central committee were to be elected. But then there was a row about the method of election, started by a motion by Peter Oola, president of the Acholi branch. For two hours the delegates argued over the motion and then threw it out – 46 votes for, 176 against.

Many of the 46 then marched out, and later declared that they had started their own party, with much talk of the Congress being merely a Buganda party. This was dismissed by the Congress spokesman as "government propaganda". And in an official statement the chiefs of Congress said that it was a battle for power in the Congress which had caused the break, and talked of an attempt to "overthrow the party". ❑

first mass meeting of the Congress was convened in Kampala on April 6, 1952, and was intended to coincide with Van Riebeeck Day in South Africa. The first resolution adopted by the Congress was an international one expressing concern over the colour bar in South Africa.

All that was fine, but the Congress was faced with real problems. Uganda had no knowledge of modern politics and the people said: "Congress is selling our country to foreigners." The old chiefs looked at it with fear and suspicion, anxious about their traditional powers. Even the British government began to fear and hate the UNC when it gained strength.

In spite of this, Congress has managed to do a lot of good. It led the struggle for the return of the Kabaka, and Mr Musazi, president of the Congress, headed the delegation to England to ask for the Kabaka's return. But that issue has now been won and the Congress has turned its attention to something else – self-government. ❑

By Joseph M Nnambale

21

BOYCOTTERS CLASH WITH POLICE

DRUM: Unpublished 1955

After nearly three months the incident-packed boycott of non-African shops led by the Uganda National Movement (UNM) reached a climax in a clash with baton-wielding police.

After a meeting under Kampala's "Tree of Liberty" addressed by the movement's fiery leaders, supporters rushed to a nearby bus depot to put the bus boycott into force by pulling passengers out of

their seats. At the first sign of violence, police charged with batons and 200 reserves moved onto the scene. The boycotters took to their heels as tear gas was kept ready. The government responded with threats of strong action and has banned all meetings of over 250 people.

In the beginning people thought the boycott idea was a big joke. They remembered how the boycott in 1954 petered out within a fortnight. But this time it looks as

if it has come to stay. In Buganda, particularly in the west, the small Asian shopkeeper has been hard hit. In one town 20 Asian shops in a row have closed down. It is only outside Buganda that the effect is not seriously felt. Recently the boycott has been extended to include Kenyan milk and eggs, and European beer and cigarettes, while buses run by non-African companies have been placed on the banned list. UNM leaders talked of non-violence while the biggest noise of all, Mr Augustine

THOUSANDS GATHER TO discuss the UNM's boycott strategy under Kampala's "Tree of Liberty" (left). The meeting decided to physically enforce the bus boycott – but the police had other ideas (below). Faced with a ban on meetings of over 250, Kamya (in car, above) staged huge car processions through Kampala's streets.

Kamya, was charged with "watching, besetting and threatening violence". Shopkeepers allege that he has stationed "watchmen" in every town in Buganda to stop people buying from Asians.

A big question mark at first was which way the Lukiko would jump. The Katikiro, Mr Michael Kintu, has frowned on the movement but some of his ministers are thought to be in secret sympathy. One of the first companies to be granted immunity from the boy-

cott was the Uganda Development Corporation which had two Lukiko ministers on its board of directors. There have been other exemptions, granted by the UNM and many of the biggest companies are carrying out better trade than ever before.

But opposition to the boycott is steadily growing. It is not just a battle between the government and the UNM now. The Katikiro has denounced the boycott, along with the non-Baganda Leg-

islative Council. The democratic political parties have been slow to actively oppose it, but Mr Benedicto Kiwanuka (DP) and Joseph Kiwanuka (UNC) have spoken out. Meanwhile shops and companies are laying off their African staff and particularly their Baganda employees. The Uganda Bus Company that was seriously affected by the boycott has sacked 150 workers. It is this rising army of unemployed that may soon force the UNM to call off the boycott. ❑

UGANDA ENJOYS ITS ELECTION FEVER

UNDER THE TREE OF LIBERTY: *Dr BN Kununka, the secretary general of the Uganda National Congress, played a major role in his party's victory.*

DRUM: January 1959

The results of the recent elections have given politicians the chance of a lifetime to build up party organisations, form a national government, and go on to work for independence.

Practically every man and woman outside Ankole, Buganda, and Bugisu had the chance to vote. And about 85 per cent of the people did. The elections were fiercely contested. Religious and political passions were literally aflame.

The Democratic Party, suspected of being Catholic dominated, gained most votes, but not the highest number of representatives. Uganda's aggressively African nationalist party, the Uganda National Congress, claimed five seats out of ten. The Democratic Party won one seat. The remainder

PAINTING POSTERS: *Abu Mayanja, London-trained lawyer.*

DEMOCRATIC PARTY LEADER: *Benedicto Kiwanuka.*

VICTORY MARCH: Thousands of UNC supporters slogged through Kamapla led by IK Musazi (with flag) and Dr Kununka.

of the representatives were independents who, however, showed strong sympathy with the political parties.

But the great thing is that the Ugandan political parties, with little organisation, had drawn together their many splinter groups and emerged as big parties.

In contrast to the spirit of optimism of the political parties was the attitude of the neo-traditionalists in Buganda, who had baulked at direct elections to the Legislative Council. The traditionalists who control Buganda are not prepared to see people voting democratically. The extremists among them say they want Buganda to "go it alone". They hope that Buganda can get its independence without the rest of Uganda. They

LOYAL SUPPORTERS: UNC faithful listen to victory speeches following the announcement of the election results.

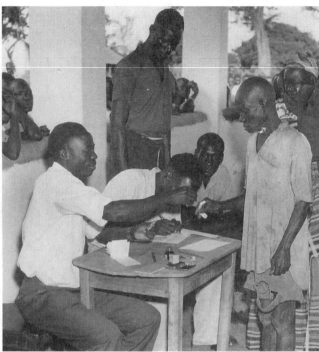

QUEUING TO VOTE: For many the first experience of democracy came after long waits in the hot sun.

want a small country to be divided into still smaller pieces. The future of Uganda's movement for independence now lies with the new members of the Legislative Council from outside Buganda.

The big question now is: Where does Uganda go from here? It still has no nationwide political organisations, nor a universally accepted leader. Also, people are not yet fully politically conscious, and are too divided on tribal and religious grounds.

But Uganda's biggest problem is undoubtedly the brake on pro-gress applied by the traditionalists in Buganda. There is no easy solution. "Uganda's prime struggle is for independence and a system of parliamentary democracy," said Abubaker Mayanja. "To do this we must have political unity, mass organisation, mass appeal, and democratic leadership." ❑

UNC VICTORS: UNC Legislative Council members and party organisers. From the left – standing: BK Kirya, JW Kiwanuka, M Obote, G Magezi, Mungoma, P Oola. Seated: IK Musazi, unknown, Abu Mayanja, Ben Otim.

THE COOL AND DETERMINED MILTON OBOTE

DRUM: July 1959

Levelheaded, determined, with a record of solid achievement behind him, Apollo Milton Obote has most of the attributes of a successful leader. Working hard in the shadow of Uganda's political glamour boys is Mr Apollo Milton Obote, the pipe-smoking politician from Lango, in the north. There is a cool consistency about him, from the calm expression on his face to the solid purposefulness of his political career.

While African leaders in Kampala have risen and fallen, exploded and fizzled out in a blaze of short-lived popularity, Milton Obote has modestly worked along his own careful path.

When Mr IK Musazi left the Uganda National Congress in a shower of bad eggs and rotten fruit, the news made such a splash that few noticed the bright-eyed, slightly-built northerner who slipped quietly into his position as president general of the party.

It was certainly an achievement for a non-Muganda to have won this important post. And, indeed, the UNC delegates at Mbale showed their true feeling for their country when they voted in the pipe smoker from Lango with a big majority.

No first-rank Ugandan leader has come from outside the kingdom of Buganda yet, but Obote may be the first such leader. Already he is becoming the central figure in politics outside Buganda, and is feeling a way towards national leadership.

He has several advantages. He avoids the backbiting and scandal to be found at the centre of Ugandan politics, and there are no po-

APOLLO MILTON OBOTE: The first top-flight politician to come from northern Uganda. Obote learned his trade in Kenya as an associate of Tom Mboya.

litical black marks against him. On the other hand, he starts with none of the natural advantages of a Baganda leader. He cannot be carried to national leadership by working up Baganda mass enthusiasm. Instead, he has the formidable task of selling them democracy. He must persuade the ordinary Muganda to abandon tribalism, and to realise that a man from another tribe has as much right to a democratic vote as a per-

son who lives on the Kabaka's doorstep.

Milton Obote lives in a simple house in Lira, capital of Lango. He seems happiest when relaxing at home, dressed in an open-necked shirt, and shrouded by a cloud of tobacco smoke. His friends, mostly members of the super-organised branches of the UNC, come streaming in. He is polite but impassive. His face is a mask of calmness, whether he is thinking of his own problems or listening to other people's troubles. His coolness goes with him to the political platform, where he can keep a crowd's attention without getting emotionally carried away.

His father was a poor farmer who worked himself up to the position of a Gombolola chief. He was determined to give his son the best possible education. Obote did not fail him, and completed a higher arts course at Makerere University College. He also became secretary of the Makerere Political Society, and it was not unexpected that he went into politics when the administration stopped him taking a District Council scholarship which would have enabled him to study overseas.

Thinking Kenya would be his best political training ground, he packed his bags for Nairobi. It was 1952. He met Kenyatta, Walter Odede, Achieng Oneko and his old friend from Makerere days, Paul Ngei, before the Mau Mau uprising exploded and swept these leaders out of Kenyan politics.

After nearly five years of politicising in Kenya he decided he was finished with his political apprenticeship. He returned to Uganda to put the politics he had learned into practice. In the first democratic elections in Uganda, Obote had three candidates standing against him. He won the seat with a majority of nearly 40,000. Foreign journalists called his election campaign the most businesslike of the election. Posters, handouts, loudspeaker vans, party uniforms. Obote used them all.

But Obote had also built up his success by really solid work for the local people. They remembered that Obote had been the first person to press the government to give boys and girls scholarships for overseas study. He had reformed the system of appointing chiefs, so that the businessmen, teachers, and farmers could become senior chiefs without working their way slowly up the ladder. And he had managed to get an unpopular district commissioner transferred.

Obote's career and character will ensure him a place in any democratically-elected council in Uganda, but to emerge as a real Ugandan leader he will have to overcome the forces of tribalism and traditionalism.

Coming from outside Buganda, he cannot accept the popular Baganda solution which entails dominance by the Lukiko or the Kabaka over the rest of the country. At the same time the Baganda cannot easily accept a leader from outside their tribe.

Milton Obote wants Buganda to play its full part in the future of Uganda, but this does not mean that he thinks it should have special privileges. He means that the Baganda should be treated the same way as other citizens of the country, and that they should be prepared to elect their own representatives to a democratic council.

But at present there is no chance of this. The Lukiko and some other groups are solidly against the Legislative Council and, as long as their opposition continues, Milton Obote will gradually build himself up as the centre of the opposition to Baganda traditionalism. ❐

By Alan Rake

SELF-RULE TO INDEPENDENCE

In late 1961 Uganda's political leaders met in London to work out a constitution for an independent Uganda. Representatives from political parties, the four monarchies and the colonial government finally reached agreement in October.

CONFERENCE DELEGATES: (l-r) Milton Obote, Mr Monson, Sir J Martin (below).
THE KATIKIRO of Buganda, Michael Kintu, signing the new Buganda Agreement, watched by Iain Macleod, at the close of the Constitutional Conference (below right).

CONSTITUTIONAL CONFERENCE OPENS: *Colonial Secretary, Mr Iain Macleod, makes his opening address.*

A NEW NATION IS BORN BY THE LAKES

ENJOYING A RIGHT ROYAL RECEPTION: The Duke and Duchess of Kent represented the Queen at Uganda's independence.

DRUM: October 1962

A new flag is flying in Kampala, Uganda, these days. Yes, yet another new nation has emerged.

Almost suddenly, and with less noise than most of its predecessors in Africa, Uganda becomes independent on October 9, 1962. And to the Ugandans more than to most, the prospects of independence may mean more prosperity, better chances on the export market and better education.

Already the group of lake kingdoms of independent-minded conservative people have much. Most people are on farms as landowners in a small way. They export large quantities of coffee, cotton, tea, tobacco and cattle hides – and their exports have been soaring higher and higher. Uganda is plunging into industrialisation too, with its big textile mills, and is mining and smelting its own copper. Probably the most valuable of all the resources of the garden country, though, is its water. It has enough hydro-electric power for a much bigger, more industrialised nation, and the

PRIME MINISTER, Milton Obote, takes the oath of office.

OBOTE BECOMES PRIME MINISTER of the self-governing Protectorate of Uganda amid much jubilation in May 1962.

great Owen Falls Scheme is steadily stepping up the output.

Of the East African states Uganda was the nation believed to be the least ready for independence only a few years ago. It has been troubled by disputes between the kingdoms, and the hesitance of Buganda, the biggest kingdom, to accept a central government. Yet Uganda is now moving smoothly into a future that seems almost rosy. The last constitutional talks seemed to iron out

OBOTE RECEIVES the instruments of freedom from the Duke of Kent, and later goes dancing with the Duchess.

THE INDEPENDENCE STATUE in Kampala is unveiled by the prime minister.

the difficulties. Buganda was granted a form of federal affiliation which seems to have satisfied the demand that no man takes precedence in Buganda itself over the Kabaka.

The Buganda political party, the Kabaka Yekka, which is devoted to the maintenance of the Kabaka's traditional position, swept the boards in Buganda at the general election this April and, allied with the strong Uganda People's Congress (UPC) formed a new government for the whole of Uganda, ousting the Democratic Party.

In the earlier 1961 election the Democratic Party had ignored a ruling by the Kabaka that no one should stand for election in Buganda as it would be challenging his authority, and gained 20 of the 21 central government seats. Mr Benedicto Kiwanuka thus became the first prime minister when Uganda gained internal self-government in March 1962 – and ruled for just one month.

Now the UPC leader, Mr Milton Obote, who is a moderate nationalist – he calls himself a "gentle revolutionary" – rules by keeping in with the traditionalist Kabaka

Yekka, but he has no overall majority by himself. The result is that, with the Democratic Party breathing down his neck politically, Obote must forget about any violently radical changes towards a too-strong central government.

Uganda's other three kingdoms and the province of Busoga exercise some internal powers under the constitution. But it was made a strict rule that no king should take precedence over any other, and that after independence Uganda should continue to regard Her Majesty Queen Elizabeth as queen of Uganda.

UGANDA'S FARMERS produce abundant coffee and tea for the export market.

One of the major points of significance about the new state, with its tiny population of non-Africans, is that its independence means the next major step towards the realisation of the plans for a vast new East African Federation of Kenya, Uganda, Tanganyika and Zanzibar.

Already many of the main services, railways, harbours, posts and telecommunications, customs and excise, civil aviation and research, are carried out jointly with Kenya and Tanganyika under the East African Common Services Organisation.

Uganda, long considered backward and slow-moving, has shown that it would certainly not be the poor relation in such a group. Financially sound, with grants and loans of over £15 million promised by Britain, it is certain to take great strides forward. Its natural resources guarantee that there will be much industry, while its excellent roads and transport system are an attraction few other African states can offer.

THE OWEN FALLS SCHEME will provide electricity for the entire region.

Like every new nation, Uganda has its problems. The odd compromises and agreements that had to be made for the constitution to be generally accepted may come under fire and the people may draw back into their tribal differences. Buganda could once more desire to pull out of the union. But there has been little indication that these things could happen, and given time Uganda could easily emerge as a nation of real economic power and help in the merging of a great new East African Federation. ❐

UGANDA MINES AND SMELTS its own copper.

DRUM

africa's leading magazine

MAY 1965 1'-

Registered at G.P.O. as a Newspaper

LUBEMBE—AKUMU—MAK'ANYENGO—MAKUWA

Battle of Kenya's
Trade Union Heavyweights

DRUM
EAST
AFRICA

Milton Obote
and the
Baganda politicians

TOWARDS A UNITED UGANDA

Independent Uganda was neither a federation nor a unitary state; neither a monarchy nor a republic: it was blandly described as "the sovereign state of Uganda". And the problems which beset the country before independence continued unabated. On the one hand, the relationship between Buganda and the central government remained strained, while on the other, the people of the three western kingdoms resented the special status accorded to Buganda. The elevation of the Kabaka to president of the whole country in 1963 did not produce the kind of national unity Obote had hoped for.

One of the thorniest problems bedevilling the relationship between Uganda's peoples was the dispute between Buganda and Bunyoro, the largest of the western kingdoms, over the "Lost Counties". At the turn of the century the British, in an attempt to punish the Bunyoro Omukama (King) Kabarega, ceded some of his territories to Buganda. At the London Constitutional Conference in 1961 it was agreed that the fate of these "Lost Counties" would be resolved by referendum two years after independence. In 1964 the Obote government went ahead with the referendum, in the face of fierce opposition from Buganda. The people of the "Lost Counties" voted overwhelmingly to rejoin Bunyoro. The Kabaka was furious and in an unsuccessful attempt to reverse the decision, refused to ratify the results of the referendum.

Although this disagreement precipitated the collapse of the UPC-Kabaka Yekka (KY) alliance, the UPC's parliamentary position was in fact strengthened by defections to it from both the KY and the DP. The defections from the KY were a calculated move by Buganda politicians who were becoming increasingly disenchanted by the obscurantism of the Buganda establishment and believed that Buganda ought to be more outward looking in its national politics.

However the UPC was itself beset by internal problems which came to the surface at the 1964 party conference. John Kakonge, regarded as a radical, was ousted from his post of secretary general, and replaced by Grace Ibingira, a cabinet minister. In addition, leftist supporters of Kakonge were expelled from the party for allegedly extremist views and the militant UPC Youth League was disbanded.

FEDERATION – THE CHALLENGE OF 1964

EAST AFRICA'S BIG THREE: Tanzania's President Julius Nyerere, Milton Obote and Kenya's Jomo Kenyatta.

DRUM: January 1964

Take a deep, deep breath all you East Africans. That glorious stuff you can feel tingling right down to your toes is FREEDOM. It's been a long time coming, but wasn't it worth all the struggle?

Tick off the list. First there was Tanganyika, setting the pace for its neighbours to follow. Next Uganda, defying the prophets of gloom who said it couldn't be done without a lot of trouble. Next on the list was lovely little

Zanzibar, beating its big, eager brother of Kenya to Uhuru by a few hours. And then, getting the finest Christmas present anybody ever had, it was Kenya's turn.

Four countries... in terms of people almost 30,000,000 souls; a huge chunk of Africa casting off its old colonial ties.

So now it's up to us. Up to us not only to show the world that we can run things in our own countries just as well as and even better than anybody else ever did, but up to

us, too, to pull off the biggest piece of Pan Africanism in the whole continent.

For anybody who can count the fingers on his hand can see as clearly that the No. 1 job for East Africa is to cast away the old imperial boundaries drawn by the British and unite those 30,000,000 souls into one great federal state.

More than anything else, unity on such a vast scale by the newly-free peoples of East Africa will show the world that Africa means business... big business. No longer will school children all over the world, and a lot of grown-ups too, fumble for the right page in the atlas trying to find where we are. With federation we'll be so important that we will stand out big and bold in everybody's mind, and speak with a voice which will command attention and respect in the highest councils of the world.

A year ago there was not a politician in the whole of East Africa who was not sold on the idea of federation. "Federation this year!" screamed the headlines of newspapers all over East Africa. It was all lined up and ready to go. All federation was waiting for was Kenya's Uhuru. Politicians from each of the territories made grand speeches, committees were set up, the Big Three – Kenyatta, Nyerere and Obote – got together and everything looked set.

But then something happened. Nobody knows quite what it was, but suddenly, almost overnight, the red-hot idea began to cool. Dates were put back, people didn't turn up for meetings, guarded statements were made about "not jumping into the dark". Nobody actually gave a firm thumbs down to federation but the tide that had been running full current began to ebb and then recede.

Kenya and Tanganyika are still solid on the idea and little Zanzibar would almost certainly fall in line if the Big Three signed on the dotted line.

The odd man out, dragging his feet is Uganda, and it is not difficult to see why. A man of the calibre of Prime Minister Milton Obote needs no convincing of the benefits of federation. Obote has made fewer headlines than most of East Africa's freedom fighters, but that is because the struggle for freedom in Uganda was hardly more than a tussle.

But make no mistake about Milton Obote. He is a great man by any standards, a superb politician, handling a situation which is more internally delicate than anywhere else in East Africa, and a shrewd tactician who knows the vital importance of timing. And perhaps more than anything else, Obote is a great diplomat in a country where tradition, tribalism and monarchies hold tremendous sway, and where a wrong word about any of them can undo years of planning.

In Kenya, Kenyatta is the boss and there's not a man who questions it publicly or privately. In Tanganyika Nyerere is in exactly the same position. But look at Uganda. Obote is the political boss all right. But sharing the spotlight is the president, the Kabaka, who is king and emperor to his devoted Baganda; and three monarchs of Bunyoro, Toro and Ankole.

Buganda long ago rejected the idea of federation, fearing its identity would be lost. It is no good Kenyans and Tanganyikans dismiss-

OBSTACLES TO FEDERATION: Three traditional Ugandan monarchs – the Kabaka of Buganda, the Omugabe of Ankole and the Kyabzinga of Busoga (above) – share the fear of losing their identity in a federation. The Baganda who have their own legislature (below) are most fiercely opposed to an East African federation.

ing the fears of the Baganda with a wave of the hand and a cry of "Pan Africa first!" The Baganda are a proud nation with a proud history and their fears of federation's ending that history, or swallowing it up, are real.

But now that the Kabaka has taken on the role of not only king of Buganda but president and the No. 1 citizen of all Uganda, the federationists in the country are hoping the Baganda will start looking outward, nationally and federally.

Now that freedom is here there is a danger that unless action is taken soon then the separate nations of East Africa will become so involved with their own problems that they may not be so eager to tackle the enormous tasks of federation. This is the challenge of the leaders of East Africa as they enter the new year which heralds a new era for 30,000,000. East Africa has shown the world that it has men big enough for big ideas and big thinking. Now is the hour for the biggest idea and the biggest thinking of all. ❒

BEN KIWANUKA WALKS THE LONELY ROAD

DRUM: April 1964

A big question mark hangs over the political career of Benedicto Kiwanuka, leader of Uganda's Democratic Party. It seems only yesterday that he was proudly established as prime minister of his country. Everywhere he went he was greeted by cheering crowds, surrounded by officials eager to please. But now Benedicto has taken the lonely road downhill.

He was recently arrested on three charges of calling and addressing an illegal meeting in the country that he had led only two years before. He was allowed out on bail the next day and when he appeared for his hearing all charges against him were withdrawn on the advice of the independent director of public prosecutions.

Mr Kiwanuka, a devout Roman Catholic who sports a small brush moustache, came to power when his party, the Democratic Party, won a rather hollow victory in March 1962 in the national election in Uganda. But a month later in the second election which was to pick a government to lead Uganda into independence, the DP was resoundingly defeated and out of parliament went Benedicto Kiwanuka. Kiwanuka suffered from being a native of Buganda.

The Kabaka Yekka gained such a hold on the kingdom that he did not have a chance of a seat in the Buganda Lukiko. So when the Lukiko nominated its own members to the national parliament it made sure that he was not returned. But neither could Benedicto, being a Muganda, pick up a seat outside Buganda.

Now, suddenly after 18 months of quiet living, in which he gave no press conferences and addressed few meetings, Kiwanuka saw his chance to leap back into the political arena. And he took it. He became the coffee farmers' friend. Uganda's enthusiastic coffee farmers – most of them in Buganda – have planted far more coffee than the country can sell to quota markets under the International Coffee Agreement. The government, not wanting to have to uproot farmers' trees, is trying to buy the coffee at reduced prices and sell it in non-traditional markets at cut prices.

But Kiwanuka has been able to rally the support of some farmers behind him by claiming that the government could afford to pay more. He has called on the farmers not to sell their coffee until the government agrees to pay more.

Feelings ran high in Buganda over this issue, and, when Mr Kiwanuka was addressing a meeting of coffee farmers in Kampala, he was arrested and riot police, with batons and shields, dispersed the crowd. Kiwanuka was shown into a police cell, with his jacket, tie and shoes taken away from him, and the next day walked to court in his bare feet. He was accused of not getting a permit to hold his meeting, pleaded "Not Guilty" and was allowed out on bail. The crowd carried him shoulder-high as he came out of the court building.

Leaders all over Africa have been warning opposition parties to be constructive in their opposition. They have pointed out that Africa cannot afford disunity or the sabotaging of the national effort. Kiwanuka's challenge is to find a constructive method of opposition.

KAKONGE – WHY I QUIT

DRUM: August 1964

Everyone in Uganda is asking what will happen to John Kakonge. What is the future of this brilliant politician? Now he has been ousted as the Uganda People's Congress secretary general, can he be expected to remain a member of the party?

No matter what the quarrel with him, his opponents remember his political dedication. He won fame when, with a degree in economics, he forgot about an easy job. Instead of enjoying a comfortable life, he chose to tramp the streets of Kampala to organise the UPC from the pavements upwards. But after years of hard organisation and work came the crisis that disrupted his political career.

His troubles really started at the annual UPC conference earlier in the year. The delegates met at Gulu, the capital of northern Uganda. In the elections for party leaders, Mr Obote was duly re-elected president of the party, but the big shock came when Mr Grace Ibingira was elected secretary general, replacing Mr Kakonge, by 738 votes against 611.

After Mr Kakonge's defeat hundreds of his supporters walked out of the conference hall and staged a protest. Their protest and confused arguments were followed by a fight and the Gulu police were called in.

It has been said among the ruling circles of UPC that the Nilotics of northern Uganda are keen to hold their hard-won political positions and thus reverse the balance of power with the Bantu. Mr Kakonge is himself a Muntu from Bunyoro in western Uganda.

TWO KINGS FACE TO FACE

THE MEETING OF THE KABAKA of Buganda and the Omukama of Bunyoro was an affable one. All smiled, including William Wilberforce Nadiope (centre). But behind the courtesies lies the pressing problem of the "Lost Counties".

DRUM: October 1964

Usually October 9 is Uganda's day of rejoicing. Children revere it as the day on which their nation was born.

But this year, as the second anniversary of the most honoured day in Uganda's calendar approaches, 6,000 square miles of shadow falls across the impending festivities. It is the shadow of the "Lost Counties".

The constitutional conference, which preceded independence, decided to shelve the problem of the "Lost Counties" for a two-year cooling-off period. The delegates from the two kingdoms contesting the disputed areas – Buganda and Bunyoro – had each declared that they would not accept the independence constitution if the counties were to be ruled by the other. Only the wisdom of the man who at that time was leader of the opposition, and is now Uganda's

prime minister, Milton Obote, prevented the conference foundering in wrath.

Mr Obote proposed that the counties be watched over by the central government until October 9, 1964, on the understanding that some time after that date a referendum of the people living in the area would be held to decide their future. Now the two years of grace is rapidly running out. October 9 is almost on us.

KABAKA AT NDAIGA: Swopping his royal robes for khaki, the Kabaka has been directing the controversial settlement of Bunyoro land by Buganda war veterans.

Kabarega was joined later by Mwanga, the Kabaka of Buganda, but the Kabaka did not have the full support of the Baganda princes.

The war was thus also a civil war in Buganda, with the British supporting the opponents of the king. When it resulted in the defeat of Kabarega and Mwanga, the victorious Baganda received the Bunyoro counties of Bugangaizi, Buyaga, Buwekula, Bugerere, Buruli, North Singo and Bulemezi as part of the settlement – more than half Kabarega's territory. From that day they have been known in the western kingdom as the "Lost Counties".

Bunyoro was at one time the most powerful of the kingdoms in this part of Africa. With the loss of the "Lost Counties", the once mighty Bunyoro became the smallest of the kingdoms. Today it has a population of only 130,000. Buganda has two million.

The "Lost Counties" number seven, but the bitterest discord is over two, Buyaga and Bugangaizi. In the other five, the Baganda now form a majority of the population. Bunyoro's claim to these five is therefore no more than a formality, and the independence agreement made no order for a plebiscite in these counties.

In 1961, in Bugangaizi three-quarters of the people were still Banyoro, notwithstanding 60 years of Kiganda rule. In Buyaga the position was even more striking. There were 15 Banyoro for every Muganda. Not surprisingly, His Highness Sir Tito Winyi maintains that his case for the re-integration of these two counties into his kingdom cannot logically be denied.

For two years the rival kingdoms have reluctantly accepted the compromise. They have been two years of claim and counter-claim, two years of bitter recrimination, of continual bloodshed. Now, as the crucial day approaches, Bunyoro waits impatiently for the date of the plebiscite. The people of the western kingdom are confident that the counties will choose the overlordship of the Omukama of Bunyoro, His Highness Sir Tito Winyi IV.

The man who lost the "Lost Counties" was Omukama Kabarega, the famous Banyoro king who revolted against the British in the 1890s; the present ruler is his son.

CAMPAIGNING FOR THE REFERENDUM: Banyoro sternly stake their claim.

REFERENDUM ROCKS BUGANDA

The Baganda, however, argue that it is undesirable to disturb administrative arrangements that have lasted so long. The counties, they say, are better run by Buganda than they could be by Bunyoro, because of Buganda's greater resources. They claim that Buganda's rule has been benign and untainted by tribalism.

To the extent that the counties have been developed, they owe their development, says Mengo, to Baganda settlers and the Buganda government; and they add that it would be unjust to Baganda landowners if they were now to suffer in consequence of a change of overlordship.

To these arguments, the Banyoro are inclined to remark that they are exactly the reasons the British used to give for refusing to hand back the Empire. A journalist who recently encountered a friend in Hoima, Bunyoro's capital, and addressed him in Luganda, was told pretty sharply not to use "that colonial language".

In face of the 1961 population figures, one might expect the result of the plebiscite – when it comes – to be a foregone conclusion, but the last year or so has seen bold campaigns to settle Baganda families in the counties on a vast scale. The most controversial is at Ndaiga, on the shores of Lake Albert, where the Kabaka himself has personally directed an ex-servicemen's settlement scheme.

The Baganda emphasize that the settlement schemes are a great pioneer project, opening up thousands of acres of hitherto unbroken land and providing homes and work for tens of thousands of families. But they do not conceal the political significance of Ndaiga. ❑

NOT ONLY DID Buganda Katikiro (PM) Kintu fall following the referendum – but one of his ministers, Masembe Kabali (above) was abused by angry crowds.

DRUM: March 1965

The "Lost Counties" referendum was held on November 4 and two days later came the shock – the counties were no more Buganda's. Angry Baganda flocked to Mengo – the Buganda capital – and demanded the resignation of Kintu and his government.

Unrest broke out and ministers were seriously manhandled. Kintu himself was saved by 14 central government police officers who had been rushed to Mengo to control crowds. The Baganda stoned the Bulange, ministers' cars and the police and their vehicles. A number of people were treated at Mulago, the government hospital. The army – known here as the tough men – were called in and they tore the crowds apart. In Buganda, especially in Kampala and its outskirts, the army were to be seen everywhere – at road-

blocks and key points like the broadcasting stations, parliament buildings, the post office and electrical installations. Two days later Kintu, his government, and the counties were cast into oblivion.

Kintu's youthful successor, Mr Mayanja-Nkangi, is a popular man. He is conscious of the acute political problems facing him. The most biting one seems to be how to strengthen the Kabaka Yekka at a time when there is a continuous loss of party men to the UPC.

The UPC now controls all the District Councils in Uganda except the Buganda Lukiko and victory will certainly be theirs in the 1967 elections. The big question is whether the Baganda can survive and maintain their dignity or whether they will go the way of all flesh and be absorbed into yet another of Africa's one-party states. ❑

OBOTE – MASTER OF POLITICAL SKILL

DRUM: May 1965

He has not made his political omelette without breaking any eggs. Some people may have lost in the process and others gained, but event by event and year by year, he has been winning his way.

At every stage Dr Obote seems to have outmanoeuvred the various tribal and political forces ranged against him. This is not just empty praise. You can take the outstanding events one by one and each time it is clear that Obote has weighed up the situation, calculated and then run a neat little circle round his rivals.

Some people ask "Where did Obote get his political skill? Did he learn from Nkrumah?" Or they think of his early days of political training in Kenya and say: "Was it Kenyatta?" But the answer is that he did not learn much from others. The skill has been developing for 40 years, behind his broad forehead and wide set eyes. It comes from within. And on the whole he has got what he wants without being dictatorial or undemocratic. He has succeeded by diplomacy and persuasion.

Essentially his big problem was to make the wealthy and educated Baganda people part of the Ugandan nation and not just an exclusive club of their own. For while Obote himself came from the Lango people, numbering just over 300,000, the Baganda numbered 2 million and historically they had always held a position of political and economic dominance at the very centre of the country.

Obote carefully studied the Baganda and all the people of Uganda. He studied and exploited their weaknesses and

PRESIDENT AND PRIME MINISTER: Obote, wisely judging that he needed the Baganda's support, persuaded his UPC to make the Kabaka president of Uganda.

AMONG HIS OWN people in Lango, Obote is more popular than anywhere else.

A WORLD STATESMAN: Milton Obote at the UN next to M Bourguiba of Tunisia.

RELAXED AND CONFIDENT: With British PM Wilson and Malawi PM Banda.

KENYAN INDEPENDENCE party: Obote built a friendly relationship with Kenya.

limitations such as their political rivalries and religious differences. He then used them to help him on his way to achieving power. Once in power Obote has constantly declared that his main intention was to build a nation. He shifted the emphasis from the tribe to the nation.

When he took over the leadership of the UPC in 1961, acute problems lay ahead. He knew that Uganda was in some things like Kenya. To rule Kenya one must have a wholehearted support of the Kikuyu, and for Uganda one must have the support of the Baganda.

He dealt with the Baganda by pledging unlimited support for all their demands at the London Constitutional Conference for Independence in September 1961. They wanted a federal state, indirect elections to the central parliament, their own police, more money from the central government and their own high court. Above all they wanted their king to be the head of state. When the Kabaka returned from the conference he told a packed Lukiko, amid applause: "We got all our things." By which he meant that they had achieved all they wanted. But did they?

In fact in less than two years they had to resort to courts to get what they claimed at the London conference. After the London conference the Baganda formed a tribal political organisation –Kabaka Yekka – to strengthen their position. Obote unhesitatingly advised his colleagues in the People's Congress to form a coalition government with Kabaka Yekka.

He used his fellow northerner Daudi Ocheng to negotiate with the Mengo traditionalists. Ocheng, a schoolmate of the Kabaka and now a Kabaka Yekka MP, called it "bridging the gap between the Baganda and the northerners". But the Baganda couldn't help feeling it was a one-way bridge for the north-erners to let themselves quietly into the Kabaka's kingdom. And so they came: Ocheng, Odaka, Obwangor, Okello, Ojera, Onama... triumphantly to Kampala.

When the UPC/KY coalition government was formed the Baganda were in full triumph. Their gifted entertainers and musicians composed songs in praise. The name Obote was lauded in many tongues.

It was at this time, in October, 1963, that Obote had to decide who should be president of Uganda. Many people in the UPC were against the Kabaka. They said because he was a Muganda he could not act in the national interest. They said he was a reactionary and always opposed to political advance. They said that in choosing him Obote would be selling the north into Baganda hands.

Looking back on it now, these views seem nonsense, but at the time many influential men held them. But Obote had sufficient breadth of vision to know that the

Kabaka was really the only possible choice. He knew and he acted. All night on October 3, he argued with his party members. Slowly he wore them down; persuaded, cajoled, until at 3 a.m., his party was solidly behind him. Obote wanted to make the Kabaka president because he foresaw that this was one of the best means of making the Baganda accept him and his party.

The Baganda never looked anywhere except to the Kabaka as symbol of their tribe and unity. The government they knew was in Mengo not Kampala. Obote realised that by making the Kabaka president of Uganda, the Baganda would be forced to change their attitude and look to the central government, in Kampala.

Again the new position gave the Kabaka a dual loyalty. For from then on he had to think of himself not only as king of the Baganda but as head of the nation. The average Muganda in the villages says: though Obote is prime minister our Kabaka is the president, and for this they compliment the man from the north.

Meanwhile more and more of Obote's political opponents were leaving their old parties and moving towards the premier's side

where the real power lay. Over went Mr William Kalema of the Kabaka Yekka. Other members of the Kabaka Yekka followed. For the Democratic Party things were still more unnerving. The party which had once ruled the country under its leader Benedicto Kiwanuka, was disunited. Basil Bataringaya already had very different ideas from his party chief. But before Obote dealt the death blow to the DP he had another issue to settle with the Baganda.

The democratic attitude of the Baganda has always made them speak with many voices and Obote found he could exploit this and divide them far more successfully than the British colonial government had ever done. In November last year came the time to decide the issue of the "Lost Counties".

The Baganda had tried everything to keep the two counties of Buyaga and Bugangaizi in Buganda. They tried to get the election declared invalid, they sent in the ex-servicemen to settle, but Obote knew that when the referendum actually came the Baganda would lose and they would have to accept their loss. This is just what happened. By holding the referendum he won many friends among the Banyoro. The Baganda, though unhappy, could do nothing about it.

JOHN KAKONGE

ALEX OJERA

BENIDICTO KIWANUKA

Now Obote could deal with the DP. He urged Basil Bataringaya to cross the floor of the house and join the government. Following the example of the Kenya opposition leader, Ronald Ngala, Basil acted accordingly. "An opposition is only necessary," he said "if it has an alternative policy to offer, but this is not the case in Uganda."

Obote only had to deliver the coup de grace. In February he said he no longer recognised the opposition. "In the constitution there is no provision for a parliamentary opposition," he said. "This post died when the former leader, Mr Basil Bataringaya, crossed over to the government side. None of the Kabaka Yekka or Democratic Party leaders is a member of parliament, therefore we cannot recognise any member of the two parties as leader of the opposition."

With every success the prime minister has acquired greater confidence and esteem. Other leaders in different parts of Africa may be just as powerful and popular as Obote, but few have revealed themselves as such consummate masters of the political game. Like a great chess player playing on many different boards at the same time, he has won victory after victory and now his opponents are in disarray. ❐

By Emmanual Dduta

DR OBOTE TAKES A BRIDE: In 1964 Milton Obote married Miria Kalule. After the ceremony they drove past cheering crowds to the reception at Lugogo Stadium.

BASIL BATARINGAYA

WILLIAM KALEMA

CJ OBWANGOR

STILL FIGHTING OVER THE UPC CONTROLS

POLICE ARRESTED SEVERAL of the rowdies who rushed into the road with bits of broken furniture and other weapons.

DRUM: January 1966

On the morning of September 14, 1965, a prominent young politician – Bidandi Ssali – narrowly escaped death in a furious fight between two rival groups of UPC youth wingers in the heart of Kampala. The scramble originated as far back as April 1964, when UPC held their annual delegates conference in Gulu.

When Ibingira took over, the whole framework of the party was altered in the interests of his supporters. Ibingira's ally, Mr Kezekia Musisi, Kampala city councillor and secretary of Uganda's Trade Unions and Labour, jumped from fame to pre-eminence. Musisi's reputation, both politically and socially, warranted the envy of Ssali and he planned to cut his rival down to size. His plan was to organise an anti-Ibingira/Musisi group of youth wingers. In December 1964 Ssali complained to Dr Milton Obote that the two men were forming a Bantu group within UPC whose aim was to oust the Nilotics from power. As a result of this claim, the leading figures of the UPC sat for four consecutive days scratching their heads about the matter. The talk, both in and out of the UPC, had it that the party was split into two irreconcilable sections – the Nilotic group, backed Bidandi and the Bantu group organised by Musisi.

One Saturday, early in September 1964, Mr Ssali organised a group of youth wingers who marched to the

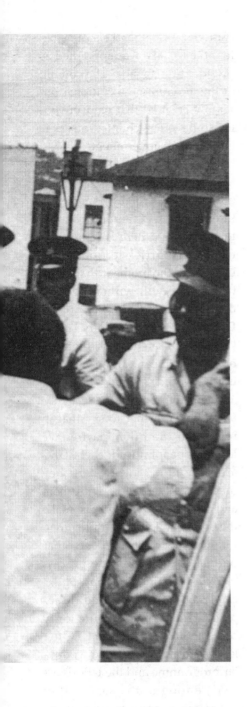

and started searching for Rukikaire to show him what was what.

The following morning Musisi's men – they called themselves the UPC Defence Force – went to Mr Rukikaire's office at the national headquarters of the UPC, determined to defend him should there be any trouble. They walked at his side to the office, where he was due to make a press statement about the menacing attitude of Ssali's boys. Immediately Rukikaire started expressing his disagreement with Ssali's political manoeuvres, a group of heavy-bodied men sprang at him. The

fell one over the other in the corners with nothing better than note books as shields. Ssali was thrown up so he hit his head on the ceiling and then an attempt was made to throw him through the upstairs window.

In this boiling struggle Musisi persuaded his boys to stop fighting. So his own angry henchmen started to punch him, tearing his shirt, to show him they disliked his intrusion into the affair. In the end the police were called upon to break up the riot. Batons were used and a number of arrests made.

KEZEKIA MUSISI'S (centre) own hotheads turned on him and tore his shirt.

European-administered Kampala Club and demonstrated against "racial discrimination". The angry young men raided the club and made away with keys from the keyboard.

Imagine Ssali's disgust when on Monday, September 13, Mr Matthew Rukikaire, national organising secretary of the UPC, issued a statement condemning the youths' barbarous behaviour at the club. Reading the statement, Ssali and his group grew hostile

time for a fierce fight, in the heart of the city, between two rival UPC groups, had come.

The office became a battlefield. Chairs were broken so they could be used as weapons. Tables were dismantled, their flaps serving as shields. Doors were taken off their hinges. The office was pillaged and office documents torn and scattered by both irate factions.

Newspapermen, who had gone to the office to attend the conference,

A newspaperman who claimed that he narrowly escaped death says: "When the fight started I rushed to the door. Before I could make my way out, a chair came buzzing overhead and rested above the door just an inch over my head. I pushed the door open but before I managed to step out a guy grabbed me by the neck and threw me back into the office, pinning my head to the door frame. I said that I was a pressman and Mr Musisi, who knew me personally, materialised my confession." ❏

47

OBOTE SPEAKS TO DRUM

OBOTE TO DRUM: "We may come to a state where we can ban a political party especially when we find that party is working for the interests of a foreign power."

DRUM: April 1966

DRUM: Perhaps Uganda's greatest problem has been the building of national consciousness and of getting the Baganda to see themselves as part of Uganda. Do you think you have already succeeded in bringing this about?

DR OBOTE: Uganda, I would say, is the same as any other developing country in Africa. We have a big problem of building up national consciousness throughout the country and for the last three years we have succeeded tremendously. The people of Uganda are very proud of being Ugandans

and we do not have the type of experiences we had a year before independence when there was this talk of what form of government we were going to have and who was going to be head of state. We don't hear that today. People are very proud of being Ugandans now.

DRUM: Would you actually say that the appointment of the Kabaka as the president of Uganda was one of the more obvious and concrete steps forward?

DR OBOTE: I think that the most important step was when we managed to bring Buganda into the

National Assembly. This came before the Kabaka was appointed as president of Uganda. The coming of Buganda into the National Assembly ensured that we were going to have one country, one parliament, one government.

DRUM: Do you feel that political unity will only finally be achieved through the UPC and do you feel that although there is liberty for the other parties to operate in Uganda at the moment that eventually they will wither away of their own accord?

DR OBOTE: Political unity. I don't know how I can describe that one, but if you mean strong national unity I would say that UPC must, and is, playing its part effectively. I would go further to say that in regard to the other parties we leave the people to judge. The UPC are very much aware that they must have the people with them and consequently they must make the people follow UPC rather than follow other parties. If the other parties disappear in the process we will be only too happy. Still, I can't say that they would disappear. That process could only come about if, firstly, the UPC follows a strong programme, a popular programme and the UPC is active enough to serve that programme, and secondly, if the people come to support that programme.

DRUM: There is no question, Sir, of the banning of other political parties or of creating a one-party state in Uganda at the present time?

DR OBOTE: Banning political parties. We don't have it in our UPC programme. We don't also follow it as a government, but of course I cannot as prime minister now, not talking as president of UPC or even as a member of UPC, say that we cannot ban a political party. We may come to a state where we can ban a political party especially when we find that one political party is working for the interests of a foreign power.

DRUM: Why do you think there has been so much political discontent among the Baganda recently?
DR OBOTE: The leaders of the Kabaka Yekka and the Mengo leaders do not see this goodwill and assume that people outside do not like the Baganda and assume that the Baganda are different from the rest of Uganda. They often do not like to tell the Baganda the truth. They call on the Lukiko members to rise and talk and complain. That's what we call leadership from behind. The future and stability of Uganda lies in everybody: the president, the prime minister and all the others upholding the constitution. I personally think the Baganda are losing their chance of leading Uganda because of their inward-looking policies. If they were really a national party they could take over the highest positions in the country, even the premiership. The day could come when we could have a Muganda premier and a non-Muganda president. But I don't think both the premier and the president should ever come from the same people. That would not work!

DRUM: Could you please state Uganda's case on East African federation. Is there any particular reason you think why this idea, which was recognised as a good idea at the time, has not come about?
DR OBOTE: We in the UPC believe in East African federation and there are some of us who want to see it soon. We are terribly disappointed that the federation hasn't come off but the fact as to

why it didn't come off is contained within the structure and the constitution of Uganda. We are not, as a party, strong enough to make certain changes in the constitution of Uganda or to carry the people with us into federation. I think this is the basic reason.

DRUM: One has often heard that one of the principal snags has been the fact that Nairobi always seems to turn out to be the centre of things and that it would be very difficult to have a federation with Nairobi as the capital?
DR OBOTE: No. I do not think it will be a big problem, at least if the people of Uganda agree to go with us into the federation even Blantyre could be the capital!

DRUM: Is there any particular line on which progress is being made at the present time? I am thinking possibly in terms of the strengthening of the common services.
DR OBOTE: Well, as you might have read in the papers, we have a commission to study the East African Common Services problem. Whether the report will bring the East African countries nearer to one another I do not know, but everybody is hoping so.

DRUM: It seems that the Ugandan economy has been doing quite well since independence. Is there any particular reason you think why Uganda has been doing so well?
DR OBOTE: We have tried to do what we considered was good for Uganda. I think there are several reasons. One was we thought of our priorities only, the type of projects we wanted to see in Uganda, and we laid emphasis on productive projects. The second was that we did not go for what you call prestige products. The third was to get everybody in government to

understand what we were able to do, and what we could not do, and decide on these matters: the UPC members of parliament know the projects we are going to do. So they do not go on promising people things which are not on the programme. We have aimed at seeing that there is money in the pockets of the people and that they have food in their homes.

DRUM: In what pattern do you see the future of the economy evolving? Over on the west coast, for instance, there is the Ghana economy which they say is a socialist economy and I think I can fairly say the Nigerian economy is a free enterprise economy. How do you see the future for the Uganda economy?
DR OBOTE: The future for Uganda's economy can only be planned on what the people of Uganda can produce, that is to say right now we are trying to build primary industries based on agricultural products. Consequently we are concentrating on the co-operative movement. We want to avoid the giving of concessions to very big and important firms and giving them a monopoly in any sector of our economy. In this respect, therefore, we try to encourage foreigners investing in Uganda to do so through the Uganda Development Corporation so our future lies between what you have described in the case of Ghana and Nigeria.

DRUM: You don't think it is necessary here to have any charter for African socialism such as the one announced in Kenya?
DR OBOTE: I always want to know exactly, when I use a word, what is the full meaning of that word. I don't understand what a charter for African socialism is, therefore I only go for what I understand. ❒

EAST AFRICAN FEDERATION – BIG TALK, NO ACTION

ALL THE PRESIDENTS (and their man) in a joyous mood: Kenya's Jomo Kenyatta, Tanzania's Julius Nyerere, Uganda's Milton Obote and his one-time tutor Tom Mboya of Kenya.

OBOTE, NYERERE, Kenyatta and President Kenneth Kaunda of Zambia.

COMRADES *together:*
In the later half of the
sixties Obote grew in-
creasingly close to Nyer-
ere and to his belief in
African socialism.

SO NEAR, AND YET SO
FAR: *As new forces came*
into play the vision of an
East African federation
faded. From the left:
Obote's new army chief
of staff Idi Amin, Obote,
Nyerere and Kenyatta.

DRUM

africa's leading magazine

APRIL 1966 1/-

Registered at G.P.O. as a Newspaper

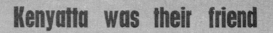

Kenyatta was their friend

DRUM

EAST AFRICA

THIS IS THE FIRST EDITION OF DRUM EVER TO BE PRINTED IN INDEPENDENT AFRICA

PLUS ZAMBIA
DR KENNETH KAUNDA

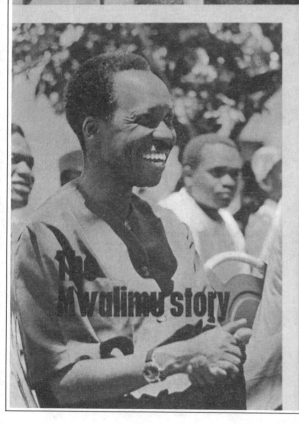

The **Mwalimu story**

Dr Obote speaks to DRUM

AND MALAWI
DR HASTINGS BANDA

PLUS SAFARI SPECIAL

THE CENTRE CANNOT HOLD

The tension building up both within the UPC, and between the central government and Buganda, came to a head in early 1966. In February, while Obote and nine other cabinet ministers were touring the northern region, senior government figures – most notably Grace Ibingira – set out to stage a "palace revolution". The plotters rekindled a 1965 allegation that Prime Minister Obote, Defence Minister Felix Onama, and deputy commander of the army Colonel Idi Amin were involved in smuggling from Zaire. They had the National Assembly pass a resolution bitterly attacking Obote's leadership. Only one government MP, John Kakonge, voted against the motion. At the same time troop movements, and counter-movements, began in Kampala. The chief of staff, Brigadier Opolot, had been requested to intervene on the side of the plotters should the parliamentary option misfire. The Kabaka, one of the leaders of the anti-Obote forces, had reportedly requested military assistance from Britain. The stage had been set for a showdown on Obote's return.

Obote returned on February 12, and at a cabinet meeting on the 14th he agreed to set up an inquiry into the alleged corruption, but refused the demand to suspend Idi Amin. He also accused his rivals of reckless political ambitions and plotting to overthrow his government. On the 19th Obote learned of extensive unauthorised troop movements planned for the following days. By midnight he had cancelled the plans but was convinced that a coup had been planned for the 22nd. On that fateful day the cabinet met, and Obote revealed what a ruthless and decisive politician he could be. As the meeting got underway, a dozen policemen burst into the room and arrested five cabinet ministers, including Grace Ibingira. The next day Idi Amin was promoted to army chief of staff.

Inexorably the confrontation continued to unfold. On April 15, Obote called an extraordinary meeting of the National Assembly, and in a remarkable exercise in parliamentary manipulation, demanded that members pass a new constitution which they had not even seen. In terms of the constitution, Obote became executive president and Buganda lost most of its federal status. Buganda was outraged. On May 20, the Lukiko declared Obote's actions null and void and passed a resolution demanding the withdrawal of the central government from Buganda soil within ten days. Four days later, government troops stormed the Kabaka's palace. After a day's fighting, the palace fell and the Kabaka began his long flight into exile in Britain.

Having defeated his rivals, Obote moved to consolidate his hold on power. In 1967 he introduced a republican constitution which abolished the four kingdoms, and in 1969, after surviving an assassination attempt, banned opposition parties, turning Uganda into a one-party state.

THE KABAKA CRISIS – A NATION IN TURMOIL

THE OLD ORDER CHANGES: The once cordial political relationship between Obote and the Kabaka soured progressively, leading to the final showdown in 1966.

OBOTE AND AMIN: Obote turned increasingly to the military as crises loomed.

DRUM: August 1966

It had to happen. Ugandans had quarrelled for too long. Their disputes had been too open, too democratic, too hard hitting. People marvelled at the way Dr Obote steered the ship of state round one jagged crisis after another. But then came Daudi Ocheng's bitter accusation. Then the news of a plot to take over government. Suddenly the dam burst carrying all before it. In the torrent many were swept from power, many went under for good, but as the waters calmed, Dr Obote was still swimming strongly with the tide.

February 4, 1966: While Dr Obote was on a tour of the north, a motion was passed in parliament demanding an inquiry into allegations that during fighting between the Congo government and rebel forces near the Uganda-Congo border early in 1965 Lieutenant Colonel Idi Amin, deputy army commander, obtained gold, ivory and money from the Congo. The accusations were made by Mr Daudi Ocheng, Kabaka Yekka MP. Ocheng produced a photocopy of Amin's bank account which proved that about £125,000 had passed through. Some ministers supported the call for an inquiry commission. Ocheng also alleged that communist-inspired underground activities aimed at overthrowing the government were taking place in a forest near Mbale. A report of the debate was rushed to Dr Obote.

February 9: The cabinet agreed to the suggestion of Brigadier Opoloto, army commander, that Colonel Amin should be arrested. The order was, however, not executed.

February 15: Cabinet agreed to

appoint a judicial commission to investigate Ocheng's allegations.

February 22: Dr Obote suspended the 1962 constitution on the grounds that the country had lost stability and that certain persons had attempted to overthrow the government with the help of foreign forces. Five cabinet ministers were arrested and charged with misconduct and plotting against the government.

February 22: Colonel Amin was appointed commander-in-chief of the army by Dr Obote.

March 2: A special declaration officially brought the offices of president and vice president to an end, and their powers were invested in Dr Obote. The Kabaka wrote to Dr Obote: "The arrest of five ministers and the suspension of the constitution has caused much anxiety. The existing tensions in the world today demand that we do our utmost to reduce them instead of adding to them in any manner."

In a speech to the nation, Dr Obote replied: "During my absence Sir Edward Mutesa, as president of Uganda, called on foreign diplomats and asked them for armed forces. The secretary to the Katikiro is out on the same mission."

April 15: The 1962 constitution was abrogated and replaced by a new one tabled by Dr Obote, who was also sworn in as Uganda's first executive president. The new constitution was approved in parliament by 55 votes to four. The new constitution decreed Uganda one united country. Among the items affecting Buganda was the provision depriving the Kabaka's government of the right to send indirectly elected members to parliament.

DAUDI OCHENG: Challenged Obote.

MAYANJA-NKANGI: Katikiro.

The Mengo government was also deprived of the right to appoint civil servants to different posts in the government, something over which the Kabaka had always had much influence. The milo-land system by which chiefs collected large sums of money was abolished. In his speech Dr Obote referred to the plot of February 22, when it had been arranged for some battalions of the Uganda army to be moved away on "training exercises".

Last weeks in April: Members of

the Lukiko reacted strongly against the new constitution, and resolved not to obey it. But the Katikiro, Mayanja-Nkangi, caught between two masters – Dr Obote and the Lukiko – spoke neither for nor against. He was all the time trying to avoid direct acceptance or rejection. Some members were so annoyed that they urged him to resign.

Mid May: In a letter to Dr Obote, Democratic Party leader Ben Kiwanuka thundered that he preferred death to being ruled

THE LUKIKO or Buganda parliament threatened to secede from Uganda.

unconstitutionally. The DP issued a statement criticising the new constitution, but in the National Assembly the DP members were instructed to take the oath in favour of it. Six KY members who did not take the oath were forced out of parliament, and some were threatened that they might be deprived of citizenship.

At Mengo the Lukiko stormed more strongly against the new constitution. Some members proposed boycott, others secession. One Ssaza chief who tabled a motion urging peaceful talks with Dr Obote, was shouted down by men in the public gallery. The quarrel intensified when the Kabaka wrote an open letter to the secretary general of the United Nations, U Thant, predicting political unrest if the UN did not intervene. The Lukiko was summoned, and a majority of members supported Sir Edward Mutesa's action.

May 20: Despite the reluctance of the Kabaka's ministers, the Lukiko passed a resolution expelling Dr Obote's government from Bugandan soil – giving May 30 as the day

for the ultimatum to expire. Sir Edward signed the ultimatum.

May 23: The central government reacted by arresting several chiefs who had apparently influenced the Lukiko's expulsion resolution. News of the arrests roused the whole of Buganda. Disturbances everywhere in the kingdom followed. In a battle at Makindye, the former Kabaka's lodge, a number of ex-servicemen raised a scratch battalion to fight against troops of the Uganda army. Two were killed and many arrested.

May 24: The day dawned amid screams and the rattle of machine guns on Mengo hill. Around the Kabaka's palace, troops under Colonel Idi Amin fought all day before overcoming the Kabaka's bodyguards. Smoke from burning houses drifted over the palace buildings and national treasures in the Lubiri were destroyed. The government claimed only 40 people were killed, foreign press put the figure at up to 1,500. Dr Obote accused the Kabaka of being the author of a "three-pronged plan for rebellion". ❐

THE KATIKIRO had much popular support, but was politically powerless.

WHAT OBOTE SAID

House of Assembly May 24, 1966

"It is my duty to inform the House that there has been an open declaration of rebellion by the Buganda Lukiko and by Sir Edward Mutesa.

The government is in possession of documentary evidence that Sir Edward Mutesa had already decided by April 12, 1966, to mount a full scale rebellion against the authority of the government of Uganda.

The method by which this rebellion was to be executed was three-pronged. The important point to note was how the mind of Sir Edward was working in the early part of April, before the House met to debate the Nationalist Consititution on the 15th. In his view the province of Buganda could secede from Uganda, which, as all members of the House know, forms the integral part of the sovereign state of Uganda.

These moves by themselves do constitute an act of rebellion, punishable under the laws passed by this Parliament. Government must be based on the will of the people and nationalism and not on the whims of one man who happens to occupy a position because of what position or status his ancestors occupied in society in the past." ❐

THE KABAKA'S FLIGHT INTO EXILE

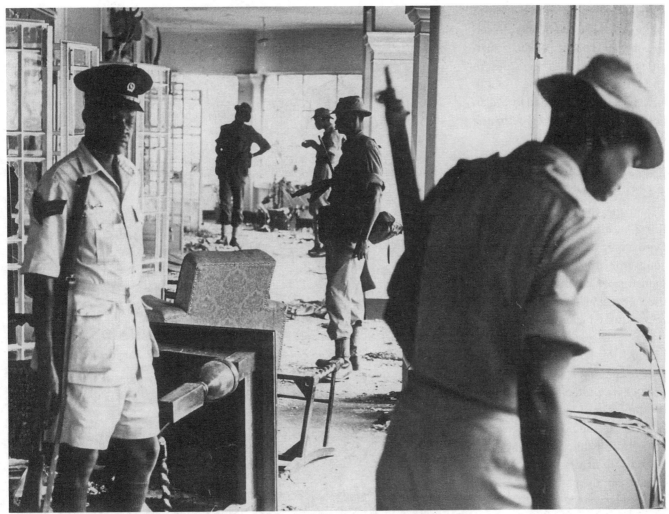

SECURITY FORCE MEMBERS stroll around the rooms of King Freddie's palace after its fall on May 24. Their presence in the ruined palace marks the final saga in the history of the 400-year old kingdom of Buganda.

DRUM: August 1966

At dawn, or rather in that black part of the night which precedes it in Africa, there was shooting. I woke up quickly and pulled on a pair of calf-length suede boots, shirt, trousers and pullover. It was only as I strapped on a webbing belt with a heavy automatic in its holster that I realised what was happening. Even at that moment the Special Force and the first of the eight infantry companies of Uganda army troops under Dr Milton Obote launched their first sortie against the Kalala Gate in the wall surrounding my palace.

It was on May 24. Within 12 hours my whole life suddenly changed.

Instead of being a king and ex-president of Uganda I was a hunted man in my own kingdom, hiding in the bush where I had once hunted big game with my friends. I would not like you to think that I am a playboy monarch from Africa because I mention hunting and palaces. The British government certainly did not make that mistake when, in 1953, they exiled me from the kingdom of Buganda.

Dr Milton Obote does not think of me as a frivolous man. A year after independence he installed me, the Kabaka of Buganda, as president of Uganda. That is why he finally mustered two companies from each of the Uganda army's four

battalions and launched them into the attack on my palace behind an advance party of the Special Force, a security shock group.

As I ran out in the dawn to find the commander of my 100-strong guard (I had always had the right to keep this armed guard), I wished that we really had a stock of arms. I grabbed a carbine, a very good one, which I think had come from behind the iron curtain.

At first my guard, ill-equipped and outnumbered though it was, did very well. The Special Force, poor fellows, forgot when they fired Very pistols to set light to the thatched huts of the banana farmers outside the compound that the

57

flames lit them up from behind as silhouettes. This made them excellent targets. In spite of their casualties the Special Force broke in and ran across the football field to join with others who had forced an entrance at the main gate to the north.

At this stage I was near the old palace. My brother, Prince Henry, joined me there carrying, of all things, an impressive and huge Rigby elephant gun which had come from my gun room. "A real manstopper," he remarked. But we did not feel as gay as this kind of remark may make us sound.

I heard the soldiers shouting as they fought a way into the old palace. As we pulled back somebody on the other side screamed: "Has he a safe in the house?" I saw two soldiers smashing my filing cabinet with their rifle butts and start tearing out the papers.

By midday the situation had become desperate and my little group, about 20-strong, pulled back to the cattle kraal, a building with mud walls and a thatched roof which I thought we might hold. The old military training learned at Warminster was coming back, and although I am a man of peace, I did not want to give in without a fight. It came on to rain, a violent thunderstorm burst, and this produced a lull in the fighting.

Then a most extraordinary thing happened. Our scout saw a procession of women emerging from the palace: my wife was there and my sister and cousins and their maids. Soon they disappeared into dead ground."Hold it," I shouted, but as they disappeared we heard two long bursts of automatic fire from that direction. "It can't be

HEAVY DAMAGE WAS *caused to palace property, including the Kabaka's cars.*

AMONG THE SHELL-DAMAGED *ruins a soldier searches for hidden arms.*

true," I exclaimed, thinking they had been massacred. But at that stage apparently the soldiers let them through. I don't really know what happened. I do know that I have little news of them.

Just to the north of our position the band of my guard company was firing away under the orders of the bandmaster. They did very well

and helped a group of my loyal followers to cover our escape. For I now decided it would be foolish to stay and get killed or captured, I would be more useful to my people if only I could get away. By this time we were almost out of ammunition, and clearly there was no hope left. Under the covering fire of these brave men we started to move back, nine of us, towards the

KABAKA: "I knew the country well and I have always felt at home in the bush."

stage of our unlikely escape in crowded comfort.

We hid for a while and I tried to work out a plan of action. I sent out scouts, one to see if my yacht on Lake Victoria could be found. He reported that the government forces had shelled and sunk it. So one escape route was closed. Eastwards, towards the Kenyan border, army patrols seemed very active, so we decided not to try that way.

The only sensible thing was to start walking westwards; to head, in fact, for the Congo. We moved off as carefully as possible. Of course I knew the country well and I have always felt at home in the bush, but moving through the bush is a slow business, and sometimes we had to take risks. A friendly Muganda gave us a lift in his car. By now there were only three of us: myself, the adjutant of my guard, Captain Jehoash Katende, and an ADC, George Mallo.

Round a bend in the road I saw with horror that we were on the Buganda border, as an army unit had set up a road block. I could even see their shoulder flashes and knew their regiment. I knew that orders had gone out that I was to be taken dead or alive, and that if we were captured everything could depend on the mood of a sergeant or a lieutenant. The driver acted quickly; he swung the car round and drove off at speed. This was only one of our narrow escapes.

Once I sprained my ankle through over-eagerness to get out of the way of a lorry. It suddenly came into sight and we thought it was an army vehicle. I leapt into the undergrowth and hurt my ankle rather badly.

12-foot high wall which surrounds the compound. The wall looked very high. Somewhere behind us three bazooka shots rang out. People shoved and pushed and I managed to get up on to the wall. For the first time I felt frightened. What should I do, where could I go? I offered a brief prayer to the Almighty and then we went over the wall. As I landed there was a

sharp pain in my back, the beginning of a long ache that lasted all the time we were on the run.

I felt dizzy and sick because of this injured back as we made our way up the hill. After a while, when I felt at my gloomiest, there suddenly appeared along the road a taxi, indeed two taxis. I promptly hailed them and we made the first

KING FREDDIE FLIES IN: The deposed Kabaka on his arrival at London airport on June 23, 1966. The royal Muganda was given a VIP reception at the airport.

On another occasion we were walking along a dirt road, rather disconsolately. I had "borrowed" a rather decrepit long mackintosh, and neither of my friends looked exactly smart. In fact, to the soldiers in the two Land Rovers which squealed to a standstill beside us, we must have looked like any other trio of shabby Africans wandering along a deserted road. They wanted to know what we were doing out after curfew. I simply explained that we were on a long journey: just how long, those soldiers will never know. Satisfied, they drove off with a warning.

Clearly my best disguise was African anonymity. It was not necessary to dress up, just to dress down.

For food we took berries and anything we could find; sometimes we had to take food and sometimes friendly villagers would give us things like sweet potatoes. But I did not want to create trouble for friendly Baganda by staying in their villages.

My back got worse and worse. I could not sleep properly when we laid up for the night in thorn thick-ets. We used to try and find a remote spot, get as far into the undergrowth as possible, and then seal the entrance to our hideout with thorn branches. The defences were as much against wild animals as against patrols. We could hear jackals screaming: we could often hear the big cats in the lonely African night.

Early in our four-week march to freedom we had decided to get rid of our weapons. We each had an automatic and ammunition, or that is what I thought until I gave the order to throw them away. Then I noticed there were four instead of three. "I had two," said Captain Katende with a reluctant grin.

The idea was that if we were captured with arms it might give the government a pretext for declaring that we were rebels in arms, and an excuse for shooting us on the spot. But later on I regretted having decided to chuck them away. We felt rather naked without them in the bush and in the great Savannah lands.

I was thankful, though, that I had learned so much about the country and wildlife on my shooting expeditions. Now I made use of my bush craft. When we thought we were being pursued, I heard a herd of elephant and decided on a plan I would never have chosen had I been hunting. The elephants seemed to be on our side. We were able to slip across in front of the advancing herd so that they obligingly trampled out and destroyed our tracks, putting off the pursuers.

For some time we hid away in the Masaka. I had a hunting lodge there and thought it would be a good place to hide until I felt better and more fit for the journey. I was tired, and in great pain because of my injured back. Unfortunately, the troops had thought about the hunting lodge and their patrols were so active in the area that we had to go to ground in the bush.

by only a stitch, and in grave danger of falling off. He could not make up his mind what to do. He kept giving orders and then, afraid of local rebels, changing those and then thinking of something else.

helpful motorists that I eventually arrived dusty and dirty in the capital Bujumbura.

The place did not seem at all strange to me for I had many friends there.

THE LONDON BED-SITTER in the shabby docklands suburb which became home to the deposed Kabaka as he lived out his second spell in exile.

After a while we felt the time had come to move again, and eventually made our way across the Ugandan border into the Congo. This is a part of the world I would not have chosen to pass through had there been any other way because fighting is still going on there between government troops and rebels and European mercenaries are active.

Before long we ran into trouble. A Congolese army patrol held us up – six men under a very sloppy and incompetent corporal. Even his stripes seemed to be held in place

No one paid much attention to him, but they seemed a rather trigger-happy lot and we were very pleased to part company with them for we really had been prisoners. Soon after that we managed to wind up in Burundi and started to make arrangements to leave Africa. I just could not take any more. My back was giving trouble and I had managed to catch a terrible fever in the bush.

Once in Burundi we felt much safer. Now it was possible to hitchhike openly and without fear. In fact it was by a series of lifts from

Naturally I know the king and members of his family. Several ministers are also among my friends. I went straight to see two people I knew and they speedily put me in touch with other people. The cabinet met and decided to give me assistance.

In London I quickly began to recover from my ordeal on the run. I even felt well enough to summon my tailor and order some suits to replace the old khaki shirt and trousers in which I arrived here at the end of the 14-hour flight. ❐

HOW DOES HE STAY ON TOP?

A GROWING ARMY: On becoming president, Obote enlarged the army radically.

DRUM: December 1967

When the central government troops attacked and captured the former Kabaka of Buganda's palace, some political observers claimed that Obote's government would not last more than six months. They argued that nobody could rule Uganda without the Kabaka and the support and co-operation of the Baganda.

Now more than a year-and-a-half later Dr Obote is still at the helm of Uganda and his government is still going strong. However, a lot has happened in Uganda since Sir Edward Mutesa's departure for Britain via Burundi on that rainy afternoon in May last year.

Uganda is now a republic. There has been a long wait since independence in 1962 for the simple reason that Uganda had four tribal kingdoms which kept her a monarchy.

Why were the political observers wrong in their judgement of Dr Obote's ability to survive? People have underestimated the ability and determination of Dr Obote and his colleagues to build one strong country.

A close study of Dr Obote, the man who has stood up strongly against the powerful Buganda monarch and his feudal supporters, shows that he has played his cards very carefully and indeed shrewdly. Above all, his strong conviction that Uganda must be one country with a strong central government and a society where there is no kind of discrimination, has helped him to prevail over his opponents.

Ever since Dr Obote came to power, he has steadily pursued the course of unification along the road that has had its ups and downs. He has been determined to knit together the kingdoms and other local administrations under the authority of the central government. From the very beginning, Dr Obote recognised that the three traditional rulers of Bunyoro, Ank-

FLED

DEPOSED

DETAINED

SIR EDWARD MUTESA

TITO WINYI of Bunyoro

SIR GASYONGA of Ankole

BALAKI KIRYA: Minister

ole and Toro kingdoms presented no serious problems. The real stumbling block was the Kabaka of Buganda, Sir Edward Mutesa, who is now in self-exile in London.

The adoption, in September 1966, of a republican constitution in theory somehow shows that Dr Obote has achieved one burning ambition. The dreams of a young militant politician have been realised. The confusion of Ugandan politics has given way to orthodox Africanism.

The feudalists have been heavily defeated. The central government reigns supreme and the old kingdom of Buganda has been divided into four administrative districts to bring it in line with other local administrations throughout Uganda.

What is Obote like and what is the secret of his success? He is a brilliant and able man. He is friendly and has a great sense of humour. He also has a tremendous personality.

If you add these qualities to his extensive and deep study and analysis of people and problems it gives you the secret of his success. President Obote is also very devoted to the cause of the common man. He took a job as a labourer soon after leaving Makerere University to study the conditions of the common man.

One of the main criticisms made against President Obote over the past year is that he has ignored his ruling Uganda People's Congress. For there have been no party activities since the political crisis last year. And the critics point to the number of friends he has lost and ministers who have resigned or been detained in the constitutional struggle.

But Dr Obote recently answered his critics with a dramatic announcement that the party was all set to establish a new image, character and vitality. President Obote said that the UPC would plead guilty for having been involved "head over heels in promoting national unity with a zip".

It would accept blame for the alleged "damage and mischief" of having expanded primary and secondary education, increased the output of teachers and numbers of Ugandans at universities, the setting up of a housing corporation and the launching of a trading corporation that would put

EVER CLOSER: Obote and Amin.

complete control of internal and external trade in Ugandan hands.

The president said UPC was not weak because it still generated the confidence of the masses. The party had no room for intellectual detachment or fence-sitting. In future it will be in the forefront of the struggle to improve Ugandans' lives. ❑

By Charles Binayisa

GEORGE MAGEZI: Minister

NM NGOBI: Minister

DR EBS LUMU: Minister

GRACE IBINGIRA: Minister

MYSTERY OF THE ATHI RIVER MURDERS

DRUM: July 1968

For days the disappearance of the two Ugandan girls made screaming headlines in the press and over the radio in Kenya. Pretty Lilian Millie, a 17-year-old Kampala nightclub hostess and Sara Massa, a 21-year-old Uganda police woman, seemed to have vanished without a trace.

Police got scant information until a week later when two heavy sacks were seen by a *shamba* woman floating on the Athi River, 18 miles from Nairobi. Police arrived and opened the bags. What they saw inside turned their stomachs.

This was no ordinary murder and the victims were no ordinary girls. They were well known to the Uganda police. Lilian was not only a nightclub hostess but also a police informer who knew certain supporters of the Kabaka Yekka intimately. Sara was a reliable member of the Uganda police force and was stationed at the Central Police Station, Kampala. Both arrived in Nairobi on March 31 last year, escorted by senior Uganda CID men, to look for Kabaka Yekka supporters who had fled to Kenya.

It all began in Uganda on January 12, 1967. On that day President Milton Obote and Vice President John Babiiha attended a reception at Luzira Prison. A group of Kabaka Yekka supporters planned to kill the president on this night. The motive was revenge for the attack by Uganda government troops on the Kabaka's palace at Mengo and his subsequent flight to London.

The would-be assassins waited in the darkness near a bridge for the president's return from the reception. What probably saved Obote's life was that he returned to Kampala an hour earlier than sched-uled. Mr Babiiha carried on officiating at the reception until the end when, escorted by security men, he left to return to Kampala.

As his car neared the bridge, several shots rang out from the darkness. All missed. Security men darted out in the direction of the shots but only heard the roar of a car zooming away.

Informants, including Lilian, named several well-known supporters of the Kabaka Yekka as the alleged plotters of the shooting conspiracy. They named Abraham Senkoma, former *aide de camp* to the Kabaka and a captain in the palace guards; Basilio Lukyamuzi, a former Kabaka Yekka member of the National Assembly; Daniel Kiwanuka, Kabaka Yekka youth leader; Andrew Kyeyune and John Oboo, former lieutenants in the Uganda army.

All the men named were Baganda except John Oboo who was a Teso Mudama. Kyeyune and Oboo were sacked from the Ugandan army during the emergency. They then switched sides and joined the Kabaka's palace guards. Senkoma, Kyeyune and Oboo fought against Uganda government troops during the attack on Mengo in 1966 and later helped the Kabaka in his escape to Rwanda.

Police launched an extensive manhunt in Uganda for these men but without much success. Information was then received that some of the fugitives had fled to Nairobi and the hunt switched to Kenya. But word of the Ugandan police's arrival in Nairobi leaked out almost immediately through Uganda's police superintendent Katerega's own mouth and the fugitives were put on the alert. From then on, the hunters became the hunted. The fate of the two girls was sealed.

Police believe Katerega leaked out the secret to Miss M, a Kabaka Yekka supporter living in exile in Nairobi. Miss M in turn informed Mr H, a freelance actor, and through the news grapevine of the thousands of Baganda exiles living in Nairobi, word reached the fugitives hiding in Eastleigh. Baganda exiles in Nairobi had formed a Friends of Buganda Society whose members kept in close touch with one another.

Once in Nairobi, Lilian toured the popular night spots to trace the wanted men. On Government Road she met two friends from Uganda. They told her they knew someone who could put her in touch with Senkoma and company. A rendezvous was arranged for the next morning at the Hotel Mandovi with this contact man – Kizito Bulwadda, a former well-known Kabaka Yekka supporter and Lukiko member. He promised to try to find the men. Lilian gave him her name and the telephone number of the Princess Hotel where she was staying.

Bulwadda hurried to Eastleigh where Lukyamuzi, Senkoma, Kiwanuka, Kyeyune and Oboo were all living with Krenima Mawanda, who claimed to be a prince of Buganda. The information that the girls were looking for them was no news to the fugitives. They decided to forestall the plans of the Uganda police. The Saturday Plan was hatched to get rid of Lilian and Sara.

That very night a call was put through to Lilian at the Princess Hotel by one of the fugitives in the name of Senkoma. It is not certain whether the caller was Senkoma himself. The caller said he had

LAST GESTURE OF DEFIANCE before oblivion: After the death sentence, Kyeyune gives the Kabaka Yekka salute while Kiwanuka raises his fist. The two men took the sentence with resigned calmness.

heard Lilian was in Nairobi and that she was anxious to meet him. It was arranged that "Senkoma" would pick her up at the Princess the next day between 9 a.m. and 10 a.m.

An ambush was laid at the Princess and police waited to grab Senkoma or any of the other wanted men who came to pick up Lilian. The girls waited, the police waited. But no one turned up. At 4 p.m. another call came through for Lilian from "Senkoma". The caller apologised for not turning up that morning. "What about meeting me near the Kenya Cinema at 8:30 p.m.?" Lilian agreed.

The girls left the Princess at 8:30. They were seen by the hotel manager heading towards the direction of the Kenya Cinema. They were never seen alive again.

Police believe the fugitives assigned Mawanda to pick up the girls because he was not one of the suspects on their list. He met the girls near the cinema and took them to the Commando Bar where the others were waiting. There, the girls entered their car, a Zephyr, for what they thought would be an entertaining evening out.

But the Zephyr headed towards Mombassa Road. According to the police, there were seven persons in it: the two girls and Mawanda, Senkoma, Kiwanuka, Kyeyune and Oboo. The girls sat in the back. On and on it drove towards the sluggish Athi River. Just before the bridge, the Zephyr veered right into a side road and came to a halt near the river's edge. The two girls were dragged out. According to a confession made by

Oboo, Mawanda and Senkoma took Sara away while Kiwanuka, Kyeyune and Oboo got hold of Millie.

"After admitting that she had come to identify us, she begged for mercy," Oboo said. The girls were then strangled. Their bodies were doubled, tied with pieces of rope and thrust into gunny bags, already weighted with large rocks. The bags were then heaved over the cliff into the water below.

In the weeks that followed the girls murder, Kenyan and Ugnadan police captured and brought to trial the five fugitives. The Kenyan court sentenced Oboo, Kiwanuka and Kyeyune to death, but acquitted Senkoma and Mawanda. However, they were arrested outside the court and extradited to Uganda. ❐

POPE PAUL'S BLESSING

THE POPE IN UGANDA: Crowds greet the Pope during his first African visit.

DRUM: September 1969

It was a day of splendour when the Pontiff, Pope Paul VI, stepped on Africa's soil for the first time. The place: Entebbe, Uganda. The day: Thursday July 31, 1969.

Thousands of pilgrims from all corners of the world poured into Kampala for the historic visit of Pope Paul. By 7 a.m., nine hours before his arrival, people began taking up their positions by the roadside, and by midday, the 21-mile stretch from Entebbe to the capital was packed with joyful sightseers.

Pope Paul was met by Uganda's president Dr Milton Obote, who introduced His Holiness to four heads of state, President Julius Ny-

erere of Tanzania, President Kenneth Kaunda of Zambia, President Kayibanda of Rwanda and President Micombero of Burundi. The Pope stressed his desire for peace, and promised that he would not rest until peace had been restored in Africa and the world. He said: "We bear witness by our pilgrimage to the sanctuary of the martyrs of Uganda, whose blood bathed the Cross planted by the first missionaries."

Half-a-million people later watched the Pope consecrate the shrine to the fallen martyrs. In the course of the ceremony the Pope baptised 22 people in commemoration of the martyrs – and announced the donation of $200,000 towards the completion of the shrine. ❐

WHEN UGANDA'S MARTYRS WENT OUT TO DIE

DRUM: February 1968

He is 107 years of age. He is like any other villager – simple and contented. Yet his name is among those to be found in the great archives of the Catholic church in Uganda, and possibly in the Vatican. For he is the only living witness to the tragedy of the 22 martyrs.

I met him just a few weeks before the eightieth anniversary of the death of the famous Uganda martyrs – now saints – at his home, Kasasa, not far from Masaka. For days I had been searching for his place through fertile valleys and forest-clad hills.

It was the first time I'd seen such an old human being. His partly-hairy ears, neck, arms and legs were all wrinkled. His coffee-like skin seemed to be going rather grey. The nails of the lazy hands and feet were brown and protruding showing his long life's hardship. His head carried no hair and his eyes were red but strong.

He told me about St Charles Lwanga, most famous of the Uganda martyrs whose birthplace is only five villages away from Musa's present home. Books have been written about martyr Lwanga, but few could have described him more vividly than the old man Musa. Very slowly he began: "Lwanga was younger than me. About nine or ten years. His family was a large one but Lwanga was my chosen companion. His father had a house one door away

CHILDREN FROM THE family of St Charles Lwanga pray at his shrine at Kasasa.

from mine. He was my cousin. We spent most of the day playing.

"Towards the end of the reign of King Mutesa I, or at the beginning of his son Mwanga II's reign, many young and strong men were commanded to leave home and go and serve the King. I was among the first to be selected for the royal service. Lwanga was not old enough to be honoured. Later on, however, he did join me, and it did not take him long to settle down. He immediately became the most popular page in the palace. He was the most jocular fellow of the whole lot and he always had something up his sleeve.

"After some time he met a White missionary who, obviously, was trying to find his way into the palace to teach the word of God. Lwanga became one of his converts. One evening Lwanga came to our home all excited. He had come to tell us about the White man and his religion. We had heard of the White man but we had never attended any of his preachings. And here was Lwanga, a boy we always referred to as "our kid cousin", who had come to tell us about the religion. We listened to him. This is something one could not resist from Lwanga. He was a first class speaker. From then on we used to attend the preachings though we were not very active like him.

"One day we learned from the court sources the king was angered by the Christians and was

planning to persecute them. The first reaction, naturally, was to go and warn our 'rebel' cousin. We found Lwanga on his way to Mapera, the White missionary. Upon hearing our story, Lwanga answered in his not-too-serious manner: 'This is my problem. Mapera has assured us that whatever happened it would be only three days before we returned. Since then I never saw him.'

"I am a fervent Catholic, and when I was strong enough used to go to church everyday to pray to Lwanga. But at the same time, Lwanga is my blood. If only he had listened and escaped with us, probably he would have been living. I really blame Mapera for bluffing them into believing the

tale of the journey that would only take three days. Now 80 years has passed and I am still waiting." ❑

MUSA NNYUMBA as he is today – the only living witness to the tragedy.

SEVEN YEARS OF FREEDOM

LOADING CRUSHED CEMENT stone for transportation to the processing plant.

DRUM: October 1969

Right in the heart of Africa is the cradle of the Nile where nine million Ugandans will this year celebrate the seventh anniversary of the day when Uganda – the pearl of Africa – took her place among the free independent nations of the world.

The 1966 destruction of the Kabakaship and the division of the kingdom of Buganda into four provinces brought in its wake fundamental changes which President Obote explained to the masses in a successful meet-the-people tour which took him to every corner of the country.

Meanwhile the ruling Uganda People's Congress has held two delegates' conferences, one in Gulu and another, attended by President Julius Nyerere of Tanzania and President Kenneth Kaunda of Zambia, in Kampala. During the latter conference, declarations were made to the effect that Uganda, while remaining non-aligned in its foreign policy, would nonetheless be "moving to the left".

Due to the country's stability, several international bodies such as the Commonwealth Parliamentary Association, the World Health Organisation, Food and Agriculture Organisation, and International Cotton Advisory Committee, have held meetings in Kampala. The heads of states in East and Central Africa have also met in Uganda to ponder on the doctrine of good neighbourliness. President Obote has made efforts

BAGGING UGANDA'S TOP foreign exchange earner – processed coffee.

THE UGANDA ENAMELLING company is

to stop the Nigerian war by hosting the Biafran-Nigerian talks.

For many years Uganda trade has been dominated by non-Ugandans, as well as the high posts in the industrial private sector. This undesirable situation has been debated in the National Assembly and the government has taken steps to Ugandanise trade and to curb window-dressing.

Through the Ministry of Commerce and Industry, headed by Mr WW Kalema, much has been achieved. Cotton ginning, which has been in the hands of Asians for several years, is now the monopoly of co-operative societies, and coffee is also following the same track. A new ministry for marketing and co-operatives has been created to make sure that crops fetch reasonable prices and the co-operative movement runs smoothly.

To give Ugandans an opportunity to participate fully in the economic progress of the country, the National Trading Corporation (NTC) was formed to assist, promote and advance Africans in the field of trade through credit facili-

ties. So far the corporation has been able to give assistance in commerce to a limited number of Ugandans and soon it will be expanded to reach as many traders as possible. The NTC has been appointed sole distributor of a number of commodities.

Uganda's trade with European Economic Community (EEC) countries is becoming increasingly adverse. In the years 1966 to 1968 inclusive, Uganda's exports to EEC countries continued to decline, from 164 million shillings in 1966 to 124 million in 1968.

One of the outstanding features of the economy over the last ten years has been the rapid development of the industrial sector, which has grown at a consistently higher rate than the economy as a whole. The expansion of industrial production is consistent with the objective of creating a balanced economy, by reducing Uganda's high degree of dependence on both imports and the export of primary products which are susceptible to fluctuating export earnings.

The strategy adopted for the development of the industrial sector

has concentrated on the creation of domestic industries which can produce goods which were previously imported, and are able to make full use of raw materials available locally. New factories which have gone into production in the past year include plastic goods, dry cell torch batteries, paper, cardboard boxes, protein foods from soya beans and the spinning and weaving of cotton.

According to last year's target of school intake set by the Ministry of Education, headed by Dr JS Luyimbazi Zake, 700,000 students were to be enrolled from primary seven, but 632,000 was the figure admitted. The shortfall was due to difficulties experienced in the introduction of the new primary seven system, which is one year shorter than the colonial system of eight years.

Since independence, the average wage for Africans has been rising steadily. The trade unions took a big stride, and nearly every worker belongs to a trade union and pays union fees. The central union, Uganda Labour Congress, was suspended due to a dispute which arose between its leaders. ❐

uilding up considerable export orders.

THE UGANDAN TEXTILE industry is largely controlled by Asian industrialists.

ASSASSINATION BID THAT FAILED

WOULD-BE-ASSASSIN Mohamed Sebaduka re-enacts his attempt to kill President Obote for the police investigation.

DRUM: June 1970

It could have been the most audacious assassination in modern Africa – an unknown taxi-driver killing President Milton Obote while he was surrounded by troops and security guards.

But it failed by the narrowest of margins; because a semi-automatic Czech pistol jammed after the first shot, and because a Chinese-made hand grenade failed to explode. President Obote suffered minor face wounds when the first bullet ripped through his cheeks, damaging some of his teeth and part of his tongue. But, to Uganda's great good fortune, the damage was slight, and he was soon back at his duties.

Ever since the 1966 crisis, during which the Kabaka fled into exile in Britain, Obote's advisers knew he was a target for assassination. He knew it himself. And he narrowly escaped in 1966 when a group of desperate men fired on the car of Vice President John Babiiha, mistaking it for the president's. Fortunately Mr Babiiha, too, escaped.

Dr Obote was shot and wounded at an historic moment for Uganda. He had just closed the annual conference of his UPC, moments after the delegates had unanimously endorsed proposals for a new "move to the left" socialist strategy, known as the Common Man's Charter, and had called on President Obote and his government to make Uganda a one-party state.

But the shooting was not sparked off by resentment at those policies. It was planned long before they took shape. The plotting began in June or July 1969, and the shooting did not take place until 10:40 p.m. on December 19, 1969.

The story of the plot came out when six men pleaded guilty in a Kampala magistrates' court to charges of attempted murder. It was a fascinating story that CID chief Mohamed Hassan unfolded for the magistrate.

The scene of the shooting was a dark area outside Uganda's Lugogo Stadium, where President Obote and a small party of his aides emerged from the brightly-lit conference hall, with the cheers of the delegates still ringing in their ears. For Dr Obote it was a great moment; the Common Man's Charter, which he himself had drawn up to give Uganda a completely new image, had been enthusiastically adopted by his party, and he had been given a clear mandate to go ahead with it.

As he emerged from the hall, he had 15 yards to walk to his waiting car. He set off along the concrete path; a few feet away, the Uganda army band was playing the UPC song, Uganda is Moving Forward. Other delegates were filing slowly out of the conference hall behind the president.

Then from a distance of only four feet, Mohamed Sebaduka, standing beside an ornamental cypress tree, raised his pistol and fired. The crack of the gun echoed through

THE NIGHT OF THE SHOOTING: *The president is seen leaving Lugogo Staduim after having his controversial Common Man's Charter adopted by the UPC. Minutes after this photograph was taken, Obote was shot.*

the night air – and the band kept on playing. Someone standing near Sebaduka grabbed him. He dropped his gun. Dr Obote's bodyguard flung the president to the ground and lay on top of him, to provide protection. Another bodyguard fired two shots at the would-be assassin, wounding Sebaduka in the head.

The shots panicked the crowd and people started running to get away from the bullets. In a crowded, confined area, with little light, it was frightening – no wonder the crowd ran. The army band dropped their instruments and ran too – they were only feet from the bullets.

OBOTE SPEAKS *on his vision of a self-reliant socialist Uganda on the fateful night.*

COMPLETE RECOVERY: Obote is wished well on his discharge from hospital.

gling in the crowd. They were all wearing UPC shirts in the party colours of red, blue and black, printed with pictures of Dr Obote. And they were carrying UPC membership cards which they had bought to ensure that they could get into the stadium unchallenged.

Outside, among hundreds of parked cars, was a stolen Anglia with false number plates. They had stolen it days earlier for the very purpose of making a quick getaway. Despite his wound from the pistol of the president's bodyguard, Sebaduka drove the getaway car. After dropping off his co-conspirators Sebaduka dumped the car and set it on fire. All the police found was the burnt out shell, and it was not until later, when the pieces of the jigsaw began to fit together, that they knew it was the car used by the would-be assassins.

In the confusion Sebaduka struggled free and joined the fleeing crowd. His fellow assassin, Yowana Wamala, standing beside him, saw him drop the gun and realised it could give them away. He reached down and picked it up, then quickly slid it into the branches of the tree beside him. He left on the gun a vivid thumb-print which was later to form part of the chain of evidence. At the same time, another man in the group threw the hand grenade. If it had exploded, it would have caused tragic destruction in that crowded area. But the providence which saved President Obote saved the other people too.

The assassination group left the Lugogo Stadium quickly, min-

The background to the assassination attempt is an incredible story. The plotters imported firearms into Uganda. The firearms were kept at Masaka, 80 miles west of Kampala. On December 18, old man Kisule (67 years old), who had recruited Sebaduka and Wamala, was sent to bring the guns and the hand grenade. He returned the next day, the very day the UPC conference was to close. At midday a meeting was held, and the arms were inspected. Then the group went to the house of Princess Ndagire, a member of the Buganda royal family, for a final briefing. Said police chief Mr Hassan in court: "This final meeting and briefing was attended by a Kampala lawyer. This lawyer was the leader of a political party now proscribed as a society dangerous to peace and order in Uganda. The plot of the assassination was reviewed and agreed on." ❒

SHOWING SUPPORT: Kaunda, Obote and Mobutu at the opening of the UPC meet.

UGANDA MOURNS BRIGADIER OKOYA

STRANGE CASE OF "KIDNAPPED" DIPLOMAT

DRUM: May 1970

Brigadier Pierino Yere Okoya, commander of the Second Infantry Brigade of the Uganda army, who was earlier this year found murdered with his wife at the couple's home in Gulu, was one of Uganda's ablest soldiers. The 46-year-old brigadier joined the then Kings African Rifles 20 years ago. He was commissioned as a lieutenant in 1962. After independence he rose rapidly in rank, becoming a captain, major and colonel in 1965. In 1968 he was made a brigadier.

In a tribute, President Obote, who was a close friend, described Okoya as a "born leader, and friend of all". His dedication to discipline was an inspiration to officers and men of Uganda's armed forces, Dr Obote said. ❑

DRUM: August 1970

By faking his own "kidnapping" – an event which caused worldwide concern because it was the first reported kidnapping of a foreign diplomat in Africa – 49-year-old British diplomat Brian Lea hoped to draw attention to the plight of thousands of Asians in East Africa.

This verdict, pronounced to the world after a six-week long inquiry by Mr Justice Russell, answered the main speculation aroused by the Lea affair in Uganda, and in many other countries. Lea claimed he was kidnapped and held in a remote jungle hut; but the other version, which the judge believed, was that he conspired with three Asians to fake his own kidnapping, and in fact spent the last weekend voluntarily on tiny Nkunze Island in Lake Victoria. Judge Russell's words were dramatic: "I can only state with utmost confidence that I find Mr Lea's account of the matter is false."

But the affair aroused important questions – far more important than Lea himself. They concerned the future of the Asians in Uganda (something like 50,000 of them hold British nationality, and expect to be ordered to leave the country to make room for Ugandans) and the future of relations between Uganda and Britain. It has certainly not improved the lot of Asians in Uganda. In fact, most Asians were shocked by the story unfolded by Lea and his accomplices. And they feared that it would harden local opinion against them, a fear which seems to be fully justified. ❑

BRIGADIER Yere Okoya with Obote.

NKUNZE ISLAND: Site of Lea's hideaway built below the dense undergrowth.

LET THE BEAT OF OUR DRUM BE THE PACEMAKER

OBOTE THE STATESMAN: Obote and his army chief, General Idi Amin, usher Presidents Nyerere and Kaunda to their plane.

DRUM: October 1970

Opening the new session of parliament, President Obote sent a message of the seventies to the nation, saying: "In our march through the decade into the sunshine of political and economic freedom, let the beat of our drum, and not the trumpets and bugles of others, be the pacemaker."

He added: "We must cultivate and develop greater courage and boldness than hitherto for the consolidation of the gains of the past decade and the creation of new conditions for the advancement of all."

One constitutional aspect of the beat of the Uganda drum, Dr Obote said, was the decision to discard the Westminster inheritance of a divided House of Parliament. And he warned members that they had to deliberate on all matters for the good of Uganda, never for the advancement of the fortunes of a political party.

The president urged members of parliament, people in the public service, and in particular teachers, to make it known and realise that the strength of the economy of Uganda would for some time to come rest on the shoulders of the farmer.

It was the sweat of the farmer that had built the towns with all the glittering amenities seen today, he said. It was the same sweat that should begin to transform, in the new decade, the rural areas into busy and prosperous localities with amenities not too different from those found in the urban centres.

Dr Obote urged: "Let us put our heads together to find a national answer to the challenges and the problems of the seventies. The call of the moment, which will continue to echo in our ears throughout the decade, is that both the political and economic power be

THE COMMON MAN'S CHARTER

DRUM: October 1970

The old order changeth, yielding place to new. That is exactly what has happened in Uganda in the new political culture ushered in by the adoption of the Common Man's Charter.

The charter, brainchild of President Milton Obote, a man who has risen from the humility of a labourer to the stature of a world-famous statesman, does not merely admire or preach socialism as a political ideology. The charter lays down a practical strategy for the fulfilment of the aspirations of socialism and enforces the view that the entire nation must be involved in, and committed to, the cause of nation-building.

To implement this philosophy, President Obote has announced new measures and proposals embodied in documents such as the Nakivubo Pronouncements, the Proposals for National Service, the Communication from the Chair, and the latest one which embodies proposals for new methods of electing the people's representatives in parliament.

The basic consideration behind the new election proposals is that representatives of the people in parliament should be elected by a cross-section of the people of Uganda as a whole, leaving no room for "any real or imaginary factionalism" in an election. It is proposed that a parliamentary candidate should contest the election in four constituencies and, if elected, should represent the four constituencies but be known as a member for his basic constituency.

On "tribal politics" President Obote's 23-page document urges the party to direct its attention to destroying the tendencies which tie any representative of the people to local tribal issues. ❐

---

vested in the people and be exercised by them.

"We must resolve now, at the beginning of the new decade, to finance as much as possible of our development programmes from local resources, and then seek from our friends in other parts of the world any necessary assistance which will increase our capacity to develop more and more of our human and material resources."

The president reported to the country that there were people in Uganda who claimed to be "immigrant settlers". He warned that the Immigration Act of 1969 applied to all such people.

Dr Obote said that these people were not Ugandan citizens and were not entitled to remain in Uganda at their own will or because they could not be admitted to any other country. These people had never shown any commitment to the cause of Uganda or even of Africa. "Their interest was to make money which they exported to various capitals of the world on the eve of independence," he said.

He observed, however, that these people were human beings and although they had shown every sign of being rootless in Uganda, "we would like their departure not to cause either them or those dear to them, or even ourselves, any human affliction."

Dr Obote's message to African leaders on Africa Day, May 25, was "listen to the people". He explained: "If we all listen to the people, we will sustain and maintain our political independence.

"If we listen to the people we will win the war for economic independence. If we listen to the people, the southern part of Africa shall be free." ❐

KIGANIRA RETURNS

DRUM: April 1968 – *After his release from prison Kibuka Kiganira, the self-styled prophet jailed for his wild incantations during the Kabaka's first exile, returned to his mother taking her in warm embrace. Although he is seen in traditional bark cloth and clutching a spear, since his release he has refrained from the messianic practises which saw him jailed twice during the 1950s.*

Above, left: Sheikh Swaibu Nsubuga, was arrested after the attempted assassination of President Obote last December.
Above, right: Minister of Education in the former Buganda Kingdom Government, Abu Mayanja, lifts his arms in delight

FREEDOM DAY!

It was a day of joy recently for 27 Ugandans. They were all released simultaneously from detention under their country's Emergency Regulations — and were met by jubilant crowds of relations who had gathered outside Luzira Prison, near Port Bell on the outskirts of Kampala. The first inkling that they were to be released came the afternoon before the joyous occasion, when Minister of Internal Affairs Basil Bataringaya simply listed the 27 names and said they would be freed. No reasons were given either for their release or for their detention when their names were announced.

The 27 included some famous personalities. There was Abu Mayanja, once Minister of Education in the former Buganda Kingdom Government and a leading opposition Member of Parliament after the alliance between his Kabaka Yekka Party and the Uganda People's Congress was dissolved in 1965. Then there was Dr. E. M. K. Muwazi, another Buganda Kingdom Government Minister; two County Chiefs, James Lutaya and Lameka Sebanakitta; and Stanley Bemba, a former Minister in the pre-independence Uganda Government formed by his Democratic Party (now banned because Uganda is a one-party State).

They all looked fit and well — surprisingly so, in view of their detention. But none of them would talk publicly about his experiences.

Below, left: relatives and friends surge forward to lift one of the released men to a waiting car. Their welcome is so enthusiastic, they almost sweep him off his feet. Below, right: another scene, typical of those enacted as old friends meet once again.

EXODUS AS 20 000 KENYANS HEAD FOR HOME

BY BUS, TRAIN OR TRUCK the refugees head for the Kenyan border.

DRUM: January 1971

With their ragged boxes and bundles around them, pitiful queues of men, women and children waited at Uganda's border posts with Kenya before straggling "home". At the same time other groups crowded the bus depots of Ugan-da's main towns like forlorn refugees. This was the tragic scene that marked the biggest exodus of its kind as over 20,000 Kenyans moved out of Uganda following the government's order to employers to sack unskilled and semi-skilled Kenyans and give their jobs to Ugandans.

It was a sad event for most of the people affected; many of them had lived in Uganda for ten or even 20 years. Most were members of the Luo tribe from Kisumu and other parts of western Kenya, the area which adjoins Uganda. For years, Kenyans have been seeking jobs in Uganda, many of them leaving their wives and families on their tribal lands, and sending money to them each month.

But in spite of the long tradition of Kenyan workers in Uganda, employers in Uganda said they had to accept a directive from the Ministry of Labour to replace their non-Ugandan unskilled and semi-skilled workers with Ugandans. The directive was sent out on the orders of Labour Minister Erika Lakidi soon after President Obote announced sweeping measures to implement Uganda's new socialist philosophy, including the government's acquisition of 60 per cent shares in leading companies.

One result of the move to the left in Uganda was the imposition of controls on cash remittances from Uganda to neighbouring Kenya and Tanzania. Until then, such remittances had been free from control, and Ugandan notes were accepted throughout East Africa.

But the new currency rules meant that non-Ugandans working in Uganda had to apply for permission to send money to other parts of East Africa, and it hit hard at the Kenyans working in Uganda who were sending monthly sums to their families in Kenya.

The Uganda government had not realised how much currency was going out of the country in remittances to workers' families in Kenya – and, to a smaller extent, in Tanzania. The size of the cash flow shocked many people, when it was reported that it ran into millions of shillings each month. Soon afterwards, Mr Lakidi's directive to sack Kenyans went out.

One Kenyan worker, Mr Paulo Muga, whose home is near Kis-

A KENYAN FAMILY waits for a bus to take them back to Kenya.

MANY KENYANS were only able to take the bare necessities with them.

umu, said as he boarded a bus in Kampala to leave Uganda: "I have worked here for ten years with a construction company, but because I am not classed as a skilled worker, I have been sacked. I don't know what I can expect in Kenya. There is already a serious unemployment problem and it will not

be easy to find a job." Many others waiting for transport to Kisumu said they had lived and worked in Uganda for many years, and had never expected one day to be forced to leave the country. They had, they said, paid their taxes in Uganda and their work had made a big contribution to the country's development.

One of the biggest worries of the Kenyans who were sacked and decided to return home was to transfer their savings from Uganda to Kenya. Many of them said they had been refused permission by the Bank of Uganda to take their money with them. There were pitiful scenes as people tried to exchange their Ugandan money for Kenyan notes, often offering high premiums in the hope of getting something they could spend in Kenya.

But perhaps the most tragic aspect of the whole Ugandanisation programme is the plight of thousands of Kenyans of low-income who streamed back into Kenya. Some of them found on their arrival at their former homes that not only did they have no shelters, no land and no money, but some of their relatives had large families and were unable to give help to those who "forgot to remember home".

One man, Aloys Ondiek, who lived in the outskirts of Kisumu and is married with four children, told DRUM: "I have learned my lesson. I was away from home for eight years. I did not even write to my relatives. When I came back I found that our land had been sold to outsiders who built houses for renting on the graves of my ancestors. Now I have nowhere to go with my children. I have no money, no land and no job." ❑

DEAR DOLLY

Pregnant Girl Left Me For Another

I am 18. I was in love with a girl for almost two years. I left her in my home town in search of employment. Luckily I found a job as soon as I got to Kaduna. I intended to marry this girl and I had paid her dowry. When I went home last December, I was informed that she was pregnant but her father had helped her to get rid of the baby. I was very shocked but the greatest shock is that she has married another man. What do you advise?

Martin, Kampala

Forget about her. Every disappointment, they say, is a blessing in disguise. Get yourself another girl. There are many good and sincere ones around.

One Girl Could Never Be Enough

I'm a 26-year-old soldier and like sex very much. The problem is that I can't just have sex with one girl. Whenever I see a woman who appeals to me I feel like seducing her. And whenever I've made love once to a girl I lose interest in her. Now, because of sex with so many girls I don't feel I can ever fall in love. I fear this may go on forever and make marriage impossible. Help me before my life is ruined for ever.

Sam Mbale, Uganda

Your answer would be to learn some self-control. Many men have erotic and sexy fantasies about other women. But they don't go around sleeping with every girl they can lay their hands on. The solution to your problem is in your own hands and nobody else's.

The Long Arm Of The Law Worries Me, Dolly

I'm 25 and working for the O.C. of a police office. The trouble is that his wife loves me very much. I have refused to have intercourse with her and she has asked me why I love only one wife and not her. Now she says that if I do not do what she wants, she will have me sent away. Please help me.

Worried Boy, Uganda

You are heading for big trouble. It would be wise to get another job quickly.

She Wants My Body, Not My (Future) Brains

I'm 14 and in love with a girl of 16 who always asks me for sex, but I tell her to allow me to finish my education in Senior II before I give it to her. Now she has threatened to leave me if I don't go to bed with her. I love her very dearly and I cannot live without seeing her.

JS Kitaasa, Masaka

You won't thank me for the advice but – live without seeing her, you must. At your age, education must come first. You've plenty of time for love after leaving school. I don't approve of boys your age becoming sexual experts, anyway, no matter what the apostles of the permissive society may say.

We Move So Well Without Words

One day I happened to meet a girl near the technical school where I am studying who greeted me in a language I could not understand. I used signs to indicate that I loved her and to my surprise I knew she had agreed. At last I managed to have sex with her.

Whenever I meet this girl we only laugh at each other as we cannot speak. The problem is that my friends say I should not love a girl with whom I cannot talk. But I love her very much because of her good behavior. As you know, actions speak louder than words.

Worried Boy, Fort Portal

I do not know, obviously, as well as you do how much louder than words actions do speak. In your case very loudly. I think your friends are plainly jealous.

Our New Baby Looks Just Like My Best Friend

I am in a dreadful state. I am married with one child and have stayed with my wife for four years. Unfortunately, I went abroad on a six-month course and on my return found that my wife was three-months pregnant, with a child which I understood fully was not mine. Now she has delivered and the boy is about five-months and resembles the man my home people mentioned was the father. Can I returned this boy to his father? Or to my wife's parents? Or shall I divorce the woman?

Confused, Moroto

Oh dear, how difficult to advise anybody in this situation. I feel so sorry for you but how much do you love your wife? And is she likely to be unfaithful to you again? If there is a chance of mending the marriage I must urge that you do so – for the sake of your other children as well as the one who is not yours. He is innocent. Do not make him suffer for your wife's sins on any account.

They Insisted I Took This Other Woman

My wife has left me – after I made another woman of 24 pregnant. This other girl was brought to me by force by her parents and while I didn't like her they threatened me with evil if I didn't accept her. So my loving wife left me. She told me that if I leave this second woman, she will return, otherwise she will never come back.

Makro, Kampala

You must think both your first wife and myself are naive. Even if you had to give shelter to the other girl through fear, you certainly did not have to make love to her. If you want your first wife back you have only one course of action open – and to do that you must defy baseless superstition. ❐

THINGS FALL APART

At 9:30 p.m. on January 24, 1971 President Obote, in a long-distance telephone call from Singapore, told his top aides in Kampala: "Get out of the parliament building. If you don't move now you will find it too late." By dawn the next day, he was no longer president, the parliament buildings had been taken, and his loyal aides were either under arrest or in flight. General Idi Amin had seized power in a military coup.

Before leaving for Singapore to attend the Commonwealth Summit Conference, Obote had thought twice about going. Kampala was awash with rumours of a coup and Obote was preparing the ground for a showdown with the increasingly desperate General Amin. Promoted out of effective control of the army in 1970, Amin's past was beginning to catch up with him. He was accused of giving unauthorised military and logistic aid to the Anya Nya rebels in southern Sudan, of misappropriating large sums of army money, and of having been involved in the murder of Brigadier Okoya, the deputy commander of the army who had questioned Amin's loyalty. The trial of those implicated in Okoya's murder was to have taken place in February and Amin had no guarantee that his role would not be uncovered. Just before his departure for Singapore, Obote had demanded that on his return he should be given written explanations by General Amin and Defence Minister Felix Onama of the fate of the missing army funds. The president then secretly ordered his close government colleagues to arrest Amin while he was away.

But in the president's absence, his deputies failed him. They acted neither swiftly nor decisively and their hesitation allowed Amin and his supporters, who had got wind of Obote's scheme, to strike first. By the morning of the 25th, Amin's small group of supporters – spearheaded by tanks and armoured vehicles from the Malire Mechanised Regiment – had taken over Kampala. The battle was over before it had begun.

The initial response of the people to Amin's takeover varied according to the region. In central region, where support for Obote had been fragile, the downfall of the old administration was greeted with jubilation. In the rest of the country, as in large sections of the army, there was considerable apprehension. Amin had to move fast to secure the people's support. Having come to power without any coherent programme, he resorted to a variety of ad hoc measures. Within days he had lifted the national state of emergency, allowed the Kabaka to be entombed in Uganda and released 50 prominent politicians from detention. Amin also announced that he would reverse Obote's policy of partial nationalisation. These early gestures earned Amin considerable popularity, especially in Buganda, and the lack of support from the outlying areas was, for the time being, of little concern to the regime.

SHAKE-UP IN UGANDA

UGANDA'S NEW STRONGMAN: Major General Idi Amin, surrounded by armed soldiers, drives through the crowded streets.

DRUM: February 1971

It all started with the rattling of gunfire throughout the night of January 24, 1971, which gave residents of Kampala not the slightest chance to sleep. Only a few people, probably only men of the armed forces, knew what was going on. The gunfire continued throughout the morning, and still there was no real knowledge of what was taking place.

Yet there was suspicion everywhere that a coup was taking

broadcasts, and an unnamed soldier read a lengthy statement announcing that the army had taken over the government. Part of the announcement read: "We, men of the armed forces have this day – the 25th January, 1971 – decided to take over power from Dr Obote and hand it to our fellow soldier, Major General Idi Amin Dada. We hereby entrust him to lead this, our beloved country of Uganda, to peace and goodwill among all."

The soldiers had acted, the statement said, to prevent the situation from deteriorating; and complained of increasing taxation, corruption among "big men", including ministers, rising crime, lack of free elections and the detention of political rivals.

It was the words: "... we men of the armed forces have this day decided to take over power from Dr Obote..." which sent the people mad and wild with joy. The entire country echoed with noise from the jubilant people shouting long live Dada, long live Major General Amin, long live the army and the new republic of Uganda.

Drums were played, horns blown, empty tins dragged along the road to produce rough noises. There was hooting, singing, dancing and jumping high up as men of the armed forces drove through the city's streets. Bottles of beer, cigarettes, bread and biscuits were thrown over to army vehicles as they passed through human walls. At times the armoured cars were prevented from moving as dancers performed in front of them.

The volume of acclaim for the overthrow of Obote was surprising to some observers. But there seemed no doubt about the

place. Many people heard the 7 a.m. news bulletin from the BBC, reporting heavy fighting and troop movements in Kampala. Radio Uganda had nothing to say. Its early morning news bulletins were not broadcast – instead listeners heard only martial music. Then at 3:45 p.m. Radio Uganda interrupted its day-long music

"AMIN, AMIN, AMIN" – This was the cry of the excited crowd which flocked into the streets of Kampala.

IN OBOTE'S RESIDENCE troops found a cache of Russian-made arms – in Red Cross boxes.

sincerity of the people in Kampala and in Jinja, Uganda's second largest town, where more demonstrations were quickly organised. There were processions through the streets, with crowds of people following army vehicles and shouting their joy.

After the first night of the dusk-to-dawn curfew, imposed by the army, people emerged cautiously from their homes. There had been sounds of heavy firing near Kampala throughout the early hours. However, traffic moved normally into the city, shops and offices opened, and crowds of celebrating people thronged the streets.

"I AM A MAN OF FEW WORDS..."

DRUM: February 1971

On the evening of January 25, Major General Amin made the following address to the nation on Ugandan radio:

"Fellow-countrymen and well-wishers of Uganda, I address you today at a very important hour in the history of our nation. A short while ago men of the armed forces placed this country in my hands. I am not a politician, but a professional soldier. I am therefore a man of few words and I shall, as a result, be brief. Throughout my professional life I have emphasised that the military must support a civilian government that has the support of the people, and I have not changed from that position.

"Matters now prevailing in Uganda force me to accept the task that has been given me by the men of the Uganda armed forces. I will, however, accept this task on the understanding that mine will be a thoroughly caretaking administration, pending an early return to civilian rule. Free and fair general elections will soon be held in the country, given a stable security situation. Everybody will be free to participate in these elections. For that reason political exiles are free to return to this country and political prisoners held on unspecified and unfounded charges will be released forthwith. All the people are to return for work as usual." ❒

ARMED SOLDIERS hold the crowds back as the people stream onto the roads.

CROWDS MILL around the parliament buildings after the coup.

BAGANDA LOYALISTS form a procession headed by a picture of the late Kabaka.

Cars and lorries decorated with green branches moved up and down throughout the day, and several thousand people gathered at the parliament building. They demanded that the army shoot down the massive medallion bearing the head of Dr Obote hanging from the Independence Arch in front of the building. No action was taken, and later General Amin announced that he would not agree to such steps. History, he said, could not be rewritten. Most shops and offices closed at midday, many of them because their workers were all away celebrating.

Within a couple of days life in Kampala returned to normal, though with a heavy military presence. Major General Amin called several meetings of permanent secretaries and then consulted the former ministers of the Obote government about forming a caretaker government. He stressed that Uganda was no longer a one-party state, as it had been since the end of 1969. All political parties were free to campaign and take part in the new elections.

And he drew widespread cheers from the Baganda when he announced that the body of former Kabaka, Sir Edward Mutesa, now buried in London, should be brought back to Uganda for a ceremonial burial. Amin also pleased many people when he said that Mr Benedicto Kiwanuka, who was prime minister of Uganda before independence, would be released from detention, and his picture given its place alongside that of Dr Obote as one of the key figures of Uganda's history.

General Amin said Dr Obote could himself return to Uganda "even now" if he wished. ❐

THOUSANDS OF PEOPLE walked miles to attend the prisoner release at Kololo.

AMIN FREES OBOTE'S PRISONERS

DRUM: February 1971

The entire country went mad again on January 27, when Major General Idi Amin Dada, leader of Uganda's military government announced the release of 55 political detainees held since 1966. Among those released were five ministers dismissed and detained by Obote, and Uganda's first prime minister, Mr Benedicto Kiwanuka. Also freed was Nalinya Ndagire, sister of the late Mutesa.

People in thousands, bearing green, yellow and blue flags and carrying tree branches, chanting Amin Oyee, Dada Yekka, Kabaka Yekka and DP, flocked to Kololo airstrip where the formal release of the detainees took place. Immediately after the midnight announcement of the release of the detainees was made on the radio, people, ignoring the curfew imposed on them two days earlier, started walking to the airstrip. By 8 a.m. the next morning they had gathered in their thousands.

Cheers of Long Live Dada, Long Live Uganda, spread all over the area as the detainees drove through human walls in a prison bus. The soldiers and the police failed to control the public when Major General Idi Amin arrived to address and convey good wishes to the detainees. Officially releasing them, Amin said: "You are joining other free Ugandans at a time of great excitement and joy in the country." ❐

A GRATEFUL SUBJECT BLESSES Amin for freeing the political prisoners.

THE POLITICAL PRISONERS on army trucks await their release by Major General Amin.

AMIN MEETS THE MEDIA: Uganda's new ruler soon struck a very strong affinity for the media, and they for him.

SOLDIERS DEMONSTRATE their strength during the release.

OBOTE FLIES INTO EXILE

OBOTE IN DAR ES SALAAM: "There is no question of any takeover. I can tell you I am going back to Uganda after I have had my discussions here."

DRUM: March 1971

An unannounced and un-scheduled Comet airliner touched down at the hectic Dar es Salaam international airport. The time was exactly 2:15 p.m., Tuesday, January 26, 1971. On charter to the East African Airways, the Comet was carrying a special guest of honour, a fallen champion of the Common Man, Dr Apollo Milton Obote.

Unarmed Field Force policemen had hurriedly been posted along the airport apron. Airport staff were in a disorderly rush to join the party of hosts. Members of the special branch mingled with the reception group. The atmosphere was so formal as to make Dr Obote forget the reality of the situation – that his eight-year span of power had come to an abrupt end.

This was about 40 hours after Dr Obote was swept off his seat as captain of the Ugandan ship of state, and that very unceremoni-ously. Wearing a light grey suit and an open-necked shirt, Dr Obote looked calm, cool and col-lected. He even had enough tran-

quility to shake hands with the air hostesses as he descended from the plane's first class exit.

The fallen Pan Africanist was re-ceived at the airport by a high ranking Tanzanian delegation which included the second vice

THE GOOD OLD DAYS: Obote and Amin together in Kampala in 1968.

ONE OF THE LARGEST demonstrations in Dar es Salaam for many years gathered to denounce Amin (above and below).

president, Mr Rashidi Kawawa, and the minister of finance, Mr Amir Jamal. After a brief sojourn in the VIP lounge, Dr Obote walked swiftly to a waiting state car. He was brandishing his thick-stemmed walking stick in acknowledgment of the spontaneous burst of hand-clapping that greeted him from the small crowd of officials.

Waving briefly to newsmen, Obote quickly stepped into the State House's shiny Rolls Royce which carried his Ugandan presidential pennon. The Uganda presidential standard stirred gently in the heavy afternoon air from one of the flagpoles lining the runway. The convoy sped through the streets of Dar es Salaam towards State House. No crowds lined the streets as there had been no announcement of the arrival. The entire operation had been carried out with quiet, unostentatious efficiency – almost as efficiently as the coup which swept Obote to Dar es Salaam.

A few hours after his arrival, the fallen leader told a press conference at State House – in the absence of President Nyerere who was still at the Singapore summit – that he was planning to go back to Uganda: "There is no question of any takeover. I can tell you I am going back to Uganda after I have had my discussions here." He added that he had not asked for asylum in Tanzania.

Amid the flashing of camera bulbs and the bright glare of television lights, the 46-year-old honorary doctor of law said dramatically: "Whatever these rebels might say, the people of Uganda believe, like many African countries, in socialism. They believe in the Common Man's Charter which has received popular support throughout the country. Now a group of traitorous army personnel have come forward to say that they know everything, that they are the saviours of Uganda, and that they must shoot and kill, not only civilians of Uganda but also their comrades in arms.

"These people, I say to you quite clearly, are the servants of foreigners." He named the Israelis as having been involved in the bloody seizure of power by the Uganda army.

Dr Obote accused the coup leader Major General Amin of having swindled over £2 million. He said the funds were lost or stolen by an army officer directly under General Amin's command. "I am of the view that what has happened in Uganda is to try and hide this very serious matter."

Meanwhile the whole atmosphere in Dar es Salaam was rife with rumours and speculation. Conflicting reports flowed in regarding the

NYERERE ADDRESSES the anti-Amin rally: "How can I sit at the same table with a killer. Jomo Kenyatta is speaking for the people who elected him. I am speaking for you. Whom will Amin be representing? I cannot sit with murderers."

Uganda turmoil. President Nyerere cut short his Far East tour to return home. He immediately went into heart-to-heart consultations with his socialist inclined friend, Dr Obote.

He also conferred with his cabinet for hours before releasing a statement: "The government and people of Tanzania unequivocally condemn the purported seizure of power by Major General Amin in Uganda. It would, if consolidated, weaken the national independence of Uganda, with inevitable effects upon the strength of the whole nation." The pungent state-

ment added that the government of Tanzania continued to regard President Obote as the president of Uganda.

A few days later hundreds of city dwellers took part in one of the largest demonstrations in Dar es Salaam for a long time. It was in support of the one-time herdsboy and labourer – Dr Obote, and it was against the self-styled head of state and one-time boxing champion, Major General Idi Amin. Nyerere told the rally that to recognise Amin as a head of state would be like inviting a gun-brandishing soldier to rule Tanzania. ❑

IDI AMIN – AFRICA'S RELUCTANT RULER

A MAN OF THE PEOPLE: Idi Amin relates to his people better than the somewhat aloof President Obote.

DRUM: April 1971

"I am not an ambitious man. I have taken on the leadership of this country to save a bad situation from getting worse..."

These words of Uganda's new head of state have now passed into history. But in many ways they sum up the character of the man who has taken over from deposed President Obote. Born of a poor family with little formal education

Idi Amin has never sought power during his long military career. But because of his natural qualities of leadership, his commanding appearance and his ability to deal with problems, he has often had power thrust upon him. And so it was that Major General Amin found himself as Uganda's new leader after the January coup. After the takeover, the people of Uganda and East Africa and, in fact, the rest of the world saw a re-

markable exhibition of restraint and statesmanship as he made his first announcements as Uganda's head of state.

Major General Amin comes from as far north as you can go in Uganda. He is a member of the Kakwa tribe which lives in an area which is partly in Madi District, west of the Nile in north-west Uganda, and partly in the adjoining Sudan. The major general is quick to point out

AMIN IN 1968: A loyal soldier?

with pride that he comes from a poor family and that his father never owned a coat. In fact, he points out, he could never imagine how his father ever managed the bride price for his mother!

Until he joined the King's African Rifles (KAR) at the age of 20, he had little formal education. But he had the physique and the intelligence which the army needed, and he made swift progress in the KAR. He was promoted, first to lance corporal, then to corporal and then to sergeant. In 1953 he was serving in Kenya where the Fourth (Uganda) Battalion of the KAR was operating during the Mau Mau. Then it was back to Uganda, and to a time of swift promotion. Amin was a keen boxer, and was heavyweight champion of Uganda from 1951 to 1960. He was also a keen rugby player.

In 1959 he was promoted from the rank of sergeant major to that of *Effendi*, when the rank of *Effendi* was created to provide promotion opportunities for outstanding African soldiers. He was made a second lieutenant in 1961.

With independence in 1962, the Uganda battalion of the KAR took on the title of the Uganda Rifles, and formed the nucleus of today's

THE NEW PRESIDENT speaks to Ugandan farmers.

much larger army. By November 1963, Amin had been promoted to the rank of major, although British officers were still in command. Then early in 1964, there was a mutiny among some sections of the army, and the British military mission was withdrawn. Israel sent a military mission to help train the army, but command of the army passed to Ugandans, with Idi Amin holding the rank of colonel, and the post of deputy com-

mander. The commander of the army at this time was Shaban Opoloto, who was placed in detention in 1966 by Obote, but released after the January 1971 coup on the orders of General Amin. Given the rank of brigadier and, later in 1969, that of major general, Idi Amin is a popular figure with the army. He is 6-feet 3-inches tall, and well built, weighing over 200 pounds. But he is gentle in his speech and manners. ❐

SIR EDWARD'S LAST JOURNEY

THE KABAKA'S WIDOW at the lying-in-state in Kampala. Flowers and tributes surround the casket.

DRUM: May 1971

He died not in a glittering palace surrounded by adoring subjects; but alone in a humble flat in the poor dockland area of London. This was the tragic end, at the age of 45, of Sir Edward Frederick Mutesa, Uganda's exiled "King Freddie" who died of acute alcoholic poisoning on November 29, 1969, two days after his 45th birthday.

Although he died a penniless exile, pomp and pageantry marked his return to the land of his forefathers. Sir Edward Mutesa, first president of the republic of Uganda and the 36th, and last, Kabaka of the defunct kingdom of Buganda, was laid to rest at the Kasubi Royal Tombs amid unprecedented scenes of military parades and Kiganda traditional rites.

Thousands of mourners braved the scorching sun to pay their last respects to the man they used to call *Ssabassaja* – Husband of the Husbands.

Gloom, tension and grief reigned at Entebbe airport as the aircraft which brought the body of Sir Edward from London appeared on the horizon. As the aircraft, escorted by four Uganda air force jet fighters, neared, men, women and children in the crowd on the tarmac, in the VIP lounge and on the airport building balcony, began to sob.

To many people in the crowd, the moment of truth had arrived because they erroneously believed that Mutesa was not dead. The crowd burst into tears when the body was carried by a special guard from the plane and was flown to Kampala by an air force helicopter.

People started assembling at the Kampala airstrip in the small hours of the morning and by 9 a.m. all invited guests, including diplomats, religious leaders, representatives of heads of state, high court judges and members of the funeral committee had arrived. The crowd cheered when the president, General Idi Amin Dada, arrived in an open jeep.

As Sir Edward's coffin, wrapped in Ugandan colours, was removed from the helicopter by four army officers, wailing gripped the airfield. Cries must have been heard miles away, as women, some dressed in black *busuti* and clad in bark-cloth pieces – traditional dress during times of mourning – threw themselves carelessly into the mud. Men stood, mouths open and enduring the pain of the scorching sun.

Although the Buganda kingdom is no longer a constitutional monarchy, Sir Edward's heir, Prince Ronald Mutebi, was there to perform an important traditional function – he laid a piece of bark cloth on his father's coffin and was later led by Baganda elders to a hut behind a fence of reeds where he was offered a chair on which he sat. He was then driven away as, according to tradition, he must not attend his father's funeral.

Amid wailings and sadness among the 30,000 crowd General Amin said: "This is a place of history. We therefore felt it right and fitting that the late Sir Edward Mutesa should come to this place for one more event of history – his return, which he foretold when he said, 'In the end I shall return to the land of my fathers and to my people.'" ❐

GENERAL IDI AMIN places a wreath while the waiting mourners weep.

MOURNERS LINE the funeral route.

PRINCE RONALD MUTEBI, 16-year-old son of the late Kabaka, with his mother.

1971 – A MOMENTOUS YEAR FOR UGANDANS

A COMMON SCENE: Amin was accorded tremendous receptions throughout Uganda during his numerous tours.

DRUM: October 1971

On October 9, Uganda celebrates, under military rule, her ninth independence anniversary. Since January's coup, politics has been outlawed in Uganda. In making this order, General Amin made it clear that this was to allow time to clear up the confusion left by the Obote regime, but he promised that he would, as soon as possible, hand power back to the politicians and go back to barracks.

There is speculation on how long it will take to make the transition back to a civilian regime. Soon after the coup, Uganda's soldiers said they wanted the military regime to remain for at least five years, but Amin insisted that he

hoped to hand over earlier than this.

There was no lack of problems for the new military regime. The problems ranged from the financial – it was revealed that the Obote regime had incurred a deficit of 350 million shillings – to those of security. It was announced that dissident Ugandans had been recruited for training as guerrillas in Tanzania, in order to carry out attacks in Uganda aimed at restoring Obote to power.

Serious incidents occurred in July when fighting took place at army depots in Jinja and Moroto, after which it was announced that guerrillas had attacked the depots but had been killed.

After this incident, Uganda closed her borders with Tanzania and Rwanda. And while the Rwanda border was later reopened, allowing normal trade to flow to and from that landlocked country, the Tanzanian border remained sealed. Flights between Uganda and Tanzania were banned, as was movement on Lake Victoria between the two countries, halting all air and steamer services.

Ugandans were also concerned by the state of crime in the country, with a large number of violent robberies. But General Amin himself called in senior police officers and told them they must do a better job. He introduced a reorganisation of the force, appointed new top men, and established a new

Police Council with himself as chairman. Within a short space of time, the incidence of crime dropped and, although incidents are still occurring, there are fewer of the daring robberies which had formerly shocked Uganda.

Shortly after the coup, the military regime was under pressure from Buganda to restore the kingdoms which had been abolished by Obote. The soldiers' reply was that they had not taken over in order to restore feudal organisations, and Uganda must remain a republic. At a meeting of elders from Buganda, Amin was faced with a virtually unanimous demand for the restoration of the kingdom. General Amin's reply was to repeat the views of the soldiers that Uganda could not restore the kingdom.

General Amin himself paid his first visits outside Uganda since the coup when he flew to Israel and Britain in July. Soon afterwards he added further trips to Ethiopia and Liberia. His regime has achieved wide recognition and acceptance % despite the refusal of Tanzania, Zambia, Guinea and Somalia to recognise the military government. Uganda was disappointed when the Organisation of African Unity summit conference in June was not held in Kampala, as had been planned, because of the opposition of some countries to the military regime. And there were serious fears for the future of the East African Community with Tanzania and Uganda unable to sit together.

There are many problems facing the country and its military ruler. But the general has shown no sign of being daunted by the size of the task he faces, and he has so far been able to astonish his people by his ability to take everything in his stride. ❏

NEWLY PROMOTED police officers pose with General Amin at his Kololo home.

GENERAL AMIN at an OAU conference in Ethiopia.

IN JULY the Jinja and Moroto army barracks experienced fierce factional fighting.

GENERAL AMIN GETS HIS GOAL

BIG LEAP BY A BIG MAN: President Amin limbers up as the cabinet team waits to be inspected by the archbishop.

DRUM: July 1972

Thousands thronged to Nakivubo Stadium, Kampala, to see the soccer match between Ugandan government ministers and foreign diplomats. The crowd was particularly interested in seeing their president, General Amin, in action with the team.

SHARP SHOOTING PRESIDENT.

The 43-year-old soldier has been known as a man of action. Hence the now popular slogan of "government by action". Having pledged to assist liberation movements in southern Africa, General Amin made an all-out effort to help raise funds for the movements in response to a special appeal launched by his foreign minister, Mr Wanume Kibedi. One of the several fund-raising functions organised by the ministry was the football match between the Ugandan cabinet and diplomats based in Kampala.

General Amin, a former Ugandan heavyweight boxing champion, captained the cabinet team and made his footballing debut at Nakivubo Stadium. The record crowd cheered wildly when he

THE FOUR WIVES OF IDI AMIN

MADINA AMIN

NORAH AMIN

DRUM: August 1972

"It is not wrong for a man to marry more than one wife provided he can share out his love equally among his wives" – that is the advice Uganda's president, General Idi Amin, gave to an army private who got married simultaneously to twin sisters.

When President Amin extended that counsel to his fellow soldier he was preaching what he practises. The general is married to four wives – Kay, Norah, Maama Maliamu and Madina.

Although the general married his latest wife after becoming head of state and commander-in-chief of the Uganda armed forces, the marriage ceremony – conducted under Kiganda customary law and Muslim religious rites + was characterised by great simplicity. It was celebrated with the minimum of pomp and pageantry which nor-

mally attends the wedding ceremony of a head of state. Consequently the ten million Ugandans under the general's leadership were pleasantly surprised when they learned of the marriage from an evening radio news.

As for President Amin's advice to the soldier on sharing out affections, he also practises what he preaches. None of his wives ever steals the limelight at the expense of the other. On his trips abroad and on official functions in Uganda, the general is accompanied by a different wife or wives, giving each and all of them a fair share of public life.

Of course, apart from being public figures, the president's wives are also housewives and mothers. Recently two of them Kay and Madina, presented the general with babies within a space of two months. ❐

KAY AMIN

MAAMA MALIAMU AMIN

scored one of the cabinet's three goals.

The diplomats, captained by the ambassador of Rwanda won the match by four goals to three. But the cabinet team had the consolation that their three goals raised no less than 16,000 shillings for the OAU Liberation Fund, paid in by donors who had pledged to pay various amounts for every goal scored by President Amin and a little less for every goal scored by any other member of the team.

It was fitting that one of the linesmen who assisted Archbishop Nsubuga in the gracious task of officiating the match, was another religious leader, the chief kadhi of the Muslim faith in Uganda, Sheikh Matovu. ❐

IDI AMIN GOES SWIMMING

AMIN SPENDS A LOT of time at the top international hotel in Kampala – drinking tea, entertaining, and above all, swimming.

UGANDA'S YEAR OF DESTINY

ON THE FIRST ANNIVERSARY of Amin's coup d'etat, thousands of Ugandans turn out to watch the massive military parade throug

DRUM: October 1972

In a dramatic 21 months since January 25, 1971, Uganda has undergone deep changes which have altered its character. From a trend towards doctrinaire African socialism before the 1971 coup, Uganda has moved to a military state where politics is forbidden.

The revolution which took place early on the morning of January 25, 1971, meant the end of the era of political leadership in Uganda

for an unknown period. The heady days which followed the coup, however, have gone, and Uganda's military regime in the subsequent 21 months has settled down to the task of running the country. It is a unique system, with President Amin wielding complete executive power. Parliament and other representative councils were suspended immediately after the coup, when the soldiers decided to bar politics, until the country could be put back on its feet.

Amin's cabinet is formed almost entirely of experts and technocrats, many of them former civil servants. Nevertheless, the army exercises its own control through the Defence Council, the supreme body of military chiefs, which sits with General Amin himself in the chair, and which decides important matters of policy. But whereas, in the weeks immediately following the coup, when the army's presence was obvious, with tanks even seen in the streets of Kampala, this is no longer so.

streets of Kampala.

The army is out of sight, but it is there nevertheless, although no visitor to Uganda would imagine from the absence of soldiers in the streets that the country was under military rule.

The army and air force is larger than ever before. General Amin has stressed that the armed forces were deprived of the opportunity to develop under Milton Obote, and it is only now that ground is being made up. However, he has also stressed that he has spent no money on new arms, buying only replacements and essential supplies for his troops. There have been no costly new machines for the army, and even the helicopters obtained for the Police Air Wing, and used extensively by President Amin and his ministers to tour the country, have a dual role to enable them to provide communications and to lift urgently needed supplies in case of floods, fires and other disasters.

Inevitably, the sharp and sudden transition to a new system of government has meant that problems have to be overcome. What happened in Uganda was that the political system, increasingly directed by one man, Milton Obote – for it was he alone who produced the nationalisation plans, the Common Man's Charter, and the national service proposals – was abruptly brought to an end.

While in most cases the civil service machinery remained intact, the policy direction changed. Instead of the arch-politician, who had moulded Uganda in its all-important first years of independence, there was a bluff, down-to-earth professional soldier.

Another basic difference in Uganda today is the readiness of President Amin to allow delicate issues to be aired. In July 1971 for instance, an American freelance journalist, Nicholas Stroh, and a university lecturer Robert Siedle, disappeared after visiting Mbarara barracks in western Uganda, where Stroh had gone to investigate reports of an alleged massacre among the troops. As a result of rumours about their fate, and under strong pressure from America to explain the men's disappearance, General Amin ordered a public inquiry into the whole affair.

When the report of the inquiry was submitted by the British judge, Mr Justice Jones, Amin immediately ordered it to be published, giving the lie to speculation that, because the report was expected to blame army units for the deaths of the Americans, General Amin would not publicise it. The report did find that the Americans had been killed by people in the army at Mbarara. Nevertheless President Amin ordered the government printer to work non-stop over the weekend to get the report out in record time.

The president then handed copies of the report to the American *chargé d'affaires,* expressing the hope that it would bring about better relations between Uganda and America. He also said his government was considering offering to pay compensation to the families of the two men.

Where Milton Obote had become more and more isolated in the later period of his rule, General Amin emphasises his approachability. He is there to serve the people, he insists, and people high and low can, and do, approach him with their problems, and invariably receive an attentive hearing.

President Amin has toured not only every district in Uganda, but every single county, involving trips to remote locations. Often travelling by helicopter, he has called meetings of tribal and other local elders, and has discussed with them their needs.

Amin has called on all parts of Uganda to send representatives to top-level discussions on such subjects as the needs of farmers or the unification of religious groups. And he has invited the people to express their views on a wide range of basic issues. ❑

DRUM

AFRICA'S LEADING MAGAZINE

EAST AFRICA EDITION 1/50
ZAMBIA   30 NGWEE

DRUM ACCUSES IDI AMIN'S REGIME

Special report on murder and brutality against Ugandan Africans

NGALA'S STORMY LIFE-EXCLUSIVE

THE TRUTH ABOUT AMIN

Within two years of the coup, Amin had created one of the most monstrous dictatorships Africa had ever been subjected to. Although Amin's rule was born of violence and he never ran shy of government by violence, in the early days he did try to engender genuine popular support for his regime. One of the ways was to keep in close contact with the people. He and his ministers gave numerous press conferences and toured the country extensively. Amin also tried to win over religious institutions and leaders. Historically, the various religious establishments had played an important social role, and Amin hoped they would use their position to bolster his regime. He donated large sums of money to all major religions and even acted as a peace broker within and between different denominations.

However, after about a year in power the regime had squandered most of the goodwill it had enjoyed in the early days. Faced by a growing crisis of legitimacy, Amin and his cohorts became extremely sensitive to any criticism and clamped down hard on opponents, real or imagined. Following the precedent he had set in July 1971 – when he had thousands of dissenting Acholi and Langi soldiers massacred – in 1972 Amin launched another "mopping-up" operation against Luo-speaking members of the army, once again killing thousands. As public confidence in the regime waned, underground opposition continued to spread, to the extent that top civil servants who had initially welcomed the coup began to openly show their disillusionment. Amin responded by dismissing 22 senior civil servants in April, and at the end of the year he sent his entire cabinet on indefinite leave.

In an attempt to find a scapegoat for the regime's dismal record, Amin turned on the Asian community. Amin identified the Asians, who were traditionally as aloof from the African community as they were well off, as the cause of Uganda's troubles. On August 4, 1972 he announced that all Asians with foreign passports – the vast majority – were to "go back" to their own countries within 90 days. The impact of the expulsion was dramatic – there was general euphoria amongst the ordinary people and Amin's soldiers moved in fast to take for themselves properties left behind by the Asians.

In September 1972, ex-President Obote launched an ill-fated invasion of Uganda in an attempt to spark a popular uprising against Amin. When the uprising did not materialise, the 1,000-strong exile force was routed by Amin's soldiers, aided by about 400 Libyan troops. Although the invasion failed, it ushered in a new and unprecedentedly violent phase of Amin's rule. Prisoners of war were publicly executed, soldiers were given more power to terrorise civilians and enrich themselves, measures were taken to greatly expand the army and a pogrom of prominent public figures was launched. Amin, a hamfisted, politically obtuse soldier-dictator, was at a loss to know how else to maintain his hold on power.

AFRICA RALLIES TO AVERT WAR

BODIES OF GUERRILLAS, claimed by Uganda to have been in the invasion force, displayed by members of the Simba Battalion.

DRUM: November 1972

Africans everywhere watched anxiously as the threat of war rumbled again on our continent.

As relations rapidly worsened between Uganda and Tanzania, on September 17, 1972, fighting flared on the border of these two members of the East African Community. African leaders were quick to try to secure peace between Uganda and Tanzania, especially as the Libyan military leader Colonel Muammar Gad-

dafi had flown troops and equipment to Uganda and pledged support for President Amin. The Uganda government announced that a force of insurgents sup-porting former President Obote had struck across the border with Tanzania and overrun several border towns before being wiped out by Uganda's Simba Battalion.

Within three days the Ugandan radio announced the invasion had ended and the towns had been recaptured. In Dar es Salaam, top Tanzanian brass denied knowl-

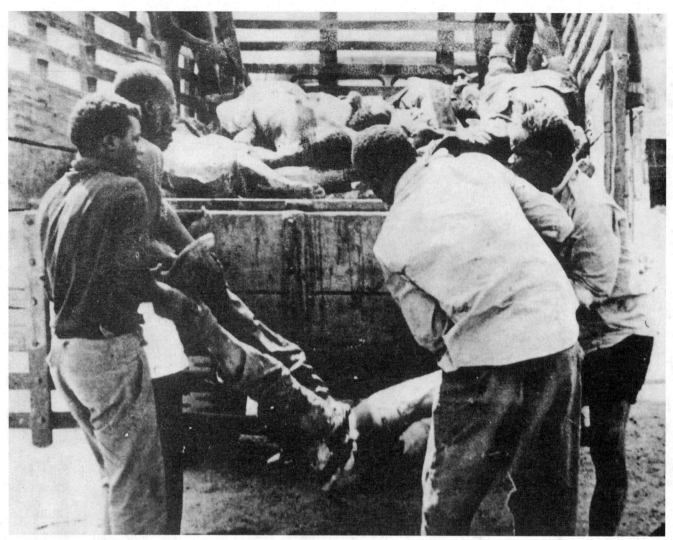

CAPTURED INSURGENTS LOAD their dead fellows onto a lorry for disposal.

edge of the attack. General Amin accused Britain and Israel of conniving in the invasion, and later the Ugandan president alleged that India had joined a plot against him. Meanwhile, the militant anti-Zionist Colonel Muammar Gaddafi of Libya had despatched five C-130 transport planes loaded with troops and equipment to Uganda to support President Amin. But as they crossed Sudan,

UGANDA ARMY TROOPS and heavy tanks at an assembly point outside Kampala at the start of the border crisis.

THE STILLBORN INSURRECTION

Sudanese jets forced the convoy to land at Khartoum and turn back. The Libyans reached Uganda in a second attempt; and their presence brought a new dimension to the conflict.

The Uganda air force replied to the border attack by bombing the northern Tanzanian towns of Mwanza and Bukoba, which it alleged were enemy camps. An air force spokesman reported that all was quiet in the towns afterwards.

As Tanzanian troops stood by, African leaders rallied to try to prevent the conflict from spreading and possibly involving other non-African countries. Mr Nzo Ekangaki, new secretary general of the Organisation of African Unity, and the foreign minister of Somalia, Mr Omar Arteh, hastened from capital to capital in the hope of finding acceptance to a five-point peace agreement drafted by Mr Arteh.

And behind the scenes, President Mobutu Sese Seko and other African heads of state made careful overtures. Then came an announcement of peace, signed by the foreign ministers of Tanzania and Uganda in Somalia. African brotherhood had triumphed, said the statement, over the continent's detractors.

Relations between Uganda and Tanzania have been strained since the coup of January 1971 in which Idi Amin came to power in Uganda after the overthrow of Dr Milton Obote, who sought exile in Tanzania. Earlier border incidents had threatened to aggravate the differences between these two members of the East African Community. This time, as the crisis was complicated by the exodus of Asians, all Africa and the world watched anxiously. ❑

PISTOL SLUNG IN HOLSTER, Amin makes a statement during the conflict.

DRUM: March 1979

When Dr Milton Obote was ousted as president he started training Ugandan exiles in Tanzania and Sudan in an effort to regain power. In fact, by August 1972, Obote had a trained force of 1,000 men ready to restore him. On September 10, 1972 the plan to invade Uganda had been completed.

The plan was to "borrow" an East African Airway DC 9 and transport 300 guerrillas to Entebbe airport, capture it and march on to Kampala to take the radio station where a prerecorded message was

WAR DAMAGE: President Amin shows visiting Kenyan cabinet ministers, including Foreign Minister Njorge Mungai, damage cause

to be broadcast over Radio Uganda. Obote calculated on making a psychological impact on Ugandan soldiers and civilians alike and getting them to rally behind him.

The contents of the message were never known as the plane did not go beyond Tanzania's Kilimanjaro airport. A ground attack was

planned to be launched through Mutukula and advance towards Masaka, while another smaller column was to cross the border into Uganda through Kafunzo and advance westwards to take the Simba Battalion stationed at Mbarra. After defeating Amin's soldiers there, the column was to join with the main force at Masaka for a joint attack on Kampala.

Obote calculated that since Ugandans were tired of Amin's mass murders of civilians, the soldiers would join the guerrillas.

On September 15, there was no indication of the guerrilla invasion of Uganda except that after midnight at the Dar es Salaam airport police and plain clothes men took over the airport at gunpoint and

Obote's insurgents during their invasion.

ordered everyone inside the buildings. Telephones and all communications in the airport were cut off. Then two Africans boarded an EAA aircraft and took off. Later an EAA DC 9 crew on a scheduled flight had gone to the terminal to continue with their flight, but their plane was not there. The plane was found at Kilimanjaro International airport with burst tyres.

On that very day, the Kenya special branch which had learned of the Obote invasion, informed Tanzania that Britain was preparing to send troops into Uganda on the night of September 17–18 when the first Asians were scheduled to leave Uganda, on the pretext of protecting the lives and property of its citizens. Nyerere summoned Obote and his military chiefs. It is not known what they talked about, but it is said that Nyerere wanted to call off the operation as he did not want a confrontation with the British.

It is not precisely clear what happened to the airborne platoon that was to land in Entebbe but rumours say it was called off at the last moment. The "black box" in the EAA DC 9 found at Kilimanjaro airport recorded that the plane took 50 per cent more time to reach Kilimanjaro airport than normal. It is thought that it had gone to either Entebbe or Nairobi. However, if the guerrillas had reached Entebbe as planned they would have been wiped out as, due to lack of co-ordination among the three platoons, the ground forces would not have reached Kampala to reinforce the airborne platoon.

The Mbarra platoon planned to cross the border at 5 a.m. but only crossed some hours later. They sent an advance party to clean up the border post where they killed all four guards and burned it to the ground before advancing towards Mbarra. The contingent, armed with recoilless rifles, a few rockets, and some sub-machine guns was commanded by Captain Oyire and Lieutenant Okot.

About 14 kilometres inside Uganda, the guerrillas met an army Land Rover with eight soldiers who fought with the invaders. All the soldiers were killed and the attackers suffered no casualties. The invaders arrived at Mbarra at about noon and when they tried to enter the barracks many were killed and the rest scattered. Only 50 escaped with only five trucks reaching the Tanzanian border the next morning, September 18.

The Masaka force crossed the border at 5:30 a.m. through Mutukula. Four trucks went ahead to clear the border post. Under the command of Captain Anach they killed all the border guards and advanced towards Kalisizo. In the afternoon they were met by planes, tanks, and armoured personnel carriers.

The guerrillas fought bravely but, having run out of ammunition, they had to retreat. Under pursuit some were able to reach the Tanzanian border under cover of darkness. Casualties among the guerrillas were high and among the dead were two former Obote ministers, Wakloli and Ojera. The cause of the failure, as the guerrillas later conceded, was lack of training, inadequate arms, lack of support and bad leadership.

Worst of all, Amin is said to have been informed of the invasion by Kenya's special branch which didn't support Obote's return to power as he had been repeatedly accused of inciting a succession in Nyanza and supporting the now defunct Kenya People's Union.

After the invasion Amin bombed the Tanzanian towns of Bukoba and Mwanza, and threatened open war. Inside Uganda everyone suspected of supporting the guerrillas was killed. Many leading personalities disappeared, were killed, or fled the country. ❐

THE TRAGEDY OF BEN KIWANUKA

BIG BEN KIWANUKA, with his wife, in his heyday as prime minister of Uganda.

DRUM: March 1983

Ben Kiwanuka, chief justice of Uganda and former prime minister, had one fatal shortcoming – he was too popular. And as a shaken Amin took stock after the September invasion, he was in no mood for such a rival. In late September 1972, Kiwanuka was hauled out of his judge's chambers, thrown into prison and, a few days later, gruesomely murdered.

The late Ben Kiwanuka's widow has given an interview with **DRUM**, providing a full account of the events of his tragic death.

DRUM: When did the real trouble with Amin begin?
Mrs Kiwanuka: In late 1972 after a high court judgement by my husband when he declared to the effect that army personnel had no power to arrest and detain somebody without an arrest warrant.

This judgement brought the fateful events to a climax.

DRUM: Why didn't your husband try to run away when he saw danger?
Mrs Kiwanuka: He was the type that could not run away. He was a man of exceptional courage and was immune to any threat. You could say he was a kind of Spartan when it came to anybody trying to challenge or deflect him from what he considered to be a moral duty. He would rather die.

I remember him telling me that if he had wanted to run away at all he would have done it way back in 1959 after his election defeat at the hands of the UPC-KY alliance. He said that if he did run away he would be betraying the trust put in him and the people would lose confidence and faith in him. He would rather die as a courageous man than run away like a coward.

He once said to me: "Sooner or later somebody has to die for a noble cause in this wicked world. If Amin kills me somebody else will take my place. But nobody will do so unless someone sets an example. We can't afford to wait for other people to undertake moral challenges when we can ourselves. If I die, I will have played my moral part."

DRUM: How exactly was your husband murdered?
Mrs Kiwanuka: Before that controversial high court judgement by my husband, intelligence reports from friends kept on reaching us touching on Amin's anxiety about my husband's mounting popularity and the respect accorded him wherever he went. Reports indicated that my husband had, as a result, become a top item on the agenda for discussion at every cabinet meeting.

This was the state of affairs before the day of that fateful high court judgement. Around 7:30 that evening, Amin telephoned my husband and, in an angry voice, demanded to know why my husband had stated in his judgement speech that, "the army had no power..." As my husband was trying to explain that that was not exactly what he had meant, that he had been misinterpreted and that Amin should look at the file first, Amin blasted away and replaced the receiver with a bang.

Amin was so furious and noisy, I could hear his voice over the receiver, roaring. I knew hell had been let loose. But my husband never showed any sign of fear or timidity at all. He remained as composed and determined as ever.

The next morning, September 21, at about 8:15 a.m. my husband was

"I SAW KIWANUKA MURDER" SAYS FORMER CELL MATE

forcefully dragged from his high court office by a mysterious gang who dumped him in a car and drove away at top speed. We knew in advance what excuse was to be given – something to the effect that my husband had run away to Tanzania.

Rumour had it that after the forced arrest of my husband, he was first taken to Makindye Military Police Station to be tortured. From there he was taken the next day to Malire Barracks at Mengo for interrogation by Amin himself. It is said that it was at Malire that important people were slaughtered.

It is rumoured that Amin himself did the deed by chopping off the head of my husband with a dagger. Before the execution we heard something that sounded like a cannon or a gun salute. I do not know what this meant exactly.

DRUM: How did you know about the manner of his death?
Mrs Kiwanuka: Intelligence people working with Amin's security forces always fed us with information either out of charity or for money. To prevent any information from reaching us, some Banyankore who were present as my husband was being butchered by Amin were killed under mysterious circumstances. But all the same, we knew.

Many people tried to help us with information. My husband had many friends. The children and I missed my husband, but so did every Ugandan of goodwill. Everybody asked to know whether Ben was still alive or not... and if dead where he was buried. It was hard to believe for many people that Ben had been murdered in cold blood by Amin. Ah, my husband... my husband. ❐

DRUM: April 1974

A ghastly account of how Uganda's former chief justice, Benedicto Kiwanuka, met his death at the hands of Ugandan trigger-happy soldiers has been given to DRUM by an eyewitness.

One of the men who was in detention with Chief Justice Kiwanuka at Makindye Military Prison, and who escaped with his life, spoke to DRUM about the death of Uganda's first prime minister.

He is a Tanzanian intelligence officer, Deusdedit Kusekwa Masanja, who was arrested in Kampala on charges of spying for his country against Uganda at the height of the military conflict between the two countries.

"We were arrested on February 21, 1972, at the Fairway Hotel in Kampala where we were staying and taken to Makindye Military Prison under army escort. We were badly tortured. The tortures included kicks with boots and I lost my sense of hearing from that day. We were locked in Cell Two, which was full of blood at the time. Due to my beating I became unconscious.

"Shortly afterwards all prisoners were ordered to stand up and form a single line. One, Sergeant A, picked five prisoners and ordered them to lie down. One soldier had a hammer while the others were armed with pistols. The soldier with the hammer ordered prisoner number one to take the hammer and hit the prisoner number two on the head. Then prisoner number three was

ordered to hit prisoner number four on the head with a hammer and he did so. After this, prisoner number five was ordered to take up the hammer and kill prisoner number one. Lastly, prisoner number five was shot.

"The other prisoners were ordered to take the bodies of the five prisoners away. We were forced to put the dead into a jeep and to wash the blood from the cell floor.

"Then Major B turned to me and said that unless I admitted that I was spying for Tanzania, I would suffer the same fate as the five prisoners. I still maintained that I was not a spy. Then they tortured me until I was unconscious. This killing by hammer continued at Makindye throughout the week, except on Fridays.

"It was in September 1972, at Makindye that I saw the former chief justice of Uganda, Benedicto Kiwanuka, at night. He was brought in wearing an army uniform. By that time he had lost weight, he was unshaven and barefoot. He looked very dirty. Some of the prisoners, particularly the Baganda, recognised him at once and crowded round him to talk to him.

"By midnight he was taken out of the common cell and pushed into his own cell and instructions were given that nobody should approach that place.

"On September 28, 1972 he was brought into our cells for his last day. He was killed by a hammer by Sergeant B. Some senior army officers watched the killing." ❐

EXODUS OF ASIANS BEGINS

AFTER TWO TIRING DAYS in the train from Kampala, these Sikhs arrive in Mombasa, Kenya, to begin their sea voyage to India.

DRUM: November 1972

At the height of Uganda's border crisis with Tanzania, the exodus of Asians began from Kampala. Idi Amin had ordered some 50,000 Asians who still held British citizenship to leave the country by early November or face the risk of being moved to transit camps. The British government immediately protested, at the same time making

MR SLATER, British High Commissioner, with Amin.

AMIN WITH DEPORTED Asians at the Kololo airstrip, Kampala.

arrangements to receive the displaced families. And India and Canada offered to take substantial numbers.

The exodus gained force as Asian families wound-up generations-old businesses and left by plane to Britain, or by rail for Mombasa in Kenya and then by ship on to India. In Kampala, British high commission officials worked day and night to issue long queues of Asians with immigration documents.

At the time of independence, some 80 per cent of Uganda's small businesses were owned and run by Asians. The situation was – and is – bitterly resented by the Ugandans who felt that the presence of these brown-skinned aliens was preventing them from ever rising out of the labouring class, either into trade and commerce or into the lower levels of the civil service.

The present expulsion order against the Asians reflects the ever-increasing pressures on the Ugandan economy as more and more Ugandans arrive in the towns from the countryside looking for jobs. ❐

BY TRAIN AND SHIP: Uganda's Asians begin the long voyage to find new homes.

FILLING OUT VISA forms.

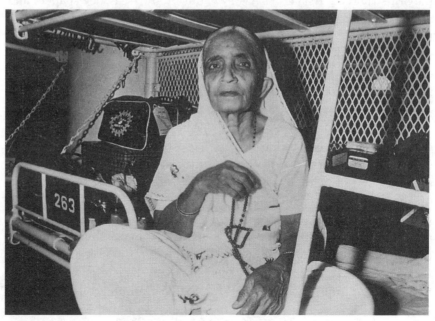

LIFE MUST BEGIN AGAIN for this deported Asian.

EXCLUSIVE – GENERAL AMIN TALKS TO DRUM

MEETING THE PEOPLE: General Amin, here with Lieutenant Colonel Ochima (third from left), has toured Uganda extensively.

DRUM: March 1973

President Idi Amin of Uganda has, in a dramatically short time, given marching orders to the Israelis, the British and the Asians. He has also taken uncompromising steps to rid Uganda's streets of armed robbers and prostitutes, and has campaigned against what he calls "phoney missionaries".

The controversial soldier-president has been criticised by the foreign press for jeopardizing the economy and of being intolerant of Christian worship, while there have been reports of disappearances of many top Ugandan people. In an exclusive interview, DRUM put these allegations before President Amin.

DRUM: Overseas newspapers have been carrying stories about people disappearing in Uganda without trace.

AMIN: We in Uganda do not depend on the sensational stories put out by overseas newspapers and even the BBC. Some of these people alleged to have disappeared are staying in the neighbouring countries. They were not chased away from Uganda, but they decided to run away on their own. Where there have been genuine cases of people disappearing – like the case of the two Americans – we have not hesitated to appoint an inquiry.

DRUM: Can you say that there has been a drop in crime in Uganda since you came to power?

AMIN: Definitely yes. *Kondoism* has died since I ordered the army to shoot robbers on sight.

DRUM: Mr President, can you explain the reasons which led you to embark on what you have described as the "economic war"?

AMIN: We embarked on the economic war because the Asians were milking Uganda's economy. Some were engaged in economic sabotage while others were busy taking their money out the country. No responsible government can allow this state of affairs to continue.

DRUM: What evidence has your government got that the Asians were sabotaging the economy?

AMIN: My government is a government of action. We have eyes and we can see things. Some Asians have been caught redhanded trying to take Ugandan money outside the country. In one instance, police raided a mosque in Kampala and found nearly two million Ugandan shillings in currency notes packed in biscuit tins. These so-called biscuits were due to be exported to Britain. Is this not sabotage? Asians in Uganda have also been sending their money to relatives and friends in the neighbouring African countries. We cannot tolerate a situation in which our economy is being milked by foreigners.

DRUM: What progress has Uganda made in winning the economic war?

AMIN: We have made a lot of progress. Shops vacated by departing Asians are being allocated to Ugandans. The banks are ready with money to give to those African traders who apply for overdrafts. There are so many African countries ready to help Uganda with personnel to replace the non-Ugandans who have left.

DRUM: Can you say something about your relations with Great Britain?

AMIN: The British are my best friends, but they are annoyed because I have kicked out the British Asians. They can say what they like. I have no time for imperialists. They have decided to cut off financial and technical aid to Uganda, but we do not worry. There are so many countries ready to help us. The British are very much annoyed with us now because they are spending between £7 million and £8 million a year in feeding the British Asian refugees in camps all over Europe. If the British want friendship, we are prepared to remain friends, but the steps I have taken to hand over the economy of Uganda to Ugandans are here to stay. We have to win the economic war.

DRUM: Is there freedom of wor-

SEALING ASIANS' SHOPS. "The Asians were milking Uganda's economy" – Amin.

ship in Uganda. If so, why are you being accused of persecuting Christians?

AMIN: In Uganda there is complete freedom of worship and everyone can follow whatever religion he or she chooses. My quarrel with Christian bishops is that some of the White missionaries in the country are not missionaries in the real sense. They are mercenaries. Some are spies. I feel that the security of the people of Uganda is my paramount task. Some of these so-called missionaries do not even know the Bible. You will understand, therefore, why I have not been disposed towards such missionaries because when trouble starts, it is the people of Uganda who will suffer.

DRUM: You frequently condemn

young women for the way they behave and dress. Do you think you are being fair to them?

AMIN: I am totally against loose living by some women in Uganda. Some of them have gone elsewhere in Africa and are doing terrible things there with Europeans. Some of them are loitering in our towns at night looking for customers. To make matters worse, some of our women are spying for foreigners. This must stop. It is no use saying that these prostitutes are a minority. As far as I can see, they are women and that spoils the image of Uganda. I have already banned the miniskirt and other sexy dresses. The next step will be to round up all town women and take them to camps in rural areas where they will be fed and made to work on the land. ❑

UGANDANS FLOCK TO PUBLIC EXECUTIONS

FEAR SHOWS CLEARLY in the eyes of Sebastiano Namirundu (left) and Tom Masaba, two of the 12 alleged guerrillas executed.

A FINAL GESTURE: Masaba's underclothes are taken from him.

DRUM: April 1973

They bound them to trees first. Then they stripped them naked in front of 20,000 people. They dressed them in aprons – white aprons, easy to see from a distance. Then they shot them dead.

And as they cut them down in the pouring rain, the bleeding bodies fell into the mud. Tom Masaba and Sebastiano Namirundu had seemed calm – or frozen with fear – before General Amin's soldiers formed a firing squad in that sodden-wet field at Mbale and carried out the public executions.

Altogether throughout Uganda, 12 men died, sentenced to death by a special military tribunal on charges of guerrilla warfare, involving, it was alleged, killing and kidnapping. Scores of thousands of people watched the first public executions in Uganda this century, carried out simultaneously in six towns by firing squads.

In Kampala traffic came to a standstill as motorists rushed to see Badru Semakula tied to a tree to face a 12-man firing squad before an estimated 30,000 strong crowd. The crowd started gathering an hour or more before the execution and a nearby main road was soon blocked with people and cars. Men stood on the tops of lorries and small boys climbed trees to get a better view. Women carried babies in arms, and small children ran around. Badru Semakula was brought from a nearby military police prison. He wore a grey hood so that his face could not be seen, and an army uniform. Soldiers roped him to a tree, and a Muslim sheikh heard his last words. The execution squad took up position and the order was given to fire. The dead man's head slumped forward, but the ropes prevented him from falling. The crowd continued talking, and then began to drift away.

The other eleven alleged guerrillas were shot in six towns, in line with a ruling by President Amin's Defence Council that each should be executed in his own home district, "so that everyone, including his parents, can see". An official warning has also been given that the family of anyone proved to be a guerrilla or anyone giving shelter to guerrillas will be destroyed. ❐

LIFELESS HOODED BODY of Masaba slumps forward.

VANISHED UGANDANS – GOVERNMENT SPEAKS

STRONG MAN in Obote's cabinet, Basil Bataringaya, is taken away by Amin's troops. He was later pronounced "missing".

DRUM: April 1973

Amid reports in foreign newspapers and rumours that many leading Ugandans – including some outstanding scholars and administrators – had been murdered in Uganda, the government of Idi Amin Dada issued a catalogue of 85 people claimed to be missing. It said six were still alive, 38 were living abroad and three were killed during the 1972 invasion, while the fate of 38 was not known.

The government also announced that, in accordance with service regulations, the usual "death benefits" would be paid to the families of missing government servants whose whereabouts were not known.

Here DRUM looks at the "explanations" given by the government for the fate of some of the missing people.

**BASIL BATARINGAYA
"Missing"**

Leader of the opposition Democratic Party in parliament (1962–64). He switched in 1965 to the UPC and later became minister of

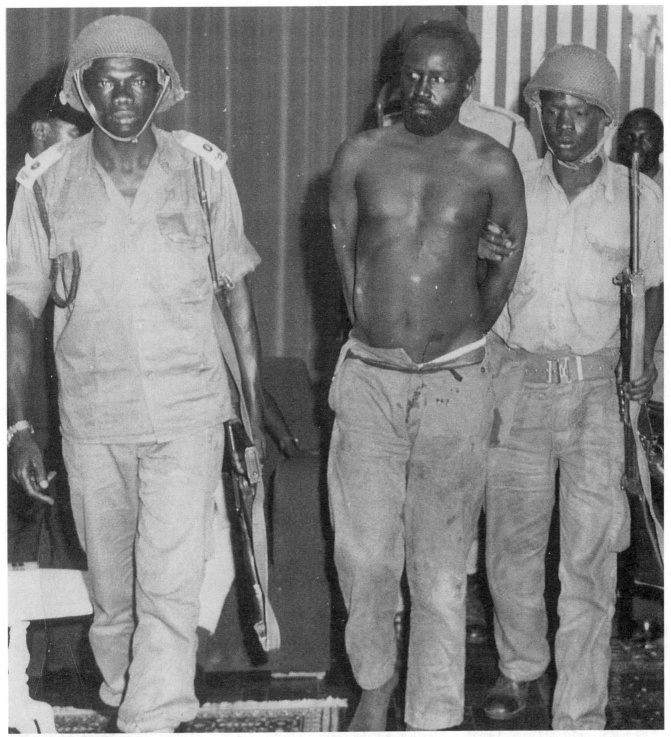

CAPTURED REBEL leader Alex Ojera at an OAU cocktail party where he was publicly interrogated by Amin.

internal affairs in Obote's government.

"Reported missing, but investigations have not revealed where he might be."

ALEXANDER ARTHUR OJERA
"Escaped Custody"

In the first independence government he was parliamentary secretary in the Office of the Prime Min-

ister and government chief whip. In 1963–64 he was minister of community development and labour before becoming minister of information in 1964.

"He was one of the people who invaded Uganda during September 1972. He was captured by members of the security forces and put under detention. But later on he escaped, together with Captain Oyile and six others."

JOHN KAKONGE
"Missing"

An active politician for several years, he was elected unopposed as the UPC secretary general in 1962, and in 1963 he became director of planning in the prime minister's office. He entered the cabinet in May 1966, as minister of planning and development, on the introduction of Dr Obote's

121

JOHN KAKONGE

new constitution. He was the country's youngest minister.

"Investigations have revealed that he is not in the country and no one knows where he is."

JAMES BWOGI
"Missing"

Formerly with the Ministry of Information, he was commercial manager of Uganda TV.

"Reported to have been arrested by the security forces, but investigations have revealed nothing fruitful."

JAMES OCHOLA
"Missing"

Chief whip of the Democratic Party, but in 1965, accompanied by Mr Bataringaya, crossed the floor and joined the UPC. He was deputy minister of information and broadcasting and tourism, until his appointment in 1966 as minister of public service.

"Not in the country and no one knows where he went."

MICHAEL KAGWA
"Found Murdered"

Educated at Trinity College, Cambridge, Barrister-at-law London. Public prosecutor 1954–56. Resident magistrate 1957–63. Senior resident magistrate. President of Uganda Industrial Court.

"Charred body found in burnt-out car near Kampala."

JOSHUA LUYIMBAZI-ZAKE
"Missing"

BA, LlB MComp, PhD. He was elected as a member of Kabaka's government in 1962. Nominated by Lukiko to Uganda National Assembly. Minister for education and the acting attorney general, 1968.

"Whereabouts not known."

JOSHUA WAKHOLI
"Died In Custody"

Elected to the Legislative Council as a member of the UPC in 1962. Parliamentary secretary to the Ministry of Health in Obote's government on independence.

"Wakholi was in the contingent that

JOSHUA LUYIMBAZI-ZAKE

attacked Uganda in September 1972. He was captured by the Uganda security forces and wounded during the exchange of fire. He died on his way to hospital."

BENEDICTO KIWANUKA
"Abducted"

In 1961 he became chief minister and for a brief period in 1962, before Dr Obote's UPC came into power, he was Uganda's first prime minister. Mr Kiwanuka was appointed chief justice by the present government.

"Was arrested at the high court by

three persons posing as security officers. Their true identities and the fate of the chief justice remain a mystery."

ERISA KIRONDE
"Not In Uganda"

Member of the Planning Commission for Uganda. Chairman of the Uganda Electricity Board. Chairman of the Uganda Red Cross.

"Not returned from official visit overseas."

WILBERFORCE KALEMA
"Missing"

Appointed parliamentary secretary to the Ministry of Education. Became minister of works and housing, later minister of commerce and industry in Obote's government.

"Investigations have revealed that he is not in the country, and no one knows where he went."

FRANK KALIMUZO
"Abducted"

Permanent secretary, Office of the Prime Minister. Head of Uganda Civil Service and secretary to the cabinet, 1962. Secretary of the Karamoja Security Committee. Chairman of the Entebbe Town Council. Vice chancellor of Makerere University.

"Disappeared after being arrested by men masquerading as security officers." ❐

FRANK KALIMUZO

WARRIORS TOGETHER

DRUM: March 1974 – *THE MUCH DECORATED General Amin takes up a spear and joins a party of leaping Masai morans during recent celebrations of Kenya's independence.*

THE TRUTH ABOUT IDI AMIN

DRUM: May 1973

In the guise of a "Champion of Africa", General Idi Amin Dada has committed heinous crimes against his own African people. Day by day, month after month, execution squads – acting for, or operating without interference from, the Ugandan military regime – have purged Uganda of hundreds of its most able and loyal citizens, and eliminated thousands of officers, soldiers and innocent people. In this issue DRUM tells the sadistic and horrifying truth about Uganda under Idi Amin.

Throughout the night of January 25, 1971, sporadic shooting was heard across Kampala. By the morning troops loyal to the general had surrounded parliament and seized the radio station. And Idi Amin, son of Amin, a northern Muslim peasant, held power. There was rejoicing in Kampala as the powerfully-built soldier-saviour released political detainees, promised to end corruption, *kondoism* and arbitrary arrests, and announced that elections would be held after a temporary spell of military rule. "There is no room for hatred and enmity – only for love and friendship between us all," Amin told Ugandans in a broadcast.

More than two years later Idi Amin's boasts remain hollow. The country he rules is seized by fear, intimidation and capricious sadism. And Uganda, with a history more violent than many African countries, seems to be slipping

back into the age of barbarism and cruelty of centuries ago.

To understand this disintegration of a progressive young nation, one can chart the disintegration of Idi Amin himself – a once bluff and amiable soldier who could speak of love and gentleness and African brotherhood with a sincerity that for a long time deceived his people and the rest of Africa. This decep-tion seemed complete during the first month of his rule. Here, it ap-peared, was a true leader of the people – not an African aristocrat, nor a product of a Western univer-sity or of the international socialist scene, nor an impeccable creation of Sandhurst Military Academy.

The coup d'etat that brought Amin to power only briefly resolved the antagonism in the army between Amin's Kakwa tribe and Obote's Lango tribe, and their relations the Acholi. While Amin was travelling to Britain and Israel in July 1971 to try to buy arms, tribal clashes broke out within the ranks at Mbarara, Moroto and Jinja bar-racks. Some 900 soldiers belonging to the Lango and Acholi tribes were believed to have been killed by Amin's supporters. Amin, with some skill, hushed the distur-

125

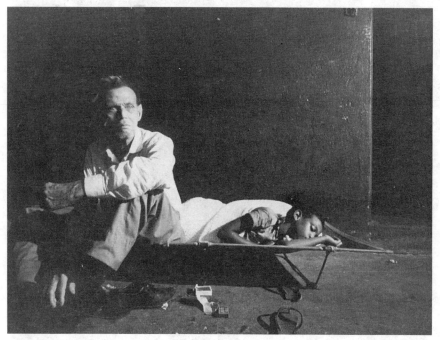

DIMLY LIT LIMBO: Two unknown prisoners in the grim Makindye Prison.

AMIN REMEMBERS the Jinja army barracks massacre in which hundreds died.

AMIN PRESIDED OVER a massive increase in the size of the Uganda army.

bances up. But early in 1972 the rumours of successive bloodbaths in Uganda were exposed to the scrutiny of the world when 23 Ugandans escaped across the border into Tanzania with indisputable evidence.

The escapees were among 500 former members of Obote's armed forces – nearly all Lango and Acholi – detained at a prison farm at Mutukula, near the Tanzanian border. Many of the men had been members of Obote's special police, who had intimidated Ugandans.

MAKINDYE JAIL, KAMPALA. *This photograph, taken by a photographer briefly detained, shows a communal cell with faeces drifting in an open sewer.*

The escapees told a press conference that 400 of the prisoners had been killed. Every day a Kakwa execution squad had taken a group of men to a wood and shot them. Officers went first, and when they had been eliminated, the executioners began on the other ranks. To break the monotony, the executioners sometimes cut their victims throats instead of shooting them. One notable prisoner, Mohammed Hassan, head of Obote's CID, had been shot in his cell because he was too ill to walk to his death. The refugees said that they had escaped in a desperate mass break-out, climbing over the bodies of some 70 of their less fortunate brothers heaped in a prison gateway.

The violence that began within the army spread quickly to the beautiful and amiable capital of Kampala, once royal city of the great southern Baganda tribe. One by one, some of Uganda's most talented citizens began to disappear. Chief Justice Benedicto Kiwanuka, a father of Ugandan nationhood, was taken from his high court by a group of men in an official car and murdered. Was it a coincidence that scores of other leading citizens who disappeared were Baganda Roman Catholics, or belonged to the Lango and Acholi tribes, or had been ministers in the Obote government?

A distinguished and outspoken academic, Professor Kalimuzo, vice chancellor of Makerere University, was soon silenced. A Roman Catholic editor, Father Clement Kiggundu, and a Muganda tycoon were found – charred corpses – in their burnt-out cars. George Kamba, a former Ugandan

MEMBERS OF THE SIMBA Battalion who massa-cred dissenters. Throughout 1971 Amin and his supporters systematically eliminated all the sol-diers who were suspected of being loyal to Obote.

PILES OF CORPSES *lie in the dust around Simba Barracks after being massacred by Amin's troops. Idi Amin was only able to retain power by a reign of terror and murder.*

ambassador to India and West Germany, was dragged screaming from a cocktail party at the International Hotel.

It would be difficult to believe that President Amin was directly responsible for every Ugandan killing. His control of the army and of government is only fleeting, and cabals of violent men are looking after the "security" of the country for him. But as the crime against humanity deepens, and as the killers continue their work unhindered, the massive responsibility rests with Amin.

To ordinary Africans throughout the continent, Amin seemed to be a man after their own heart – a leader who could deal unceremoniously with the neo-colonialists, the Zionists and the Asian dukawallahs. Amin's place at the front of the stage was cleverly winning him time. Yet the promises he had made to Ugandans were unfulfilled. The high taxes had not been cut; the standard of living had not improved; his "economic war", for all its superficial victories, was dismantling all that had been achieved over the years.

Amin had begun to run out of scapegoats when he turned his attention again to the guerrilla threat. The Uganda army had without difficulty put down an early invasion of guerrilla supporters of ex-President Obote. Now a new guerrilla movement emerged, calling itself the Front for National Salvation (FRONASA). One of the group's leaders, 27-year-old Yoweri Museveni, had earlier worked for Dr Obote. Although FRONASA announced that it was not fighting for Obote, but to free Uganda from Amin's grip, the discovery of its first camp near the Uganda-Kenya

border gave Idi Amin the pretext to begin a witch-hunt for "Obote guerrillas", whom he saw lurking in every corner.

Villagers suspected of giving minimal help to the small band of Chinese-trained guerrillas were arbitrarily rounded up by Amin's troops and publicly executed in several Ugandan towns.

The guerrilla bogey was used as a well-worn disguise by Amin's regime for the rumblings of unrest throughout the country. To try to counter it, Amin sent trusted officers to the provinces with extraordinary powers of suppression.

One of the amazing achievements of Idi Amin during these dark days was his instinct for survival. He ensured this by surrounding himself with northern tribesmen related to his own Kakwa. Many of them, who hold key positions in the army, are not Ugandans at all but Nubian mercenaries from the Sudan. From the beginning, Amin replaced well-trained officers with wilful and dangerous men, who found themselves promoted from lowly rank as privates to grandiose positions as senior officers. And in recent months, an indolent rabble of civilians have formed themselves into a private army around Amin.

Lurking behind dark glasses and wearing paramilitary clothes, the part-time squads prefer to operate quietly by night in the seemingly amiable capital city. Their visits to Ugandan homes mean more disappearances – always officially denied. They like to kill people by bundling them into the boot of a car and executing them with pangas. Amin protested at first about some of their activi-

ties, but their deadly vigilance continued.

A well-used dumping ground for corpses is the lonely shores of Lake Victoria. A British television technician reports that he found bodies floating in a lakeside inlet. The victims had been bound hand and foot, and their stomachs were slit. In some cases severed genitals had been stuffed into the victims' mouths. Fishermen have reported finding bodies cut open and filled with rocks to make them sink. This year the authorities in Zaire complained that corpses were being dumped by Ugandans over the Zaire-Uganda border.

President Amin, having crushed the judiciary, the police and the civil service, eventually turned on the civilian ministers whom he had appointed when he took power. Minister of education, Edward Rugumayo, fled to Kenya, while the foreign minister, Amin's brother-in-law, Mr Wanume Kibedi, who had striven to keep up with his president's capricious sallies in foreign policy, was admitted to a Nairobi nursing home. When Amin became impatient with his cabinet's growing reluctance to play follow-my-leader with a man of his equivocation, he sent them all on indefinite leave.

The men now behind the throne are the most forbidding and ruthless military command ever to emerge in Black Africa. Towering above them is Lieutenant Colonel Ozo, more enormous even than Amin. Ozo hurtled up through the ranks to command the infantry battalion at Moroto. The most powerful soldier in Uganda after Amin, is Lieutenant Colonel Asumani Mussa, commander of the 5th Malire Specialised Mechanised Regiment. If Amin fears anyone, it is Mussa. ❐

THE MIND OF AN AFRICAN TYRANT

"AMIN'S IMPATIENCE and wilfulness has led, directly or indirectly, to the murder of innocent people" – DRUM editorial.

DRUM: May 1973

One day when the graves are counted and the grisly evidence is put together, Africans will try to find out what pushed Idi Amin Dada, this seemingly affable and tolerant man, into tyranny.

Perhaps part of the answer goes back to his early years in the isolated north-west of Uganda. His tribe was so backward that it had no chieftaincy system, nor the kind of local democracy that many other African people take for granted. Strong personalities counted more than the wise or compliant ones.

When Amin first went south to Kampala he came across tribes like the Baganda who, despite a violent history, were literate and politically sophisticated. They were also Roman Catholic. He could only have been ill at ease. As a soldier of the British, Amin was isolated for most of his career from these political subtleties. He was taught that loyalty and action mattered most. When total power was given to him after the coup, he tried to run a complex nation, which had already embraced modern economic ideas, as an army battalion. He failed completely to follow the patient example of soldiers like General Gowon of Nigeria, or experienced statesmen like President Kenyatta of Kenya. Whatever Amin wanted, he wanted it now.

His brand of instant government soon made monkeys of the qualified civilians whom he appointed to his government. Life in the ministries became a bemused pursuit

133

THE PRESIDENT, General Idi Amin, with education minister, AK Mayanja.

of Amin's whim. The politicians who flourished were the sycophants, who were in frequent attendance – drinking endless cups of tea at Amin's Kampala home, suitably called the Command Post – waiting uncomplainingly while Amin disappeared for one of his frequent dips at the pool of a Kampala hotel.

The politicians who suffered were those who saw the extent of the disintegration of government, and who had to listen to Amin exchange sergeants' mess banter about the state of the nation with crude military cronies. They also had to learn to live with Amin's visits to the local oracle.

Those close to Amin spoke of his disturbing pride. It was the pride of a simple man – the kind that turned to petulance and vindictiveness if hurt. During one of his adventures abroad at the beginning of his rule, Amin's pride was injured by both the British and the Israelis within a few days. Beaming with goodwill, Amin asked Golda Meir, the Israeli premier, and Sir Alec Douglas-Home, the British foreign secretary, for sophisticated strike planes and ground-to-air missiles.

Why did he want the planes? the amazed foreigners asked. To attack Tanzania, he said. One source reported that Amin intended not only to snuff out Obote guerrillas who, he claimed, were training in Tanzania – but he wanted to capture the Tanzanian port of Tanga for Uganda! When Mrs Meir and Douglas-Home rejected Amin's request, the Ugandan's bonhomie vanished. He had been made to feel a fool in the diplomatic world, and he was not to forgive either the British or the Israelis.

All the time, Amin was very sensitive to the reaction of his fellow African statesmen. Many of his blunders in foreign policy had been due to his enraged determination to prove what a good African he was. Amin knew, as most Africans do, that foreign domina-

FRIENDS NO MORE: Amin with British military advisors in his first year in power.

tion of the economy and the double-face presented to White southern Africa by Britain and other major powers were a challenge to independent Africa. Ordinary Africans throughout the continent warmed to Amin's forthrightness. But the worldly wise and the national leaders soon realised that Amin was a bull in a political china-shop. And they feared that his impetuous actions could put their hard won national security in jeopardy.

At home in Uganda, Amin made a few dramatic gestures towards national unity. His funeral of the Kabaka of Buganda was a masterpiece of stage-management. In the cause of religious unity, he sent two of his sons to a Roman Catholic seminary to become priests. But he was thwarted in his brief pursuit of unity. Nothing seemed as simple as life in the battalion.

Amin was particularly unnerved by the raucousness of the British press, who were enraged by Amin's short treatment of the British. Again Amin's good intentions turned to petulance and mistrust of fictional foreign "enemies" who planned his downfall.

In recent months the enemies of Amin have grown in his imagination until they lurk in every government ministry, every church and every provincial town. Every other foreigner was a "spy". Every Asian possessed a suitcase full of ill-gotten Ugandan money. Even his own ministers were disowned.

Amin is at the end of his tether. Many of his symptoms are the classic symptoms of tyranny, and have been well charted in other men down the ages. More lasting than the tragedy of Amin, is the

AMIN WITH Union Jack during his controversial stint in the King's African Rifles.

tragedy of his country. Although Uganda was a divided country under Milton Obote, the worst excess of Obote's rule could not add up to

what has happened in any one month of Idi Amin's republic. It will take a decade at least for the wounds to heal. ❐

BIRDS OF A FEATHER flocking together: Amin with fellow despot Bokassa.

LETTERS TO THE EDITOR

Defence For Ugandan Asians
I take this opportunity to air my views on the expulsion of Asians from Uganda and the unfair criticism that has been levelled against them. Why weren't the posts of business manager, accountant, teacher and cashier given to the Africans at the time of independence, when there was every possibility of it? Why weren't the Asians asked to leave the country at that crucial period and let the Africans do the job?

Naturally, and it is only fair to say that there were no suitable Africans at that time to take up these posts. Now that time has passed and the hard work of the Asians has produced the required fruits, the role they have played in the country's economy seems quite unimportant to those who harbour prejudice and ill-feelings against innocent people.

Anjans A Panday, Dar es Salaam

Amin – True Son Of Africa
People should stop criticising President Amin. He has got rid of the people who were taking the fruits of independence. Amin, a man of action, suggested that Africans should unite forces and simply fly once over South Africa and Rhodesia in a show of strength that would free our brothers. Did any leader come up with support? Amin is a true son of the black race. Let us all unite and liberate our brothers in the south now.

Ricky John, Nandi South, Kenya

A mere show of strength would be unlikely to dislodge the entrenched rulers of South Africa. The consequences of a Pan-African war would be dreadful. – Editor

Tough For Us In Uganda
I am one of the oppressed Uganda women and I feel our government is doing more harm than good to us. Minis were banned, along with wigs and trousers.

These ruthless army men have harassed the women. You pass a policeman and he stops you, measures your dress, finds it's the right length, lets you go. But before you walk two yards you come across an army man. He stops you, and before he has measured the dress he has started beating you, saying your dress is too short and pushing you to the jeep which takes you to the police station.

Nobody can say anything unless she wants to see another world. We have been standing it, but just recently we were shocked and dumbfounded when we heard of the ban on cosmetics!

We're tired. Why should we wait for these ruthless nuts to harass us again. Soon they'll make it an offence to have vaseline. Hey women, why don't you wake up and protest!

Concerned Ugandan Woman

I Am Ashamed Of Being A Ugandan Today
I am currently living outside Africa. I have noticed great changes in the attitude of Africans, Europeans and Asians who once had nothing but praise for my country. In the days when I was first a student, Uganda was considered to be the "Pearl of Africa" and people respected our policies. How can any Ugandan travelling overseas justify the killings now taking place in our beloved country?

Many Africans in Uganda are disgusted with the policies of Amin. Not many of them were worried when he told the British and the Israelis to quit. After all, other African countries have fought with the British and the Israelis. But what finally turned many against Amin was his policy of killing-off rival tribesmen and staging executions – held after false trials had taken place. People have kept those photographs, so proudly given to the world by none other than the Ugandan government.

Do those foolish people in Kampala think that such pictures are Christmas cards to be sent through the post like presents?

Ugandan-In-Exile

Were These Executions Legal
In the begining many Africans looked to General Amin as a source of inspiration. It seemed when he took over that he would do a lot for the average man, even though he was a soldier. Most people could understand, too, when he expelled the Asians.

But recently Amin and his friends have been shooting fellow Africans without open trials so that the people can judge whether they are enemies of Africa and Uganda or not. My question to you is this: were the executions in Uganda trials or not? I cannot see how they were because there was no judge.

BA McJohn, Lira

Thanks to the 3,200
It is almost impossible for me to find suitable words to express my happiness to you for publishing my photograph in the Pen Pals column. So far I have received about 3,200 letters. What amazes me is that although it is months since my photo appeared I still receive new letters and I am still pleased with every letter I get. I would like to convey my heartiest thanks to all those wonderful people who have written to me. And I promise that no matter how long it may take, I shall try to reply to every one. ❏

THE NEW NAME OF SHAME

As the regime failed to put into effect any of the reforms it had promised, its popular support dwindled. Amin's response was to short-circuit the normal procedures of government, resorting first to rule by decree, and then to outright repression. Lacking popular support, Amin concentrated on keeping the army under his control – through skilful public relations, by narrowing the army into a Sudanic-speaking Muslim force, and by continual intimidation and juggling around of top military officers. Amin also manipulated the theme of the foreign threat to the country to distract people from their domestic problems, while constantly resorting to violence as the ultimate means of extracting compliance. Members of Amin's special security branches, the State Research Bureau and the Public Safety Unit, began to penetrate almost every sector of society. With such pervasive surveillance, and because Amin's agents ruthlessly eliminated dissidents, there was no way in which people could organise against Amin.

Following his 1972 trip to Libya, Amin launched a major drive to Islamise the country. Henceforth the regime began to actively use Islam as a criterion for recruitment and promotion in the army and the civil service. Because of Amin's professed faith in Islam and his recently acquired anti-Israeli stance, Arab countries, notably Libya and Saudi Arabia, underwrote the cost of sustaining Uganda's paralysed economy and burgeoning army.

Ugandans were suffering not only from the terror, but also from the effects of the counter-productive "economic war" which decimated industry and badly weakened agriculture. Shortages of essential commodities such as salt, sugar, matches, cooking oil and bread were endemic. In the face of these problems, farmers in outlying areas withdrew further into subsistence farming. Those closer to urban areas switched to cash crops, such as coffee, which were invariably smuggled out of the country.

The regime's attempts to use international diplomacy to offset internal problems were greatly boosted by the hosting of the 1975 OAU Summit Conference in Kampala and the election of Idi Amin as OAU chairman. Zambia and Tanzania boycotted the summit for they felt Amin did not deserve the respectability it bestowed upon him. Amin's preoccupation with African affairs during his year as chairman allowed Ugandans a relatively quiet 12 months. However, the spectacular Israeli raid to rescue Jewish passengers held hostage by Palestinian hijackers at Entebbe airport shocked Amin out of this relative benevolence. A humiliated Amin struck out against civilians who had taken delight in the army's embarrassment, and against Kenya, whom he thought had helped the Israelis. A bitter verbal war broke out between the two countries and Amin ordered that Kenyan nationals in Uganda be identified and eliminated.

BIG DADDY'S ECONOMIC WAR – IS HE WINNING?

SIGN OF THE TIMES: What were once Asian shops have fallen into the hands of African traders new to the business.

DRUM: February 1974

At first glance, you cannot avoid being impressed by the changes in the streets of Ugandan towns. All businesses – even the most sophisticated like pharmacies – are run by Ugandan Africans.

One of the most striking features of Uganda's economic state is the ruthlessness with which the military deals with business malpractices like overcharging or hoarding of essential commodities. It could result in not only loss of a trading licence but, in extreme cases, in the business being allocated to someone else. The military regime also ensures that once a trader has been allocated one business he cannot acquire an-

other one, or turn the original business into a shop dealing with different commodities.

There are widespread shortages of essential commodities because of the disruption caused to factories and to the supply network by the sudden eviction of Asians. Uganda, which used to export sugar, has now been forced to import it from Kenya. There are reports of widespread smuggling of goods across the border to Zaire and the Sudan by African merchants who want to make quick money outside Uganda.

Idi Amin's government has given stern warning to traders against the hoarding of commodities like cooking oil, salt, sugar and even

maize-flour, and has directed the State Trading Corporation and the district commissioners to crack down on malpractice. Despite these warnings, the situation appears to be getting worse. This can be judged by hundreds of Ugandans who stream into Nairobi week after week in search of essential items.

The worst aspect of the hasty Africanisation of trade in Uganda, are the skyrocketing prices the new African traders charge for goods. Some of the traders are nicknamed *mafuta mingi* or "much fat". A locally made shirt which costs 30 shillings in Nairobi, is sold in a Kampala road shop at 105 shillings; a cheap safari suit that costs 80 shillings in

Nairobi, is sold at 285 shillings in Kampala.

It is a question of take it or leave it for many Ugandans, as they have no choice. Restrictions imposed by the Bank of Uganda do not allow Ugandans to leave the country with enough money to make many purchases outside the country, and the penalties for smuggling Ugandan money can be severe. To make matters worse the ordinary peasant who wants such essential commodities as soap, sugar, bread or cooking oil has to dig deep into his pocket to be able to buy them.

The country relies very heavily on Kenya for goods. Black market trade has enriched the traffickers. Lack or shortage of wagon trucks and the delays at the border for commercial vehicles seem to have hit the trade very hard. Social life in Uganda has had a tremendous jolt with restrictions placed on the drinking hours and on the manner in which the girls can dress. Gone are the miniskirts and the trendy gear of the younger generation; gone too are men's beards – for the major general does not believe in the "revolutionary" look that is the feature of students in most other countries.

It seems that a few Ugandans have benefited from the economic revolution – some are members of the armed forces or members of the government, some are traders from the rich areas of Buganda and Busoga.

Things seem to have quietened down on the political front; people simply do not feel inclined to talk against the military government. In the pubs the big conversation is all about the economic war. Many pub talkers believe

AFRICAN TRADERS *took time to adjust to the new order.*

Ugandans are winning the war, and praise is poured on Major General Amin and his "government of action". Idi Amin's economic war will face its severest test in 1974. We hope that all Ugandans will eventually share in the success – and not a few handpicked people who find themselves men of property because of their connections and not because of their ability for hard work. ❐

CONFISCATED TYRES.

HINDU TEMPLE *becomes a school.*

AMIN HITS OUT AT COWBOY SOLDIERS

DRUM: May 1974

They call him the "Bulldozer of Africa". Idi Amin Dada, the tough-talking general who rules Uganda, is a man always in the news. Hardly a day passes without the press carrying a story of his latest pronouncements on almost every subject.

DRUM visited Idi Amin in Kampala's Makindye Lodge for this exclusive interview.

DRUM: Your Excellency, what do you see as the main achievements of your controversial government during the past three years?

AMIN: All people of Uganda are revolutionaries and this includes members of the armed forces. Everything in the country is shared by everybody so that they can enjoy the fruits of the revolution of January 1971. We have already won the economic war and all the businesses formerly owned by foreigners, who were milking our economy, are now in the hands of Ugandans.

DRUM: But there are complaints from some Ugandans that the soldiers have grabbed businesses in the major towns?

AMIN: I have already warned that senior army officers, particularly provincial governors, who have many businesses and houses, will be dismissed at once from their services so that they can go and do business. I have stressed since the declaration of the economic war that no one should own more than one business. It appears, however, that some army officers try to own

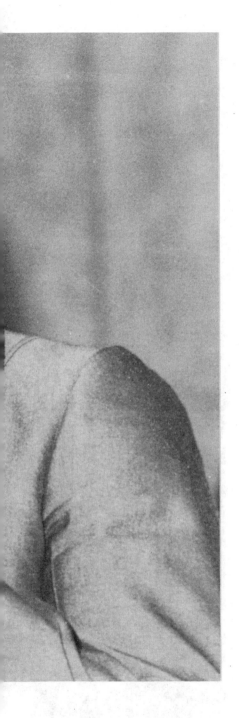

and will continue to fight corruption and other ungodly tendencies in all their forms. Uganda is now steady and peaceful. All the incidents of hijacking and killing are being reported only in Buganda. Because of the seriousness of the matter I have decided to call Baganda chiefs so that they can discuss the issue and find ways and means of stopping crime. Intensive investigation intended to unearth the mysteries of disappearing people in Uganda has been started.

DRUM: Is it true that some army officers have been involved in the kidnapping and disposing of innocent people?
AMIN: We are a government of action. If we have evidence that an army officer is guilty of kidnapping and murder then he will face justice. There is no evidence to back up such a serious allegation.

DRUM: How is discipline in the armed forces? There are reports that some soldiers behave as if they were the president of Uganda?
AMIN: Our soldiers must behave themselves and not think that they are above the law. I have discovered of late that when some army officers are promoted they run for big cars and stop buying suits. Some of them dress like cowboys in bell-bottom trousers. This applies also to some Makerere University students who do not comb their hair, pretending that they are reading books, and have no time to shave. On the other hand, you find that these students have time to go to bars and drink.

DRUM: Mr President, how popular do you think you are with the people of Uganda and Africa as a whole?
AMIN: I am the only president

GODFREY BINAISA: In exile.

WANUME KIBEDI: In exile.

who drives alone. If a leader is liked by his people, then his security is taken care of by the people themselves.

DRUM: When you speak of your popularity in Uganda, how is it that some of your ministers have decided to run away and seek refuge in other countries?
AMIN: My former minister of education, Mr Edward Rugumayo, and my former minister for animal resources, Prof Banage, as well as a former attor-

a house in every town in Uganda. This is capitalism and I will not hesitate to dismiss such officers as they are spoiling Uganda's name.

DRUM: There have been reports of people being kidnapped and put into car boots and later killed. How far is this true?
AMIN: It has taken us less than three years to fight the social menaces such as highway robbery to the extent that the evil is no longer a social menace in Uganda. We have been fighting

THE PRESIDENTIAL SALUTE.

NOTORIOUS KONDO, Emmanuel Mala, killed by villagers.

ney general in Obote's government, Mr Godfrey Binaisa, and another lawyer, Mr Kazzora, are all out of Uganda, but they are not bad people. They were among my best friends because they were carrying out their duties efficiently, but they were confused by a few bad elements who advised them to run away. Nobody would do harm to them if they returned to their mother-

land. I am happy that all of them are employed wherever they are.

DRUM: How about the future of Dr Obote and his supporters now living in exile?
AMIN: They are free to return to Uganda anytime they want.

DRUM: Has your government any plan to expand the economy?
AMIN: My aim is to revolutionise Uganda and see that all Ugandans are very rich in the future. When I decided to transfer the economy of the country to Ugandans, the British approached me and offered me 200 million shillings so that I might rescind my decision. The British also told me that if I refused, I would be assassinated with the help of some Ugandans, but when the Ugandans knew I was working for their interests they refused to kill me.

DRUM: There have been accusations that your government is giving more help to tribes in northern Uganda, including your own Kakwa tribe. How far is this true?
AMIN: Tribalism is the biggest enemy in Africa today. Many people confuse the word tribalism with tribe. When we say we do not want tribalism, we do not mean that there should not be a tribe. Tribes are here to stay. In Uganda today there is no tribalism being practised as the government appoints only people who are able to do their jobs. My own family is an example. My four wives come from different tribes in Uganda.

DRUM: Perhaps, Mr President, we can discuss some international issues. You were one of the African leaders who took active interest in the 1973 Middle East war. What are your views on the Arab-Israeli conflict?
AMIN: If Arabs had not been

confused by Dr Kissinger (that arch-murderer) to stop fighting and had continued to fight for five more days they would have captured the whole of the Sinai and the Golan Heights. I have decided to form what will be known as a suicide squad and if Israel does not want to withdraw from Arab land, members of my suicide squad will drop on Tel Aviv and Haifa to fight from there.

CELEBRATING THE COUP: General Amin addresses the nation at a gathering in Kampala on the first anniversary of his coup.

The people of Uganda and Africa as a whole will continue to give the necessary support to our Palestinian brothers and sisters at the frontline in their just cause for survival against the Zionist and imperialist forces.

DRUM: You recently banned the wearing of wigs in Uganda. What prompted this decision?
AMIN: African culture is very im-portant to me. Following the ban of wigs in Uganda our women now look more beautiful and very natural. I had to give this directive because I do not want to see Ugandans wearing dead hair from dead imperialists or wearing hair from those who have been killed by the imperialists in Vietnam.

Any member of my family who wears a wig will not be regarded as a member of my family with im-mediate effect.

DRUM: Many Ugandan women do not seem to be happy about the decree which forbids them to dress as they wish. What are your views?
AMIN: As I have said, they must look natural and this is final. But I am concerned over the way the men are dominating women. ❑

BIG DADDY MAKES IT A HAPPY LANDING

BIZARRE HOLIDAY SNAPSHOT: General Amin, the liberated passengers AND their hijackers pose happily together.

DRUM: June 1974

It took Africa by surprise – the first case of air piracy of its kind over African soil. An Ethiopian couple seeking refuge because of the political situation in their country attempted to reach Libya by hijacking an East African Airways plane to take them first to Libya and then to Moscow.

Uganda's President Amin personally intervened to put a prompt end to the drama when he persuaded the Ethiopians to surrender at Entebbe airport, Kampala.

The two Ethiopians, armed with a pistol, had seized an East African Airways Fokker Friendship F27 on its way from Nairobi to Malindi. Holding the crew at gunpoint, they ordered the pilot to change course and fly to Libya, "or be shot". The aircraft was carrying 31 passengers, most of them tourists, and four crew. Captain Penfold changed course and put down at Entebbe, it was believed to refill.

The airline appealed to the Ugandan authorities not to intervene hastily. But when he heard of the hijack, President Amin dashed to

the airport and was waiting there when the plane landed. Ugandan troops ringed the aircraft. General Amin made a successful appeal to the two Ethiopians, and the passengers, all fit and well, were released.

The hijackers were taken into the airport building, along with the crew, and President Amin conducted an on-the-spot inquiry.

"At the airport the president strode up to the cockpit of the plane and began talking with the Ethiopian at pistol point," said a passenger,

CAPTAIN Penfold: Kept cool.

CO-PILOT Omar: Flew at gunpoint.

they were headed for Moscow. "The captain was very diplomatic in persuading them to go to Entebbe first," Mr Kuiper said.

The drama began when the hijacker left his seat as the stewards started to serve breakfast. He went into the cockpit, pulled off the earphones that Capt Penfold and the co-pilot had on and shouted: "It is a hijack. It is a hijack." He then ordered the pilot to head for Moscow "without any fuss". His wife was standing next to him. They held a

brief conversation in Amharic, after which the man said that they would fly to Moscow. The pilot told him that the aircraft did not have enough fuel to fly direct to Moscow. He then demanded to be flown to Libya. He was told the plane could not fly to Libya either without refuelling. He then said it should fly to Uganda for refuelling. Mr John Cherrey, another passenger, said the hijacker had talked to the passengers and given them the reasons behind the first African hijacking. ❏

Dutch businessman, Mr HJ Kuiper. "The gunman then threw his pistol from the plane onto the tarmac, and he and his wife surrendered to the president." He said the Ugandan leader allowed the hijackers to hold a press conference where they denounced Emperor Haile Selassie of Ethiopia for "perpetuating 3,000 years of slavery" in his country.

Mr Kuiper said the captain had a pistol at his head during the flight. The Ethiopian hijacker told passengers, "almost apologetically", not to leave their seats and that

UNLIKELY LOOKING HIJACKERS: Mr Katsete and his wife – Ethiopian dissidents who hijacked the plane in a bid for freedom.

THE RISE AND FALL OF PRINCESS ELIZABETH

DRUM: February 1975

Top international manne-
quin, barrister, actress and
then diplomat. That was
the impressive background of the
Ugandan beauty whom General
Amin selected to be Uganda's foreign minister. But after barely
eight months in her jet-set job,
Princess Elizabeth of Toro has
been sacked and humiliated by
her one-time patron.

The top international hotels of
New York, Paris, London, Rome
and Nairobi were "home" to
Uganda's famous Princess Elizabeth. Rich, cultured, intelligent and
beautiful, she graced the cover of
Harper's Bazaar, then the top
American society magazine, focal
point of international high fashion.

In Britain, where she studied, she
mixed with royalty and was a
guest at the 21st birthday party of
the Queen's cousin. High society
craved her attendance at important functions in whatever capital
she was passing through. Ambas-
sadors invited her to their parties.

Then came her downfall. She was
dismissed by Amin and placed under house arrest. Now her whereabouts are a mystery. It was rumoured that she had had her hair
shaved off and had been imprisoned, but Uganda's Bonn ambassador, Miss Benedicta Olowo, gave
an assurance that the Princess was
free to come and go as she pleased.
However, sources close to Uganda
believe that she may still be in
prison. The body of her predecessor, Michael Ondonga, was found
severely mutilated in the Nile a
few days after his dismissal.

*MODEL PRINCESS: Elizabeth combined
a successful international modelling career (above) with her duties as Uganda's
roving ambassador (below).*

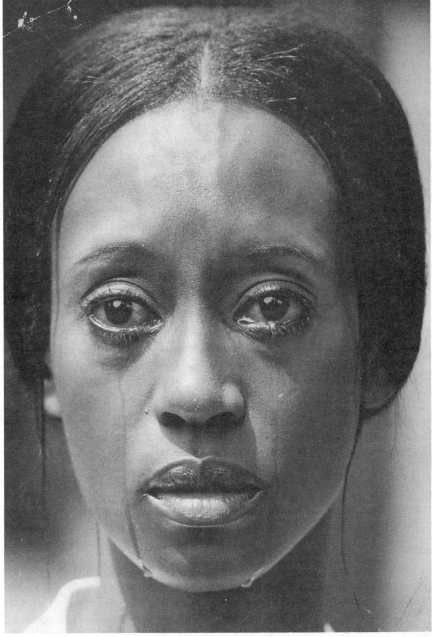

Princess Elizabeth, the daughter of Omukama George Rukidi III of Toro, was at the summit of her checkered career when Amin sacked her last November. Educated in England, the Princess mixed with British royalty. Prince William of Gloucester, a cousin of the Queen, invited Elizabeth to his 21st birthday party at St James Palace. After living in London for eight years, she returned to Uganda in 1965 on being called to the Bar, becoming the first woman barrister in East Africa.

Many people believed she was the power behind the throne of her brother, Patrick Olimi, now 31, who was deposed as King of Toro in 1967 by ex-President Milton Obote.

After his fall, Princess Elizabeth left Uganda to live in America where she became a model. Acting parts followed in the film "Bullfrog in the Sun", shot in Nigeria, and "Cotton Comes to Harlem".

The Princess – calling herself Elizabeth Bagaaya as her title had been abolished – returned to Uganda in 1971, after President Obote's overthrow. She was appointed Uganda's roving ambassador and delegate to the United Nations, where she made her first speech wearing a stunning golden robe. Then, in February 1974, she was appointed Uganda's foreign minister.

Her dismissal came eight months later on November 28, 1974, and the Princess was placed under close house arrest. Two days later General Amin assumed the post of foreign minister. ❐

FOR BETTER AND for worse: Princess Elizabeth with Amin soon after her appointment (above), and with tears streaming down her face (below).

THE JOKE THAT TURNED SOUR

DRUM: September 1975

If the Hollywood adage is true that there is no such thing as bad publicity, Field Marshal Amin is one of the world's great public figures. While his posters proclaiming victory in the economic war may be doubtful in their veracity, and the stories of missing Ugandans may be true, his skill in commanding the limelight is unequalled.

One example of this was at the OAU conference in Ethiopia in June 1974. When it came to his turn to speak he said that other leaders read their speeches whereas he scorned notes and spoke from the bottom of his heart. His address

was so funny that he soon had his audience rolling. President Nyerere of Tanzania at first listened solemnly, refusing even to look at the Ugandan leader. But he too was soon overcome by the humour of the Ugandan leader. As General Amin left the rostrum he turned on an impulse and shook President Nyerere by the hand – the first time the two had been photographed thus.

The general is, among more terrible qualities, a man of mirth. But this year, many African leaders refused to attend the Kampala summit, and perhaps Idi Amin is regretting that no one takes him seriously enough. ❑

THE AMAZING ANTICS OF PRESIDENT AMIN

ALL SMILES as two British envoys pose for photos after being given gifts by the Ugandan leader. It was a case of British diplomacy losing face in order to save one man's life (above). British Foreign Secretary James Callaghan, Amin and Denis Hills after his release (below).

DRUM: September 1975

Lieutenant General Sir Chandos Blair, Britain's personal envoy of the Queen, emerges from a traditional Kakwa hut in Arua, Idi Amin's birthplace in northern Uganda. Lieutenant General Blair and another envoy, Lieutenant Colonel Graham, had gone to the Ugandan leader on the plight of a British lecturer, Denis Hills, sentenced to death by a military tribunal – although later reprieved – for calling Amin a "village tyrant". Amin had the hut built to ensure the two British officers had to crawl on their knees to enter. Lieutenant General Blair was obviously vexed by the exercise. Field Marshal Amin told DRUM later he was the only African leader who had managed to get the White man to kneel. ❐

WHITE MAN'S BURDEN: *Field Marshal Idi Amin is chaired by four Kampala-based businessmen at a reception to mark the Ministerial Session of the OAU summit held in Kampala. A jovial Bob Astles cheers them on (right).*

THE BULLDOG OF AFRICA.

A HAPPY Amin amongst his people.

AMIN TAKES *a wife under the watchful eyes of Libya's Gaddafi and Queen Elizabeth.*

ONE OF THE BOYS: *Amin takes time off to play his favourite accordion.*

UN chief, Kurt Waldheim, with Amin.

THE BLUFF BUFFOON OF AFRICA

"AFRICA OYEE, AMIN OYEE, UGANDA OYEE" chant this large crowd, unfazed by their leader's penchant for controversy.

DRUM: Assorted

Uganda's soldier-president is a man of many words. His pungent comments on world affairs have amused many, and infuriated others. His "friends", the British, have been the butt of many of his pronouncements. Here DRUM presents an anthology of President Idi Amin's sayings.

On Obote

Obote is like my brother. He would not have remained in power until January 25 if it had not been for my help. Up to January 25 I still trusted Obote, and was going to give him a big welcome on his return from Singapore.

I will try to help Dr Obote to get back his old job as a clerk when he returns. Obote used to be a good clerk before he joined politics.

Obote knows that I am his best friend. He knows that he has lost a great friend.

On Foreign Exchange

Amin's minister: Sir, we have run out of foreign exchange.
Amin: Then print some more.

On Britain

The British are my best friends but they are annoyed because I kicked out the British Asians. They can say what they like. I have no time for imperialists.

If Britain wants compensation for its businesses which were taken over because of the economic war, the British prime minister or the Queen must come personally to Uganda.

President Amin raised £2,400 for his "Save Britain Fund" and explained that the aim of the fund was to "save and assist our former colonial master from economic catastrophe".

I am the only African head of state who has managed to get the British to kneel down and bow.

On Israel

I have sent a telegram to Golda

Meir telling her that I am not a person who fears anyone. I am six-foot three-inches tall and a former heavyweight boxing champion.

Arab victory in the war with Israel is inevitable and the prime minister of Israel Mrs Golda Meir's only recourse is to tuck up her knickers and run away in the direction of New York and Washington.

The world is now convinced that I was right when I said some time ago that Hitler was right to burn six million Jews during the Second World War.

The imperialists will face fire when I lead the OAU. They will

fear that under my leadership we will be able to free Palestine from the clutches of the Zionists.

To Richard Nixon
I am sure that a weak leader would have resigned or even committed suicide after being subjected to so much harassment because of the Watergate affair. I take this opportunity to once again wish you a quick recovery from the Watergate affair, and I join all your well-wishers in praying for your success in recovering from it.

On Prostitutes
I am planning to act drastically against these girls. But men must also contain themselves. There would be no prostitution if men refrained from talking to them.

Even prostitutes can do some work – reporting the subversives.

On Women
Women should not sleep while men are working.

On the Expulsion of the Asians
The Asians only milked the cow, but they did not feed it to yield more milk.

There are now Black faces in every shop and industry. All the big cars in Uganda are now driven by Africans, and not the former blood-suckers. The rest of Africa can learn from us.

On Zambia's Kenneth Kaunda
President Kaunda is the greatest two-faced double dealer of our continent.

On Southern Africa
All progressive African countries should form one high command. What we need is to put all our armies together under one leader. As a field marshal, I am not afraid. I

have always been in the frontline and I will continue to do so. I was in the frontline during the 1973 Middle East war. If Africa wants me to lead such a high command, I will not let Africa down.

On Food Shortages
This is just temporary. We are in the final stages of stocking all shops in Uganda to capacity with all sorts of goods. People should not think Amin is asleep. The country is stable and nobody should confuse our people.

On Monthly Cabinet Changes
Changes in the cabinet are necessary to ensure that there is new blood and that ministers do not sleep. Ugandan planners have been told to stop indulging in paper work alone without putting ideas into action.

On his Security
I fear nobody except God. I am not like some leaders who are surrounded by bodyguards. Whether people like it or not, I have made history. This has been recorded.

On the Angolan Civil War
We cannot sit idle while fellow Africans butcher themselves because of the stupidity of their leaders.

If South Africa is fighting in Angola, then it is time an OAU force was despatched to Angola. I will personally lead such a force.

On the International Media
There has been too much anti-Uganda and anti-Africa propaganda in the Western press. Imperialists and their news media always hate true African leaders like myself. They forget that the more they publicise their anti-African propaganda, the more popular these true leaders become. ❐

WHY WE WERE READY TO FIGHT

"WE HAVE FOUGHT before and we will fight again," President Kenyatta told a huge crowd at Uhuru Park, Nairobi.

THE PLACARDS CARRIED at the rally tell their own story.

DRUM: April 1976

When Idi Amin laid claim to parts of Kenya, President Kenyatta warned him that his countrymen would not give up an inch of their land. They were prepared to fight for it, he told a mammoth rally in Nairobi.

Feelings ran high in Kenya when President Amin claimed that parts of Kenya belonged to Uganda. After Kenya had sealed her borders and stopped goods bound for

Uganda via Mombasa from getting through, Amin withdrew his remarks. But the damage had been done.

President Amin's outburst was condemned by Kenya's foreign minister, Dr Munyua Waiyaki, who told DRUM: "Kenya will not surrender an inch of her territory to anyone. We will guard our boundaries with all the resources at our command."

Amin's claims not only extended to Kenya, but also to the Sudan. He claimed large chunks of both countries, which, he said, were historically part of Uganda. He also revived his threat to go to war if Uganda's access to the sea was threatened. Speaking near the Sudanese border, Amin accused British colonial administrators of transferring large chunks of Ugandan territory to Sudan and Kenya early this century. This territory, including one region stretching from the current border to within 32 kilometres of Nairobi, still rightly belonged to Uganda, Amin said.

He said Uganda's Defence Council had approved a plan to "follow up this matter so the British will have to explain why they did it. The British made many mistakes in this matter. If the peoples of these territories were not happy they should be allowed to have their own governments. My job is to liberate all Ugandan territory and right the mistakes of the British," Amin said. Amin did not pinpoint the countries he might go to war against, but in past statements he has talked about creating a "corridor to the sea" through either Tanzania or Kenya.

Kenya was quick to hit back at Amin. A government statement

KENYANS WERE ANGERED by Amin, but they did not lose their sense of humour.

said Kenya would not part with an inch of territory. "Kenya respects the sovereignty and territorial integrity of all its neighbours – including Uganda – and expects Uganda, which is a member of the OAU and whose president is the current chairman of the organisation, to adhere to the OAU charter and respect her sovereignty."

Claims by Uganda on parts of Kenya were not only provocations of the highest degree, but also went against the charter of the OAU, which recognised all boundaries in Africa drawn by the colonial powers in 1895. It is recognised that the balkanisation of Africa left much to be desired. People of the same tribes or ethnic origins were divided into different countries without regard for their languages, common amterests or even blood relationships. But this was not the fault of the Africans. They inherited the present boundaries, and if peace is to be maintained the present boundaries have to remain. ❏

FIELD MARSHAL IDI AMIN RIDES AMOK

SHOW OF STRENGTH: The 5th anniversary parade smokes through Kampala.

DRUM: July 1976

Uganda is in turmoil. The assassination attempt – which is thought to be connected with Amin's purge of the police force, the deterioration of relations with Kenya, and the collapse of Uganda's economy are all adding to local unrest.

With outrageous prices becoming the norm and lack of confidence in the Ugandan shilling, illegal dealings across the border have flourished, with dire consequences for the Ugandan economy. Many Ugandans at the border smuggle foodstuffs to Kenya and sell them for Kenyan currency, creating shortages of all sorts of commodities in Uganda. And the wounds caused by Amin's claims to parts of western Kenya will be hard to heal.

Although Amin backed down, saying that he was only referring to "historical facts" after reading a book by Sir Harry Johnston, a pioneer British administrator, Kenyans demonstrated in their thousands against Amin. Dockers in Mombasa boycotted Ugandan goods, causing long queues in Kampala. Essential goods, like sugar, milk, salt, bread and oil disappeared.

Consumption, investment, government spending and exports have dried up. Uganda has run out of foreign reserves and there is no cash even for spare parts on maintenance equipment. Nearly all the buses in Kampala are out of action. Doctors, including highly qualified specialists, went on strike because of low pay and shortages of medical supplies. They ended their strike only after President Amin intervened personally and promised help. He told them that he truly sympathised with their plight since he was a doctor himself. Sources in Kampala said that the strike was not really about pay, but about the lack of medicine and equipment.

But perhaps the main problem is Uganda's soldier-president – an unpredictable military despot who could resort to anything to achieve his ambitions. He has armed the country out of all proportion to her defence needs. He knows that his country is facing economic chaos and wants to divert the people's attention from his mismanagement.

Amin is now running into trouble with his former friends as well. When Kenya insisted that Uganda should pay in cash for the goods passing through Mombasa, Amin turned to his Arab friends, Saudi Arabia and Libya, for help. He was told that he could expect nothing. Saudi Arabia has been Uganda's biggest source of money. Two years ago, the Saudis gave the country £12 million cash aid, half of which paid for the military hardware bought from the Soviet Union. Amin's reaction to the Saudis' refusal was bitter: "I have given my life for their cause."

The future looks grim with Uganda nearing economic collapse and Amin wavering from one extreme to the other. ❐

TOO CLOSE for comfort: Even Libya's Gaddafi, an old ally, has cooled to Idi Amin.

FIELD MARSHAL IDI AMIN, VC, Conqueror of the British Empire, inspects his air force on a bicycle because there is no petrol for his motor car.

ENTERTAINING AMIN, SHAMING AFRICA

THE FIRST TANZANIAN leader to visit Uganda since the 1971 coup: Vice President Aboud Jumbe.

THE TERRIBLE TWO-SOME: Idi Amin and the Central African Republic's Emperor Jean-Bedel Bokassa (left).

WHEN THE CAT'S AWAY... In July 1975, while in Kampala, Nigeria's General Gowon was unceremoniously thrown from power (right).

IN HALLOWED COMPANY: *Amin walks in the footsteps of two African father-figures, Emperor Haile Salassie of Ethiopia and Jomo Kenyatta of Kenya.*

BRITISH PRIME MINISTER *Edward Heath with Idi Amin, 1971.*

LIBERIA'S *President William Tolbert grants Amin a Liberian knighthood.*

HOW AMIN GOT RID OF THE DISABLED

THE DEATH PLOT THAT MISFIRED

DRUM: January 1987

Kampala and its environs has very few physically handicapped people today. This was not the case until 1975 when, under Amin's orders, physically handi-capped people were rounded up in lorry loads and dumped into the crocodile infested Nile River at the Owen Falls Dam. The incident which led to this inhuman act was witnessed by Odhiambo-Ogutu:

One morning around 10 a.m. Amin drove into Kampala's main car park in his Citroen. He was accompanied by some of his ministers and bodyguards. He got out of his car and started walking around the car park. He entered one of the shops that surrounded the car park and found a group of men playing *ajua*. Amin requested that he join in the game and one of the players relinquished his position for the president.

The game resumed and word went round that the president was playing. A crowd gathered to watch. It was soon apparent that Amin was a good player. He was cheered by the crowd as he beat one man after another.

Now in the middle of the jubilation, there came into the crowd a crippled man by the name of Wandera Maskini. He was very well known in Kampala. Wandera pushed his way through the crowd with his crutches and went and collapsed in front of Amin.

He glared at Amin and started insulting him. He called the president names and told him that he should not have sent away the Asians because the common man was now suffering. "We don't have commodities in the shops yet you call yourself a president. Son of a bitch! Kill me if you want," said Wandera Maskini.

One of Amin's bodyguards raised his hand to strike Wandera, but Amin restrained him. "Shoot me!" provoked Wandera. "I hear you are a murderer and shoot people with your gun. Shoot me now!" Amin quietly got to his feet and left the crowd, followed by his ministers and bodyguards. Three days later Wandera was seen being hauled into a military vehicle. Up until today nobody knows what happened to him, but your guess is as good as mine.

That same evening, Radio Uganda announced that anybody who was lame, blind, had no hands, and anybody who felt that he was so poor and disabled that he needed help, should report to the nearest police station. The government, claimed the announcement, would offer them jobs, free accommodation and free food in Jinja.

The following morning thousands of cripples and other disabled turned up in Kampala's police stations. They were loaded onto military trucks and driven to Jinja. At Jinja, they were unloaded like sand into the Nile River. Those who could not hold on to the lorries fell into the river, while those who had hands and held on were shot and they too fell into the river. ❏

DRUM: October 1976

At dawn, Thursday, June 10, 1976 was just an ordinary day. By sunset it had qualified for a place in Ugandan history, for an abortive attempt was made on the life of Uganda's head of state, Dr Idi Amin.

It was about 6 p.m. at the Nsambya police grounds, barely two kilometres from the centre of the capital city of Kampala. President Amin had inspected a colourful police passing-out parade. As the soldier-president walked to his military jeep to depart, three grenades were hurled at the jeep. The crowd scattered in all directions as the grenades exploded, injuring 37 people including the co-driver of the presidential jeep, Sergeant Musa Abbas.

With great presence of mind, President Amin jumped into the jeep and drove the injured sergeant to Mulago hospital some eight kilometres away. The rear tyres of the jeep had been punctured by the grenade blast but this did not stop Amin from delivering Sergeant Abbas to hospital. Abbas later died in hospital.

The news of the assassination attempt spread through the capital city like a bush fire. The following day, a statement, attributed to a military spokesman, blamed "the enemies of Uganda" for the incident, but urged Ugandans not to be "alarmed nor listen to rumours of those who want to disrupt the stability prevailing in the country".

AMIN CONGRATULATES the Defence Council for declaring him life president.

The Defence Council was immediately convened to appraise the situation and held prayers to thank God for having "miraculously saved the life of President Amin". The cabinet met on June 14 and both collectively and individually the ministers pledged loyalty to President Amin. Two weeks after the attempt, the Defence Council made Field Marshal Amin life president.

Speaking at the funeral of Sergeant Musa Abbas, General Adrisi, chief of staff of the Uganda armed forces, warned that any other attempt on the life of President Amin would be "an invitation to the soldiers to teach the country a lesson it would never forget".

It was reported that Palestinian experts confirmed the grenades were of a type currently in use with only the Americans and the Israelis. The

president himself later said: "The plan was by the CIA who wanted me dead before the next OAU summit."

Abraham Sule, a State Research officer, witnessed the assassination attempt. "I was patrolling the area around the barracks when Amin came to attend a passing-out parade and inspect a guard of honour. He always suspected an attack, so it was our duty to patrol around any place he went to.

"Amin arrived driving his own jeep, but afterwards, when he left, his driver was at the wheel. Someone hurled a hand grenade and it landed on the driver's side. If Amin had been driving, he would have been killed when it exploded. As it was, Amin grabbed the wheel and drove the jeep to Mulago hospital. I think he was slightly injured by the shrapnel."

Then, Sule says, came tragedy, as soldiers and bodyguards fired wildly into the crowd that had come to watch the parade. Between 50 and 100 people were killed, and many others badly wounded, he remembers. ❐

CHIEF OF STAFF: Mustafa Adrisi.

AMIN'S BLOODY PATH TO AFRICAN BREAKUP

AMIN GREETS KENYAN Cabinet Minister Peter Kenyatta. Despite the bad feelings, Kenya maintained a working relationship.

DRUM: August 1976

Life for Kenyans living in Uganda has been a pageant of hell. Following a week of mayhem, eyewitnesses and victims claim that nearly 60 Kenyans from Jinja and Makerere village outside Kampala were shot or bayonetted to death by Ugandan soldiers who went on the rampage – looting, raping and killing every Kenyan they found.

Speaking to DRUM at the lakeside Kenyan town of Kisumu, Aloo Otiende, who has been a businessman in Jinja for seven years, said: "Armed soldiers went through villages in Jinja looking for Kenyans, especially Luos and Kikuyus. They asked everyone to prove his or her identity. Those who resisted were shot on the spot. Others had their belongings and property loaded onto army trucks and taken

away. They were beaten and told to leave for Kenya.

"I managed to escape with my wife and two kids by hiding in a bush. The shootings and ransackings went on for nearly a week. The trouble was sparked off by some soldiers who demanded free beer from a shop owned by a Kenyan at Jinja. The bar-owner refused and the soldiers resorted to violence. The man was shot dead."

But the soldiers did not have it all their own way. Kenyans armed with pangas battered a number of soldiers to death, another eyewitness told reporters at Kisumu. "We were desperate. We were fighting for our lives and the lives of our children," said Maurice Owinga. "Two soldiers entered my house at Makerere village and told me at gunpoint to get out.

"The soldiers then stripped my wife naked and sexually assaulted her in front of our three children. After taking away all my property they told me to go to Kenya if I valued my life. I sold some of my clothes and those of my wife. Putting the money together we managed to get fares for the bus to Busia."

According to eyewitnesses, the attacks on Kenyans appeared to have been sanctioned from the top, because neither appeals to the provincial governors nor the police brought any response. "They were out to get our blood. Even the police feared to intervene. The soldiers are ruthless. They don't hesitate to mow down the police."

It was the worst week of violence involving Kenyans since Idi Amin Dada took over power in January

1971. There have long been cases of sporadic vio-lence against Kenyans, including kidnapping involving workers in the East African Community, but nothing as serious as the latest mayhem.

The number of Kenyans living in Uganda at the time of Uganda's independence in 1962 was estimated at 45,000, but most of them left following the expulsion order by the Obote regime in 1969 and in the wake of thuggery which followed Amin's power grab. With the departure of the Asians in 1972 following the declaration of economic war, many Kenyans also left, some taking with them the little cash they were allowed to take, while others left behind everything, including livestock.

Another eyewitness of the bar brawl which started the trouble told DRUM that a sergeant was knifed to death in the fracas. After the incident lorry loads of soldiers arrived at the bar in search of Kenyans. Those found were shot on the spot while others fled for their lives. "People were lying dead all over the place," he said.

A Kenyan who fled the unofficial death squads arrived in Nairobi to tell of the Jinja massacre and the continuing terror campaign. James Otieno said soldiers marched into Makerere village on June 19. One of them stormed into the house of a Kenyan businessman and sexually assaulted his wife in the husband's presence. The husband was attacked when he tried to intervene and he finally slashed the soldier on the head with a panga. Other soldiers rushed to the scene and gunned the man down, Otieno reported.

The next morning truckloads of troops arrived to the sound of

AMIN WAS more at home with Zaire's President Mobutu and the Congo's Bokassa.

trumpets, and announced they were "hunting for Luos". They first seized a fish trader from Siaya, dragged him into the street, and bayonetted him to death. They moved on to another Siaya man, ordered him out of his house and executed him.

Otieno, who was himself injured in the attacks, said the soldiers continued to move from house to house, singling out Kenyans and executing them in public. The sol-diers then seized the village sub-chief, Mr Ogola, a Kenyan. They fired shots into his house and demanded to know how many Kenyans were in the area. Ten more people were subsequently "collected" and have not been seen since.

Otieno said: "When they came to my house they hit me several times with the butts of their rifles. I was left lying on the ground when the others were taken away." ❏

AMIN AND OAU OFFICIALS watch his jet fighters attack, and miss, their targets.

ENTEBBE – NEW NAME OF SHAME

AMIN THE MEDIATOR: The president greets a group of hostages released after his appeal to the hijackers to free them.

DRUM: August 1976

In the early hours of July 4, 1976, Israeli troops swept through the heart of Africa, turning Entebbe airport into a battlefield to free 102 hostages hijacked on a flight to Paris by Palestinians. The hostages had

DORA BLOCH: Murdered in anger by the Ugandans after the Israeli raid.

been detained with the spectre of death for six days. Such a rescue feat had not been accomplished before.

In the raid by the Israeli commandos, three hostages died and all seven hijackers were killed. Twenty Ugandan soldiers died and several others were wounded. Several of President Amin's MiG fighters were left in flames.

The plane, which had 250 passengers aboard, was hijacked from Tel Aviv. There were 83 Israelis aboard. It was forced to fly to Benghazi in Libya, then to Uganda. The hijackers demanded the release of scores of prisoners held in jails in several countries. Among those the hijackers wanted freed included 40 people held in Israel, six in West Germany, five in Kenya, one in Switzerland and one in France. Demands for the release

of the prisoners were made by Radio Uganda, which said the prisoners had to be produced at Entebbe airport within 48 hours.

Monday, June 28

The hijacked plane arrived at Entebbe. The five hijackers carried grenades and other weapons. The crew were refused permission to leave the jet and food was taken to them aboard.

Tuesday, June 29

During tense negotiations on the baking tarmac of Entebbe airport, the hijackers hurled abuse at Western countries. They were later disowned by the Front for the Liberation of Palestine – the group they claimed to represent. Fears were growing of a bloody ending to the two-day hijack as reports from Athens said that mass murderer Carlos "The Jackal" Martinez might be leading the Palestinians.

166

President Amin and the French ambassador in Kampala, Pierre Renard, persuaded the terrorists to let passengers and crew leave the aircraft for the transit lounge.

Wednesday, June 30

Kenya denied it was holding any Palestinians. Israel, France, Switzerland and West Germany all rejected the hijackers demands. At Entebbe, the 250 hostages sat crammed in the tiny airport lounge waiting while the five governments and the seven gun-toting hijackers haggled over their fate.

Thursday, July 1

The hijackers threatened to blow up the jet and its hostages if their demands were not met. Earlier in the day, they released 47 women, children and sick people. An Air France plane left Entebbe for Paris with the released hostages. The release of the 47 had been sought by President Amin on humanitarian grounds.

Friday, July 2

The hijack saga took a new turn when the hijackers said they would kill about 100 Israelis and crew by noon on Sunday if their demands were not met. This forced the Israeli government to break its long-standing policy of refusing to make deals with guerrillas, and concede to negotiate. The guerrillas earlier released another 100 hostages, but kept Israelis, Jews and crew members under the threat of death.

Saturday, July 3

Israeli officials refused to comment on whether any jailed terrorists were to be exchanged for hostages at Entebbe.

Sunday, July 4

Israeli Hercules planes stormed into Entebbe airport, turning the

THE AIR FRANCE PLANE at the end of the runway at Entebbe airport.

THE CHARRED REMAINS of Uganda air force planes destroyed by the Israelis.

CHEERING ISRAELI CROWD welcomes the returning rescue commandos.

UGANDANS MOURN: The bodies of the 20 Ugandan soldiers killed in the Israeli raid were publicly exhibited.

UGANDAN SOLDIERS ATTEND a funeral ceremony for their fallen comrades at Kololo airstrip, Kampala.

A HUMILIATED AMIN addresses mourners at the funeral of the Ugandan soldiers.

area into a battlefield, before rescuing the hostages. The attack took Ugandan troops and the guerrillas completely by surprise. The airborne Israeli mission swept the hostages to safety – and only hours later they were being greeted by relatives and friends in Tel Aviv.

In a radio broadcast from Kampala, President Amin said that in addition to the 20 Ugandan soldiers killed, 13 had been seriously injured. Amin said two Israeli soldiers were killed when they tried to enter the Presidential Lounge at the airport. Amin later protested to the United Nations and the OAU about alleged Kenyan complicity in the airborne commando raid. ❐

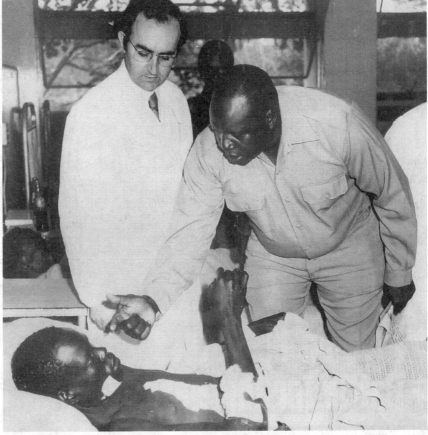

A LESS UNFORTUNATE victim of the Israeli raid is visited by Amin in hospital.

DRUM

AFRICA'S LEADING MAGAZINE

September 1977

EAST AFRICAN EDITION 3/-
ZAMBIA 60 NGWEE
U.K. PRICE 50p.

EXCLUSIVE

I was in Amin's death camp

PLUS:

▶ Pele on his future
▶ Battle for the Horn

THE BUTCHER OF AFRICA

In February 1977 an event occurred which signalled the beginning of the end of the Amin regime. By 1977 the excessive use of violence by Amin had become almost random. The military's vicious control of the state left Ugandans almost no room for criticism or dissent. The Christian church was the last remaining refuge in the midst of this repression. And yet even it was destined to come under attack from Amin. On February 5, 1977 members of the army raided the official residence of the archbishop of Uganda, Rwanda, Burundi and Boga-Zaire. At gunpoint they demanded information from Archbishop Luwum about an alleged conspiracy to overthrow the regime. In response to this incident the bishops of the Church of Uganda published an open letter to Amin condemning the government's abuse of human rights. This letter was to be Archbishop Luwum's death warrant. On February 17 he was arrested, accused of complicity in the coup plan, and killed – probably by Amin himself.

The archbishop's murder marked a crucial turning point in Ugandan history. It galvanised internal and external opposition to Amin's regime while at the same time triggering a series of increasingly desperate moves by Amin. It was a combination of these forces which was finally to topple the military regime. The archbishop and the two cabinet ministers murdered with him were all Luo-speakers. It was not surprising therefore that, following the archbishop's death, the massacre of Acholi and Langi escalated dramatically. Archbishop Luwum's murder also triggered a widespread persecution of Ugandan Christians. Within months Amin had banned 26 Christian organisations. There soon began an exodus from the country of Ugandans of every ethnic, language and political background.

The flight of thousands of Ugandan political refugees not only bore stark witness to the reign of terror in the country but also profoundly affected the way the world perceived Amin. The Commonwealth refused Amin permission to attend its London summit and strongly attacked the violation of human rights in Uganda. The United States banned trade with Uganda and a number of African states broke off diplomatic ties. These events provided a rallying point for opposition to Amin among exiled Ugandans and a number of anti-Amin organisations sprang up in America, Britain and Kenya.

The rapidly worsening crisis around Amin left him gripped by paranoia. And well he should have been, considering the by now numerous assassination attempts, coup plots and mutinies aimed at unseating him. Indicative of Amin's panic was his decision to seal Uganda off from European tourists – whom he suspected of being spies – and his attempt to kill Mustafa Adrisi, his brother-in-law, who was vice president and defence minister. Although Amin announced that 1978 would be a "year of peace", it was clear that he was neither capable of reforming himself nor of stopping the killings.

THE ARCHBISHOP AMIN LOVED AND KILLED

ARCHBISHOP LUWUM WITH AMIN: Publicly they were always on good terms, but privately Amin wanted him dead.

DRUM: April 1977

None of the violent deaths which have disfigured Uganda's recent history have shocked the world as savagely as that of Anglican Archbishop Janani Luwum.

Since President Amin came to power, the Church had walked the tightrope between maintaining a good relationship with Amin, and at the same time defending its human flock. After six years the rope gave way. On February 17, 1977, Archbishop Luwum and two senior cabinet ministers were arrested for their alleged complicity in a coup plot. Their arrest came after 3,000 soldiers had chanted at a rally: "Kill them, kill them" when they heard charges supposedly implicating the three in the plot. President Amin stopped the soldiers and told them that there would be no summary executions. The alleged plotters would be given a proper trial before any sentences would be passed, he told the troops.

Then, according to the official Uganda government version of the incident, Archbishop Luwum, the interior minister, Charles Oboth-Ofumbi and the land minister, Lieutenant Colonel Erinayo Oryema were killed in an accident as they tried to overpower their driver in an unescorted security forces' Range Rover. A spokesman said their vehicle hit a car and overturned and that they were dead on being pulled out of the wreckage.

However, there have been many conflicting reports as to what actually happened to the archbishop. The Tanzanian *Daily News* gave a graphic account of the archbishop's murder. According to the paper, the archbishop had, during interrogation by Amin and a number of other officers, refused to sign a confession and was ordered to lie on the floor. "His cassock was pulled up. He was then undressed. Two soldiers in turn whipped the archbishop. The archbishop started to pray. But the prayers seemed to incense Amin for he shouted wildly and started to use obscene language and then he struck the archbishop."

The report went on: "The archbishop's ordeal was halted for 30 minutes – while Amin broke off to hear the BBC's "World News" and "Focus on Africa" programmes. Finally a furious Amin pulled out his pistol and fired twice into the archbishop's chest."

According to another account – related exclusively to DRUM by a businessman, Ben Ongom, held at the State Research Bureau headquarters at Nakasero at the time of the archbishop's murder – it was Major Moses Okello-Safi who actually fired the fatal shots. "The three were thrown roughly into the cell,"

BRAVE DEFENDER OF human rights, the late Archbishop Janani Luwum.

KILLED BECAUSE THEY knew too much: Ministers Oryema and Oboth-Ofumbi.

he told DRUM, "and the iron gate slammed shut. Oryema and Oboth-Ofumbi were running with sweat and obviously very shaken. The archbishop was quite calm and appeared wholly composed. There was a brief conversation between the ministers and some of the other inhabitants of the cell, whom they knew well. Then the archbishop called for silence and told them that they should pray. In a quiet voice he lead the cell in several minutes prayer. He prayed for peace and he prayed that the president should see that the rule of law be returned to the country. Not only did this have an astonishing and calming effect on the terrified ministers, it also seemed to shatter

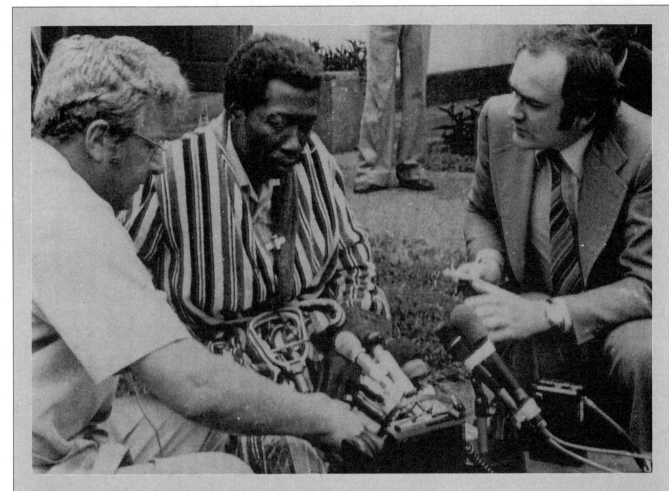

The car accident, in which the archbishop and the two ministers were alleged to have lost their lives after struggling with the driver, Major Moses Okello-Safi, to escape, was arranged just outside the State Research building at Nakasero. Apart from the obvious discrepancies in the damage to the two cars, one of the drivers, having placed his car up against the other one, got out in his suit and with a briefcase and walked back into the State Research building.

But perhaps the most telling gap in the story comes from the fact that, although this "accident" took place just outside the officers' mess, no officer or indeed anyone else, heard any cars crashing.

the guards who stood open-mouthed at the gate watching this remarkable sight."

At about 7:30 p.m. according to Ongom, several unusual things began to happen at Nakasero. First a large motorcade arrived,

which could only be Amin. Then the usual noise of beating and shoutings upstairs totally ceased. At this point the archbishop and the ministers were taken out of the cell upstairs. Ben Ongom's group heard several shots from inside the room just above the cell. This

was the first and last time people were killed by shooting at Nakasero. It was all most unusual. The next morning one of the guards told Ongom that Major Moses Okello-Safi had shot all three men with Amin in the room watching.

President Idi Amin has vehemently asserted his innocence and has denied the report that he personally shot the archbishop. The archbishop, he said, had plotted with others to overthrow his government and had died in a car accident "as a punishment of God".

At a press conference the president said that 16 smugglers had been arrested and that they had said that their mission was to organise confusion by killing prominent people. Then foreign paratroopers from the United States, Britain or Israel were to fly in from aircraft carriers and land in several Ugandan towns where they were to capture Ugandans.

The official version of the deaths has been flatly dismissed as a pack of lies and sparked a wave of international protest by church leaders in Africa and Europe. Canon Burgess Carr, the West African leader of the All-Africa Conference of Churches, said: "We are alarmed and terrified by indications that the murder of the archbishop may be part of a terror campaign unleashed against Christians in Uganda."

Mr Andrew Young, the American ambassador to the United Nations, described the archbishop's death as "an assassination" and likened it to the reported suicides of prisoners in South Africa.

What was the personal relationship between the archbishop and Amin? According to Mrs Rice-Oxley there was a mutual respect. "They each had their respective roles. Socially they were friends and they never openly clashed. In fact they often met and the archbishop was always invited to state functions. The

> ## Extract from the open letter sent to President Amin by the Anglican bishops of Uganda
>
> We have buried many who have died as a result of being shot and there are many more whose bodies have not been found. While you, Your Excellency, have stated on the national radio that your government is not under any foreign influence and that your decisions are guided by our Defence Council and cabinet, the general trend of things in Uganda has created a feeling that the affairs of our nation are being directed by outsiders who do not have the welfare of this country and the value of the lives and properties of Ugandans at heart.
>
> The gun which was meant to protect Uganda as a nation, the Ugandan as a citizen and his property, is increasingly being used against the Ugandan to take away his life and property.

archbishop once said to me that we had to love the president who was a child of God.

"Archbishop Luwum used to weep with the people if they were being hurt in any way. And he would go to any end – he would go to the president, he would go to ministers. If a lady came in and said: 'I've not seen my husband for a week. I don't know where he is. I think he's been picked up by the police,' he would go to no end of trouble to help that person," Mrs Rice-Oxley said.

Events leading up to his death indicated that a clash between the archbishop and the president was imminent. His willingness to help those who complained to him must have incensed many officials and this would no doubt have been drawn to the attention of Amin.

Last Christmas he spoke on the subject of true Christian victory which he described as "suffering love". His sermon was unceremoniously taken off the air because he was "making political comment". The archbishop threatened to lead a march through the streets of

Kampala to the president to protest against the harassment of his flock and clergy.

A week before his death the archbishop and the 18 other Ugandan bishops addressed an open letter to President Amin protesting at the deaths of many Ugandans. This letter may have been his death warrant. President Amin has never been one to accept public criticism and the letter's criticism of Amin's security forces must have put the archbishop in the firing line.

The deaths of the two ministers is also significant, for they were the last survivors of Amin's original cabinet. Both men had worked closely with ex-President Obote but both appeared to support Amin's coup. Lieutenant Colonel Oryema was Obote's inspector general of police but he was later appointed minister of mineral and water resources in Amin's first cabinet. While the arguments rage as to whether he has killed 100,000 or 300,000, one thing is certain: Amin is responsible for the death of the archbishop. A man of whom he once said: "I love". ❐

WHY AMIN KILLED LUWUM

DRUM: June 1977

President Amin shot and killed Archbishop Janani Luwum and ordered two cabinet ministers killed because he feared they would expose his plan to take the funds set aside for a Church of Uganda centenary monument.

A Ugandan, who said he had friends amongst President Amin's bodyguards, said one of them told him Amin was badly in need of the money for the construction of a Muslim mosque in Kampala.

Amin had approached Luwum and told him he wanted to have some of the British money for the church's centenary monument channelled to the Muslim Supreme Council to finish the mosque, because the Supreme Council members had squandered the money sent from Saudi Arabia. Luwum told Amin the money was for the use of the church he headed and that he had no authority to order it to be spent on other projects.

Amin, his bodyguard was quoted as saying, sent Lieutenant Colonel Erinayo Oryema, minister for land and water resources and one of Amin's henchmen, to convince Luwum that the president was serious about the issue and to persuade the archbishop to yield.

The minister was unable to convince the archbishop. Oryema was an Acholi, like Luwum. So Amin sent his internal affairs minister, Mr Charles Oboth-Ofumbi, also an Acholi, to try again. But the archbishop remained adamant.

Amin was afraid that when the international church authorities attending the Church of Uganda's centenary celebrations arrived in Uganda, he might be exposed for having threatened the archbishop over the money. With this fear rising in him, Amin had to take action. When an alleged plot to overthrow Amin was reported, the president took the opportunity to implicate the archbishop.

The archbishop was arrested and taken before Amin. Amin said he just wanted to check whether he had relented. He gave Luwum more time, telling him to go away and think again.

Then Oryema was arrested and taken to Nakasero. There he was saved by Major Farouk, assistant head of the State Research Bureau. Farouk, the bodyguard was quoted as saying, was ready to die for Oryema as he knew him well, and knew he had nothing to do with the anti-Amin plot.

But as Oryema was returning home he was waylaid by a group of Amin's men who re-arrested him despite his plea that he had just been released from Nakasero. He was taken back to Nakasero and, in the absence of Major Farouk, he was left without allies.

Charles Oboth-Ofumbi was called in by Amin because he was a Christian and therefore closer to Luwum.

The three men were taken to Amin. Amin was angered by the behaviour of the three, particularly of the archbishop. When the archbishop did not respond to the president's "requests", Amin squarely incriminated him in the coup plot. Amin, the guard said, then shot the archbishop in the room. The two ministers also had to be killed because they were witnesses to the whole affair. ❐

CHRISTIAN CHURCH UNDER SIEGE IN AMIN'S UGANDA

DRUM: April 1978

On February 17, 1977, the running battle between Amin and the Christians in Uganda climaxed in the shooting to death of Janani Luwum, archbishop of the Anglican Church of Uganda, in the Nakasero State Research Building.

When Amin seized power on January 25, 1971, he had gone out of his way in the post-coup euphoria to appear to be involving all elements of society in the new regime. At that time he really needed everyone, including the Christians, to consolidate his position. Obote's tribesmen still greatly outnumbered his own supporters in the army. He had therefore piously urged all Ugandans to be faithful in worship at their church or mosque.

He even showed an apparent interest in the internal affairs of the Anglican church. In 1971 there had been dissension among the top leaders of the Anglican Church of Uganda – one diocese was threatening to secede and another was blocking further discussions on the church's constitution. Much of this had its root in politics. Luwum's predecessor as Anglican archbishop was Eric Sabiti. Sabiti

IN DELIBERATE CONTEMPT of the church, Amin went to a 1975 ceremony in honour of the Catholic martyrs dressed as a Muslim imam. When asked to speak, he advised all those present to remember that Uganda had its Muslim martyrs too.

177

DEVOTED Ugandan Christians in Namirembe Cathedral – little did they know that they were being spied on whilst at prayer.

was a strong supporter of former President Obote and was disliked by the Baganda.

In November, Amin intervened and summoned all the bishops and diocesan councils to a meeting in the International Conference Centre in Kampala, saying he did not intend to have a divided church in his country. The meeting was highly successful in its imme-

diate objectives, though there was some doubt, among all except the president, whether the credit was due to Amin or God.

Later, in 1972 and 1973, army headquarters invited the churches to preach the love of God in all army barracks. Transport was provided, all ranks were commanded to attend. Yet amidst all this lip-service to the importance of the

spiritual life was the continuing slaughter and tightening oppression in the country. One hand was trying to pacify and gain influence with the Christians, while the other openly acted to turn Uganda into a Muslim state.

It was a dangerous and unpredictable situation, especially in a country where the Christian church had been born in the blood of martyrs and had even become institutionalised as part of the kingdom of Buganda, whose major political offices had been allocated on a religious basis.

An explanation of Amin's actions at this time must be sought in his personal motivation. He believed everything in life – religion, sex, money, friendship – should be exploited to enable him to seize, maintain and extend his grip on personal power. This end of absolute personal rule did, and would, justify any means.

Before the coup he was very much a token Muslim, perfunctory even in his attendance at the mosque, and today his children are educated at Christian schools. Even now, if he has a "religion" to guide his personal actions, it will be found in his strong retention of elements of the superstitious beliefs of his Kakwa ancestors and his wide-ranging consultations with rural and urban witchdoctors. But then, open support at the right time for the propagation of Islam and its concomitant hostility to Israel, had clear international advantages, especially when Amin's expulsion of the Asian entrepreneurs in his 1972 economic war had effectively sabotaged Uganda's natural prosperity.

Support for the Muslims, however, also had obvious internal disadvantages. The Muslims were about 10 per cent of the population; 20 per cent followed ethnic religions while the rest were Christians, divided about equally between the Protestant and Catholic faiths. Many of the Muslim schools taught little but the Koran and academically were, and are, no match, as Amin has himself realised, for the Protestant and Catholic education programmes. With numbers so drastically against him, the Islami-

sation of Uganda was one battle he could not easily win, for it was men's minds he needed more than their bodies.

Once committed, for political reasons, to a strong Muslim stance, Amin inevitably became increasingly anti-Christian. He only really trusts his Kakwa Muslim people. Even Kakwa Christians can never be wholly in his confidence. In his own mind his increasingly anti-Christian attitude was surely justified by the fact that all the abortive coups against him had been led by Christians.

The murder of Chief Justice Benedicto Kiwanuka, first prime minister of Uganda until 1962 and leader of the Catholic Democratic Party, was undoubtedly meant as a deterrent to the Catholics. However, by 1974 Amin saw the Protestants as a bigger threat than the Catholics. In March of that year, Amin said on Radio Uganda that there was only one Christian church in Uganda, the Roman Catholic. He asserted that the Protestant church of Uganda only came into being because the priests and bishops wanted to marry. The Protestant churches laboriously prepared a memo for him explaining the history of the church and the meaning of the Reformation. How Amin must have laughed!

Meanwhile, for political reasons, he continued to court Kaddafi of Libya and even persuaded King Faisal of Saudi Arabia to visit Uganda, now proclaimed as the new East African headquarters of Muslim missionary activity.

On June 19, 1974, Bishop Janani Luwum, an Acholi from Kitgum in northern Uganda, became archbishop of the Church of Uganda. It

was a well-deserved promotion and, although he was from the north, he rapidly became a highly respected and influential figure throughout Uganda, including Buganda. Over the next two years Amin's reign of terror in Uganda continued and, inevitably, most of those affected were Christians. But all this time Christian enthusiasm, and church attendance, was increasing rapidly throughout the country. Places like Makerere University had become centres of Christian activism.

Christian elements in the army, as an alternative focus of power, were an obvious threat to Amin's rule and now needed the closest supervision. In 1973 and 1974, Amin had deliberately issued a provocative instruction that all commissioned officers, the majority of whom were practising Christians, should undergo a 90-mile route march over Christmas. It was almost as if he was trying to flush the opposition out into the open. There was clear dissent over this order and Christian officers were remarking openly that the same order should be given at Ramadhan.

In 1975 a memorial was opened near Kampala to the Roman Catholic martyrs put to death by Kabaka Mwanga in 1885 under the advice of his Arab Muslim advisors. In deliberate contempt of the church, Amin came to the ceremony in the full robes and headdress of a Muslim imam. When asked to speak, he cryptically advised all those present to remember that Uganda had its Muslim martyrs too. Some Muslims say that Amin has, by this and other actions, done irreparable harm to the Muslim cause in Uganda.

By 1976 the growing Christian grassroots strength was contrasted

179

AMIN WITH MUSLIM LEADERS: Before the coup he was a token Muslim, perfunctory even in his attendance at the mosque.

adversely by Amin with the continuing comparative ineffectiveness of the Muslim appeal to Ugandans. His reaction to any apparent defeat of force is always to use more force. We believe that by 1976 he saw a real threat to his power in the Christians and had decided to take the most positive steps necessary to remove that threat. That is not to say there was a deliberate long-term plan to shoot Archbishop Luwum. But there was an increasing willingness to take any steps to lessen the power of the church. Amin is the supreme opportunist and by the end of 1976 opportunity and will were to come together.

In early 1976, Amin gave instructions that the State Research Bureau personnel should attend and make reports on all church services. His fears could only have been increased by the reports he received. Major Kimumwe attended one service at Namirembe in 1976 in which a Muganda priest delivered an openly anti-government sermon, saying it was high time the government stopped buying Russian MiG jets and bought salt and sugar instead. Kimumwe decided it would be wiser not to go there any more.

His wife attended a service at the Protestant All Saints' Cathedral where Bishop Festo Kivengere, an emotional, fiery, outspoken preacher, delivered an outstanding address on the sanctity and value of human life. He said he knew the State Research Bureau people were there in the church and he did not mind if they took him away as soon as he stepped out of the pulpit. They did not on this occasion, but many people have been arrested and grabbed by the State Research Bureau in churches.

However, the immediate signal for a major confrontation with the Protestant church came at Christmas, 1976, when Amin said that some Christians were preaching hatred and bloodshed, not love. One of the tragedies of Uganda is that so much intelligence information is extracted under torture and the leaders of the intelligence organisations are under such pressure to produce results that bad information is mixed with good, the important with the trivial, until the country's top leaders are bemused by a miasma of suspicion and persecution. They find it easier to shoot 20 innocent people to make sure one guilty one dies than to tackle the difficult task of finding out which is the guilty one.

It seems, however, that by Christmas, 1976, Amin was already receiving the first indications of another coup attempt inspired by Obote and the whispers were even then involving members of the Church.

We say this because, after our arrest in June 1977 and our arrival at Nakasero, we joined, in Cell No 2, 16 people who had been arrested in February and March and were to be charged with treason. Among them were three of the leaders of the attempted coup that led directly to Luwum's death – Abdulla Anyuru, 60, Langi, former chairman of the Uganda Public Service Commission; Ben Ongom, 40, a Langi businessman; and John Leji Olobo, 40, Langi, a senior industrial relations officer in the Ministry of Labour.

Ben Ongom was a rather special case and we took full advantage of the opportunities we had to question him about the Luwum affair. As a result we can, for the first time, throw light on a number of issues.

First, Ben Ongom told us that he, Anyuru and Olobo were couriers between Obote's people in Uganda and Obote in Dar es Salaam. Their job was to organise caches of arms inside Uganda which would be available for use by the internal elements when the external elements began the decisive push. He told us that although Amin's group had found some of these arms, there were many other caches which had not been found,

BISHOP IMATHIU *called on the OAU to condemn Amin at a service for Luwum.*

some of which, because of the cell-like nature of their organisation, he did not know the whereabouts of. There was a plot and there were arms. Amin's people were right to that extent.

Second, Ben Ongom told us that the plot was discovered as follows. On instructions from Dar es Salaam he had involved Obura, the 45-year-old Langi commissioner of police. Obura had become a member of their committee. It seems that Obura's motives were probably mixed. As commanding officer of Amin's police Public Safety Unit, he had been responsible for the deaths of thousands of people, many of his own Langi and Acholi. He would be among the first victims of any successful coup by then. Perhaps at first he

genuinely considered that he could reinstate himself with his own people this way. More likely he was betraying the group from the start and it's Dar es Salaam that should explain who chose him and why.

Be that as it may, a meeting of Ongom, Olobo and Obura had been arranged to take place at the Odeon Cinema Bar where the details for the imminent infiltration of some highly-trained guerrillas and saboteurs from Tanzania would be discussed. They walked out of the bar into the arms of the State Research Bureau people. Anyuru was arrested at his home later that night.

Obura knew that the arms had been brought in but he had not

A PROCESSION OF church leaders at a memorial service for the late archbishop.

ing mess in any old clothes he could find. He was in agonising pain throughout.

Ben Ongom also told us that he and others had gone to the archbishop's house at Namirembe some months before to tell him the situation in their districts and that they had hinted to him that there was an organisation which was developing in certain directions. Ongom said they did this because Luwum was their kinsman and they thought he would be sympathetic to their cause and even be of help to them. However, the archbishop told them flatly and very firmly that as a spiritual leader he could not involve himself in matters that were of a political nature and he, in fact, advised them very strongly not to implicate themselves in such activities, which would certainly endanger their lives.

been told where they were. However, under torture Ongom revealed that his consignment of arms was at "Namirembe, Namirembe where the Anglican archbishop's residence is, at the archbishop's house". Ongom told us that he implicated the archbishop because he thought that once they had searched Luwum's house they would leave Ongom alone. He also, of course, knew that Olobo's consignment was in-

deed at Namirembe, in the servant's quarters of the residence of Dr Lalobo, the medical superintendent at Namirembe hospital and John Olobo's brother.

It is hardly surprising that Ongom talked. After one session upstairs he came back to the cell with his scrotum cut open and his testicles showing. They were left like that for a week before he was stitched up. He used to wrap the suppurat-

Eventually the second consignment was found in Ben Ongom's own flat after he had also falsely, but as a result of torture, implicated the bishop of Bukedi, the Rt Rev Yona Okoth, in an attempt to divert the State Research Bureau men away from the real hiding place.

By the end of January 1976, Amin had concluded, with some justification, that he had unearthed a major attempt by the Langi and Acholi to oust him. He personally interviewed all Langi and Acholi officers at Malire and Entebbe and found evidence against a number of them. After the murder of the archbishop, Amin took a typically ruthless and sweeping decision: all remaining Langi and Acholi soldiers were to be eliminated forthwith. There were at least 50 in each of the 15 major units and 25 in ten minor units. Well over 1,000 Langi and Acholi were killed during this period. ❑

THE NEW ARCHBISHOP, Silvanus Wani, congratulated by his nephew, Idi Amin.

APPEALS TO ISOLATE AMIN

DRUM: July 1977

The murder of Uganda's Archbishop Janani Luwum at the hands of Idi Amin's regime shocked the world. And for the first time it triggered off open resistance by the thousands of Ugandan exiles who, hitherto, had been content to live in anonymity wherever they felt they could settle safely.

Overnight, like mushrooms, resistance movements have sprung up in several capitals of the world. Their message to the international community is an appeal to isolate Amin's regime.

In the United States there are three flourishing movements. One body, Freedom for Ugandans, is led by Godfrey Binaisa QC, an attorney general in Dr Milton Obote's government. His organisation, which is one of the largest in the United States, is based in New York City and has attracted thousands of Ugandan exiles and students.

The Uganda Passive Resistance Movement is based in Kenya and the Front for Salvation of Uganda (FRONASA) has its headquarters in Tanzania, and is led by Yoweri Museveni, a lecturer at Dar es Salaam University. Although Museveni actively belonged to the old UPC led by Obote, FRONASA has no connection with the former president. Museveni once accused Obote of lacking political will and said that if FRONASA toppled Amin, Obote would never be allowed back to power.

At one time Museveni claimed that his movement had bases in Uganda, but observers now believe that FRONASA is not equipped to fight a guerrilla war. Following the abortive insurrection in 1972 of Ugandan exiles and the retaliatory bombing by Amin's air force, Tanzania has suppressed Museveni's efforts to invade Uganda, and he has since resorted to verbal warfare.

The Uganda Group for Human Rights (UGHR) operates in London, led vigorously by Dr George Kanyeihamba, a former lecturer at Uganda's Makerere University. UGHR has attracted wide support in Britain and has been working closely with the Uganda Freedom Committee formed by the Young Liberals led by Peter Hain.

They have been picketing Amin's cargo plane which flies to England with full loads of coffee and tea and returns to Kampala with essential foodstuffs such as sugar, salt, processed tea and coffee, powdered milk, and luxury goods like whisky and cosmetics, intended for Amin's household and his troops.

Alongside the UGHR is the Uganda Action Group, led by Paul Muwanga, once a prominent politician.

Inevitably political differences have started emerging among the exiles. There is a definite apprehension within the emigré groups about the true intentions of former politicians in Uganda who, it is thought, would like to take power when Amin's regime is toppled.

Christopher Twesigye, the organising secretary of UGHR, has said: "It will be a good idea if we united and have branches everywhere in the world, then later have a convention where we will perhaps form a government-in-exile. But we do not want politicians to use us for their own ends." ❐

FRONT FOR SALVATION OF UGANDA'S Yoweri Museveni.

FREEDOM FOR UGANDANS' leader Godfrey Binaisa.

UGANDA ACTION GROUP'S Paul Muwanga.

"AMIN WILL NOT LAST 18 MONTHS"

TAKING A STROLL DOWNTOWN: Amin likes to claim that he doesn't fear his people, but ex-Minister Odaka has a warning for [

DRUM: July 1977

Sam Odaka was minister of foreign affairs in Obote's cabinet and left Uganda in 1971. He watched President Amin develop in the year before he came to power, and now waits for the military ruler's eclipse. He gave his views to DRUM in an exclusive interview.

DRUM: Don't you agree that the regime of President Amin is deeply entrenched in power?
ODAKA: This idea that Amin cannot be removed is preposterous. In fact, several attempts have already been made on Amin's life and he is a man living in fear. That is why he is always heavily guarded. We es-

timate that Amin's rule will not last another 18 months.

Conditions in the country are such that continued rule by Amin and his henchmen will not be tolerated for long. The cost of living alone is one factor that is bound to bring down Amin's government. Smuggling of essential commodities has reached such a scale that Amin has now decreed the death penalty for smugglers. But this is no solution.

The fact is that Amin has mismanaged the economy to such an extent that it will take another eight years to put the country back on to its feet. When Amin organised the 1971 coup, Uganda had 800 million

shillings in foreign reserves. These have now been squandered on buying arms, first from Israel and later from Libya and the Soviet Union. As the world knows, these arms have been used in the massacre of nearly 100,000 Ugandans. And the slaughter continues.

DRUM: Where do you get the figure of 100,000?
ODAKA: This is no secret. Amnesty International has given this figure in its latest report on Uganda. We also have our own sources. In fact, the number of people murdered by the army in northern Uganda alone is more than 80,000. There seems to be a deliberate plan to wipe out the Acholi and

AMIN BLESSES JUMA'S ASIAN BRIDE

DRUM: July 1977

One of the resentments which prompted Idi Amin to expel the Asians was the inviolable state of Asian women. For generations Asian men had chosen Black brides, but it was a one-way arrangement – until June this year when the first marriage between an African bridegroom and an Asian bride was celebrated in Gulu. Several VIPs attended, including Amin, the Indian high commissioner and the Pakistani ambassador. There were only a few Asians left to witness the occasion. ❐

Langi tribes who were the major supporters of Milton Obote.

DRUM: Have the killings been restricted to the Langi and Acholi, or have all tribes been affected?
ODAKA: No tribe in Uganda has not been affected by Amin's terror – even his Kakwa tribesmen. Although Amin first directed his wrath to the Acholi and Langi he has not spared the Basoga, Banyoro, Baganda, Batoro and other tribes.

DRUM: On what do you base your optimism that Amin will be toppled in 18 months?
ODAKA: Amin is rapidly being isolated internationally. He is re-

garded as the leper of Africa. In different parts of Europe and the United States groups of Ugandan exiles are already organised with a view to toppling the dictator. I cannot tell you our actual military logistics since these are secret but I can assure you that we will soon hit Amin very hard. The revolution will start from within the country. Amin knows it and that is why he is ruthless. That is why he suspects everyone, even clergymen, of planning his overthrow.

DRUM: What support do you think the anti-Amin forces have within Uganda?
ODAKA: Practically everyone in

the rural areas – and even those in the urban areas – are against Amin. He is kept in power mainly by the Nubian mercenaries and his Kakwa puppets, but even these have been astounded by his excesses. Who can trust a man who can order the killing of his own ministers and an archbishop.

DRUM: Do you think Milton Obote will be able to return to Uganda as leader again?
ODAKA: The immediate task facing all Ugandan exiles, Obote included, is not who will rule Uganda next. The problem is to get rid of the fascist regime of Amin, to stop the bloodshed, to revive the economy. ❐

THE ODD MAN OUT

DRUM: July 1977

The Commonwealth summit which ended in London recently was the first international meeting to come out openly and denounce Idi Amin's regime. Despite the deaths of more than 300,000 Ugandans even the Organisation of African Unity and the United Nations have kept official silence on Uganda's abuse of human rights.

The summit's final communique, though strongly worded, did not mention the Ugandan leader by name. In a carefully worded statement the conference said: "Cognisant of the accumulated evidence of sustained disregard for the sanctity of life and of massive violation of basic human rights in Uganda, it was the overwhelming view of Commonwealth leaders that these excesses were so grave as to warrant the world's concern and to evoke condemnation by heads of government in strong unequivocal terms."

A sharp clash of views on how to react to Amin's record of atrocities prevented the heads of government winding up the main business at the end of the final session, which ran one-and-a-half hours behind schedule. As the leaders began their closed-door meeting on human rights, with only heads of delegations present, it soon became obvious that demands to have Amin roundly condemned in the final conference communique were unacceptable to an influential minority of African countries – notably Nigeria, Mauritius, Sierra Leone and Malawi. They were

AMIN MISSED THE PHOTOCALL, and no one grieved: Commonwealth leaders pose with the Queen during the 1977 summit.

joined by India, Sri Lanka, Malaysia, Barbados, Trinidad and Tobago, Malta and Cyprus in arguing that an attack on Amin in his absence was not proper. But Zambia, Tanzania, Kenya, Botswana, Lesotho, Swaziland, Ghana, and Gambia were joined by Jamaica, Guyana, Bahamas, Papua New Guinea, Singapore, Australia, New Zealand, Britain and Canada in demanding that Amin should be censored by the Commonwealth.

President Kenneth Kaunda of Zambia, the arch-enemy of Amin's regime, had condemned him even before the summit opened. He said when he arrived in London that Amin's regime was a shame to the African continent and to all mankind. He added: "Look brother, we condemn terror wherever it is. I have been condemning Amin since he took power. I condemned him when he was the chairman of the OAU, and I will continue to condemn him until the people of Uganda get rid of him."

While arguments and counter-arguments about Amin were going

on in and outside Lancaster House, the Ugandan president kept his bluff alive by insisting that he intended to visit London for the conference. In Kampala he hid in one of his houses while his chair in the London conference remained empty. His vice president Mustafa Adrisi ordered Radio Uganda to announce in every news item that he was on his way to London.

The whole of Europe was plunged into hysteria. An Aer

Lingus plane on a test flight was refused a landing at Dublin airport. In Brussels, where Amin said he would land, police and troops cordoned off the airport in case Big Daddy turned up on his way to gatecrash the summit. The British sent orders to sea- and airports to see to it that Amin was not allowed to land. The British press ignored the more sensible leaders already in London and carried Amin's story. To them Big Daddy is good copy. ❐

AMIN'S FIERCEST critics: Jamaican PM Michael Manley and Zambia's Kaunda.

THE PLOT THAT NEARLY WORKED

AMIN WAS MOST PROUD of his air force which he lavishly pampered – and yet segments within it have turned against him.

DRUM: September 1977

It was only one of a long string of attempts to assassinate Idi Amin. But it was the most elaborate of them all. And it was only by the narrowest of margins that Amin escaped from the would-be assassins.

Behind this latest plot in June 1977 were a large number of officers from Idi Amin's – or to give him his official title, Life President Field Marshal Alhaji Dr Idi Amin Dada, VC, DSO, MC, CBE (Conqueror of the British Empire) – own army and air force: men sickened by the indiscriminate slaughter that has marked Amin's reign,

and who decided it was time to remove him. With them were a substantial number of small businessmen, mostly from the Kampala and Entebbe areas. Others in the plot were some of the Ugandan exiles now living in Kenya, Tanzania and Zambia.

The assassination attempt was planned for months, and unlike previous plots, this one was hatched in total secrecy. Not even Amin's intelligence agents, operating in Uganda and in other countries, had been able to pick up the details. Until that is, a few hours before the plot was due to go into action. Then an intelli-

gence agent heard a whisper, and alerted Amin at 4:30 on the fateful morning K not enough time for him to head off the attempt on his life, but long enough to take evasive action.

The plotters called themselves the Uganda Liberation Movement. They worked slowly and determinedly to build up the arms supplies they knew they would need if they were to eliminate Amin. Most of their arsenal of weapons was stolen from Amin's army. Other weapons were smuggled in from other countries. The stocks were hidden in small shops in Kampala and Entebbe.

A key aspect of the plan was the support of a number of Uganda air force officers. This produced the most dramatic part of the plot – a plan to bomb State House from the air when President Amin was inside. The flight to State House, which lies half a mile from Entebbe airport, would take only seconds – and a low-level attack could reduce the rambling building to ruins. But an air attack was not enough, and the plan was for a simultaneous attack on State House with mortars, machine guns and rifles.

Eventually all was ready, and the word went round: "Tomorrow is the day." Last minute preparations were made, and all seemed set for the most dramatic attempt to assassinate President Amin since he came to power in January 1971.

Those in the plot knew the risks they were running. If they were caught, they would face the prospect of hideous torture and possibly a show trial designed to demonstrate to Ugandans the futility of trying to overthrow President Amin. But the conspirators were not deterred. What they did not know was that someone had talked. And at 4:30 a.m. on June 16, Amin was warned of the plot.

Amin did not hesitate – he immediately began to organise his own defence. He quickly switched his plans, throwing the carefully-prepared timetable of the conspirators into confusion. He learned of the involvement of the Uganda air force and sent some of his trusted supporters to the Entebbe air force base to round up the suspects, and to immobilise the aircraft.

President Amin hurriedly left State House, heading for Kampala in a convoy of security cars. He

LIFE PRESIDENT Field Marshal Alhaji Dr Idi Amin Dada, VC, DSO, MC, CBE.

planned, by making this unexpected move, to throw the plotters off balance. And he succeeded.

Nevertheless, a small group of the supporters of the operation staged a desperate attempt to salvage the plot. They waited for President Amin's convoy to pass them on the Entebbe-Kampala road. The spot they chose was near the village of Baitababiri, two miles from Entebbe. But it was a good spot for an ambush.

The main handicap for the plotters was the lack of knowledge of which car President Amin was using. It was unlikely that he would

travel in his official Mercedes – that would be the decoy, they knew. But which of the other cars? There would be no time to see who was in them. The attack would have to be made blindly, in the hope that the right car was caught in the crossfire.

As the convoy accelerated out of Baitababiri, hand grenades were thrown at it. The presidential Mercedes was hit, careering off the road. Other cars in the convoy were hit too, but several escaped damage. The presidential bodyguard poured out of the halted cars and took up positions alongside the road, mounting an imme-

AFTER YET ANOTHER coup plot, Lieutenant Ben Ogwang reads a "confession". He has since been reported dead.

diate attack on the plotters. And President Amin escaped serious injury – although according to reliable sources, he was injured as his car screeched to a halt in the attack, its windows shattered. The plotters made off through the undergrowth and were out of sight before the presidential bodyguard mounted a search.

The people of Baitababiri suffered the most. There was an intensive search by Amin's troops. Houses were ransacked, doors were kicked down, belongings scattered. Hundreds of innocent Ugandans were rounded up and carried off for interrogation. Some of them never returned – their relatives left with no knowledge of their fate.

And the plotters? Some of them, including an air force major who claims to have been the ringleader, escaped. A group of the main conspirators made their way to the Kenyan border and crossed before Amin's orders to seal the border could take full effect. Others disappeared into the bush.

A wave of terror for thousands of Ugandans followed. With the knowledge that members of the Baganda and Basoga tribes had been prominent in the plot, President Amin ordered a purge of these tribes. Hundreds – and probably thousands – were rounded up. Many were completely innocent, but probably some of the plotters were caught in the net.

President Amin disappeared. His radio station made no mention of him, giving rise to rumours that he had either been flown out of

Uganda for medical treatment or was in hiding. According to former State Research officer, Abraham Sule, when Amin went into hiding a fat Nubian soldier, Sergeant Mohammoud, was ordered to dress in one of the frightened dictator's suits and take a "joy-ride" through the streets of Entebbe and then Kampala in a presidential limousine. Mohammoud, Amin's double in appearance, was posing for Amin, the intention being to draw the fire of any other ambush party.

Later Amin surfaced and calmly announced that he had been spending a delayed honeymoon with his 19-year-old wife Sarah on an uninhabited island in Lake Victoria. Speaking soon after the plot, Amin blamed the colonialists, imperialists and Zionists for the assassination attempt. ❐

DEATH
IN THE AFTERNOON

TWELVE brave Ugandans faced the firing squad at Kampala's Clock Tower on September 9, three days after their conviction by a military tribunal on charges of treason.

It was death in the afternoon sun as thousands of fellow Ugandans flocked to the stadium to see the men paraded before clergymen to say their last prayers.

The men were said to have planned to overthrow the government of Idi Amin in the latest abortive attempt on Amin's life. They looked thin and showed signs of having been tortured by Amin's State Research Bureau. According to the proceedings of the military tribunal, reported in full in the September 6 issue of the *Voice of Uganda,* the official mouthpiece of Idi Amin, all the 12 had pleaded guilty to treason.

Two men, John Ejura, the former principal of Aboke High School near Lira, northern Uganda, and Apollo Lawoko, a former controller of programmes with the Uganda Broadcasting Corporation, were freed.

Two other men, Boy Lango, a former ticket examiner with the Northern Province Bus Company, and John Obinu, a former hotel waiter, were each sentenced to 15 years' imprisonment by the tribunal.

The proceedings were held at the Kampala City Hall and the tribunal was made up of Lt. Col. Juma Ali (chairman), Captain Sebi Ali Kill Me Quick, Captain Fulgyensi K. Byabagambi, Captain Kiharamagara Kanoke, and Lt. Nyati Kabagwire. The State case was presented by a senior principal attorney, Mr Lulume. Here, pictured below, are the latest victims of the Amin regime.

SHOT: John Kabandize, former senior superintendent of prisons in charge of Mubuku prison farm.

SHOT: E. N. Mutabazi, former superintendent of prisons, prisons headquarters, Kampala.

SHOT: Peter Atua, former principal officer, Murchison Bay prison, Luzira, Kampala.

SHOT: Daniel Nsereko, former assistant commissioner of police and under-secretary at the Ministry of Internal Affairs.

SHOT: Lt. Ben Ogwang, former military intelligence officer, Malire regiment.

SHOT: Y. Y. Okot, former chief inspector of schools, Ministry of Education, Kampala.

SHOT: John Leji Olobo, former senior industrial relations officer, Ministry of Labour.

SHOT: Elias Okidimenya, former general manager, Lake Victoria Bottling Company, Kampala.

SHOT: Abdalla Anyuru, former chairman of the Uganda Public Services Commission.

SHOT: Ben Ongom, former Kampala businessman.

SHOT: Julius Peter Adupa, former teacher at Lira Polytechnic Institute.

SHOT: Garison S. Anono, former principal, Bobi foundation school, near Gulu.

I WAS IN AMIN'S DEATH CAMP

THE BASEMENT OF the State Research Bureau in Kampala – Idi Amin's death cell where thousands of people have been killed over the years.

DRUM: September 1977

Thousands of Ugandans have died in detention camps since Idi Amin took power in 1971. John Sekabira spent 14 months in various prisons in Uganda. In this exclusive interview, he tells DRUM of his torments and of the days he was near to death:

Three friends and I, on our way to Canada, were arrested on January 6, 1976, at Entebbe international airport. We were taken, with our faces covered, to the State Research headquarters in Kampala. When we reached the headquarters we were taken underground and they started beating us. They applied lighted cigars to our fingers. We yelled, but they continued beating us and asked us where we were going. We explained that we were going away to study. We showed them the documents we had.

After beating and questioning us for about three hours, my friend George Nsubuga mentioned that we acquired scholarships through sponsors from abroad. When they heard the word *abroad* they started beating us and poured urine in our faces. Nsubuga and Mike Sebirumbi started bleeding from their noses and ears. When Nsubuga asked for water an officer gave him urine.

The following morning at around ten, the condition of my two friends was deteriorating and they seemed near death. At around eleven the commanding officer, Colonel Francis Itabuka, came into our underground cells on his routine check. When he saw Sebirumbi and Nsubuga in a pool of blood he told the officers who were on duty to remove the two. I expected him to have my friends

taken to hospital, but his order was the opposite. After taking away my friends he ordered that I must be taken to another cell where I found different people being tortured. They were being beaten up with batons and they were using some electrical shocks on them.

After staying at the State Research headquarters for one month the commanding officer ordered his juniors to take me to Luzira detention camp. I arrived at Luzira on February 5, 1976. In the detention camp the inmates ask me if I had been interrogated by the Naguru Police Safety Unit – Amin's killing unit. I told them I had not. They told me if I had seen the unit I would also have died like my friends.

At the detention camp officers from the State Research Bureau came every morning and interrogated people. In the camp I met men such as Semei Nyanzi, former chairman of the Uganda Development Corporation. They used to collect him every morning and give him his black suit, and take him to his office under heavy escort.

I also met William Sewava, former chairman of the Foreign News Agency and a cousin of the late king, Sir Edward Mutesa, Tucker Lwanga of Uganda Television, Colonel Suleman, former general manager of the Uganda Transport Company, Mr Mulyanti and Mr Mubiru, both of the Uganda Development Corporation.

Many of the detainees had lost their hearing as a result of beatings. I also met Robert Wabwire, an air force captain who was alleged to have been found in the company of some American tourists in a hotel in Kampala. One of

his eyes was removed during interrogation.

On April 2, 1976, after spending three months in the detention camp, a State Research officer came and put some framed charges to me. Instead of taking me to court so that I could defend myself, I was taken to a room next to that of the officer in charge of the detention camp. I was surprised when a signed commitment warrant in my name, sentencing me to 21 months imprisonment, was produced. I asked one of the officers if that was the new system of sending people to prison. He told me: "You were lucky. The order was to finish you. Go and serve that, maybe you may come back alive."

I was taken to Murchison Bay Prison, a few yards from the Luzira detention camp. At the prison officers immediately started beating me. I was told to strip. After making a list of my belongings the prison officers told me that I would be working at the printing workshop.

About two months later I heard inmates talking about the space surrounding the prison fence. It was reserved for the burial of people killed by security officers. One morning, early, the corporal warder in charge of my ward, C2, told us that there had been some shooting at Nsambya police grounds. At around 11 a.m. four military policemen with machine guns came to the printing workshop. They told the warder that they wanted ten prisoners for an urgent job. I was one of the ten.

We were taken to a military Land Rover and I was shocked to see in it 12 people, all badly beaten and obviously dying. Some had their hands chopped off. Others were wearing military uniforms of the Uganda air force. We were told to start digging graves for the bodies. The whole area was full of skull and human bones, many of them newly buried. After digging two big graves we were told to start putting the bodies in. Nine of the people were dead but three were still alive. One of the three asked for water – instead he was bayonetted. After covering the bodies with soil, I asked the military officers what the people had done. They told me they were thieves. For our work we were each given a packet of cigarettes.

Not even two days had passed before the military police came again. This time they were in a big lorry almost full of bodies. I did not go to the burial but those who did told me that the dead were well dressed people. One inmate who had been at Murchison Bay Prison since 1970 told me that he had been burying prominent people for some time. He told me that the body of Ben Kiwanuka was taken there, and that of Joe Kiwanuka, former member of parliament.

In June, 1976, after the Israeli raid on Entebbe airport, I saw more than 200 bodies of senior figures from the army and the government taken there for burial. On August 20, 1976, the body of an elderly European lady and that of a policeman were brought in by three military officers. It was believed to be the body of Mrs Dora Bloch who was left at Mulago hospital after the raid.

After the death of Archbishop Luwum and the two cabinet ministers, officers of the State Research Bureau started an operation in government and the armed forces,

police and prisons to clear out the Acholi and Langi officers. On March 1, 1977, State Research officers came to Murchison Bay and the nearby prison department. Very early in the morning, we were told that we would be working half a day because all the staff were wanted at the Luzira Prison Training School grounds by a certain "big man" from the government. At 3 p.m. all the staff started arriving. Instead of the "big man" addressing the staff, State Research men arrived with heavy machine guns and a list of those they wanted. They ordered everybody to sit down and they told them that anybody trying to run away would be shot.

The first man on the list was Mr VI Okurut, senior superintendent of prisons and the officer in charge of Murchison Bay. He was followed by another superintendent, Mr Katabazi, from prison headquarters. Principal Officer Ondong was shot dead when he tried to run. On that day about 50 people were taken. After three days the bodies of 20 of those were found. Some of the bodies had no heads, some were impossible to recognise as acid had been applied to their faces.

From that day State Research officers carried out different operations, clearing out Langi and Acholi in both the private sector and in governmental organisations. Those who were taken were killed and their bodies taken to Murchison for burial. Within three weeks the place was full of bodies.

In May 1977 the vice president of Uganda, General Mustapha Adrisi, visited Murchison Bay. He addressed the officers and told them they should not be worried. Those who were taken were the

bad elements in the government and he told them that if they were called to attend a meeting they should not run away. Two days later the officer in charge of Murchison Bay received a message that all senior officers in the prison, police and army would be meeting the army chief of staff at Amin's Paradise Beach – an island off Port Bell.

On the day they went to the beach, there was plenty of drinking while they waited for the "big man" to address them. Instead of the chief of staff, Colonel Maliyamungu came in with State Research officers. He told them that there were still some bad elements and those elements would not leave the island alive. Then Major Faruk, the present officer in charge of the State Research Bureau, produced a list of 150 names. Those on the list were handcuffed and put in motorboats, never to be seen again.

On June 13, 1977, my release came all of a sudden. I was in the workshop when the corporal who is concerned with the release of prisoners told me that I had been given a remission from my sentence and I would be released that day. After my release I returned to Makerere University where I was in my third year as a medical student. I was shocked when told that there had been a directive that I should not be re-admitted. I started planning to leave Uganda.

When I remember those killings at the headquarters of the State Research Bureau and Murchison Prison, I get nightmares. People in Uganda must wish they could be animals because at least animals have societies which fight for their iives – such as the Society of the Prevention of Cruelty to Animals. ❏

SEVEN DEADLY DAYS WITH THE MAD COLONEL

DRUM: September 1977

Colonel Maliyamungu (God's property), or otherwise known as Isaak Lugonzo, strikes observers of Idi Amin's Uganda as the field marshal's power base, and the most likely man to assume power if there was a vacuum. He combines ruthlessness and courage to fan off those who try to block his rise.

This true disciple of the teachings of Professor Idi Amin told me that he has turned down cabinet posts to remain in the barracks, ostensibly organising "machinations" of the rule of the gun that keeps Amin at the helm. I spent a week tailing the colonel and pretending to be a link-man in the coffee smuggling near the Kenya-Uganda border.

"You know what, I have often been tipped as the likely man to succeed the field marshal, simply because I can boast as one of his loyal officers who carries his orders out to precision," Colonel Maliyamungu told a group of women in eastern Uganda. The women began to relax as he assured them in fluent Kiswahili that he believed that their business pursuits in Uganda would be rewarding, but cautioned them not to become involved in coffee smuggling. "By depriving Uganda of one of her foreign exchange earners, you will be committing treason," he said.

Asked what he would do if he found himself in Idi Amin's shoes, the colonel replied: "Just wear them and not glance around. I would continue to propagate his teachings and live and let live." He was asked who in the army was responsible for liquidating undesirable people. "We in the Uganda government don't eliminate people. People disappear yes, because

TRIGGER-HAPPY Colonel Maliyamungu boasts of having killed thousands.

some run away from creditors, while others abscond after hitting big money now that our economy is foreigner-free. Those who disappear don't want to share *their* fortunes with the rest of us. I personally don't like them."

A drunk soldier stormed into the hooch den we were in, and on seeing the dreaded colonel he stormed out, but before he could disappear, one of Maliyamungu's aides grabbed him and brought him before the "one-man tribunal". Sentence was pronounced: a kick in the ribs for being insolently drunk.

Here is a detailed account of my trip:

I arrived at the border on Saturday June 11 at 9:30 a.m. I was asked what tribe I was by the Ugandan police. I told them, Turkana, and they let me through. I had lunch at a makeshift hotel and, while I was eating, Uganda army men came in. Panic-sticken people started running away. I went on eating my meat which I shared with the soldiers. During the night I moved with the soldiers after becoming friends.

On June 12, the Land Rover would not start and with some of the army men we started on foot for Bukwa, 15 kilometres away. At Bukwa we found a civilian vehicle, a Toyota Landcruiser. It was ordered to Kapchorwa to meet the colonel. We met the colonel outside the Kapchorwa administrative office and we were introduced by one of the soldiers. Again I said I was a Turkana tribesman and he treated me in a friendly way.

We met three Kikuyu women at Kapchorwa. The colonel immediately ordered drink and food and the "party" went on throughout the day. The women were told to wait for their consignment of coffee from Uganda.

On Monday, June 13, an apparently drunk soldier staggered into the house in which the colonel, the women, and the other soldiers were staying. He spoke to Colonel Maliyamungu in a language which I could not understand. The

colonel lost his temper, unholstered his pistol, and shot the soldier dead.

As the day progressed 550 bags of Arabic coffee were brought to Kapchorwa in an army Land Rover and handed over to the colonel who in turn sold them to the three women. After the deal was clinched the women remained behind and joined the soldiers in a day-long drinking spree.

On Wednesday 18 bags of Blue Mountain coffee arrived in a helicopter and these, with the 550 bags, were taken to Kapchorwa forest ready for transport to Kenya. On Thursday, June 16, the bags were loaded onto Trans-Ocean trucks and later they left for Kitale on their way to Mombasa. The three women and I were given an army escort to Suam. ❑

By Joe Getheere

AMIN'S ROLL OF DEATH

DRUM: December 1978

Amnesty International is getting ready to take President Idi Amin to the International Court of Jurists on charges of genocide. The proposed action follows the organisation's report which reveals that as many as 300,000 people have been murdered in Uganda.

The Amnesty International report is based on events of the last 18 months. It describes the murder of politicians and civil servants, religious leaders, academics, teachers and students at Makerere University, businessmen and foreigners, including nationals of Kenya, Tanzania,

Rwanda, Zaire and Ghana. White citizens are also included in the report.

In Uganda it had become very difficult to get accurate figures of people who have disappeared because of fear of reprisals against relatives of murdered people. Earlier this year ex-President Obote said in London that the Uganda regime was conducting mass executions and that several thousand people from his area had been executed. Even more recently, several thousand Madi tribesmen were murdered after they demanded to know where the vice president Gen Adrisi, who has not been seen for months, was. ❑

IN THE FACE OF DEATH

DRUM: January 1978

Normally when death strikes people are bewildered and tears abound. On the day of the executions, death was in the air, but people were strangely dry-eyed. These were important deaths and they had been announced days ago. The weepers, it appeared, had done their job in advance.

That the candidates were criminals, there was no doubt, for his lordship the chief justice had himself declared them so. That the men were not highway robbers, nor killers of any kind, nor petty thieves was all by the way. The Uganda law found them guilty and the tribunal meted out justice. They were found guilty, to use the words of President Amin, of being a "breeding ground of subversive inclinations against the state".

Most people thought that the candidates were guilty of publicly and unashamedly proclaiming that uhuru had not yet come to the republic. Furthermore they were also guilty of frequently pointing at the swollen stomachs of the people in power. But when it leaked to the government, a decree was passed that whoever was suspected of being a "breeding ground of subversion against the state" was to face the firing squad.

ON THE DAY of the executions death was in the air but people were dry-eyed.

The morning sun had travelled higher in the sky. The rays had lost their blood-tinge. The hovels vomited people into the winding lanes. These trickles flowed to join others and the streams of people thus enlarged found their way to the main road – Queensway.

From here the heaving tide swept on slowly towards Katwe near the Clock Tower. Arriving there the mass stood together like a pack of cards, but each one like a single card withdrawn into himself – this was no place to exchange opinions. Two miles away a military police lorry laboured painfully from Makindye Military Prison through the crowd. By this time all other vehicles had been stopped. It was obvious that the one still moving was carrying the expected victims.

At the execution place, the commander was standing waiting flanked by other officials. Only a blind man would have had trouble in picking him out. He was an impressive figure, one you would not forget. It was as if the crushing state responsibilities had necessitated a counter balancing flesh buildup. His stomach was swollen and his navel was forced to mark its position three feet away from his strained spine.

A pistol shot seemed to go off as the rusty doors of the truck were opened. Soldiers were seen to advance. Between them walked the condemned men at gun point. There was nothing heroic about them. If anything, their eyes looked lifeless, glazed. "Don't blindfold me," Dan Nsereko, a high ranking police officer, said in a hoarse voice as they came towards him with that unmistakable cloth. "I want to see."

"Fire!" The command came harshly. The word seemed to have touched some hidden knob inside the prisoners. A split second before the firing, Dan Nsereko tossed himself forward miraculously escaping the deadly hail. What followed is impossible to describe. A thunderous explosion seemed to go off in the middle of the firing squad. The other 14 bewildered condemned men were tossed into the air. They didn't stay up long and when they descended, it was in the form of fragmented limbs and skulls scattered generously all over the place.

The sergeant cursed Dan Nsereko under his breath with the vilest names his tongue could manage. He looked at his superior inquiringly, expecting another try. Crack. That was the end of him and more bullets followed.

The crowd acted like a nest of ants into which a heap of live coals had been thrown. People from the front ran backwards in horror and those at the back ran forward. Bodies hit against bodies and toppled over, the weak were trampled. Eventually some semblance of order seemed to descend upon the crowd and the people went home. ❐

By Renny Ssentongo

OUR ESCAPE FROM AMIN

DRUM: March 1978

Early in 1977 officers in Field Marshal Amin's army and air force decided to overthrow his regime. The coup was to take place on June 18. Some parts of the plan were, however, leaked just before it was implemented. Some of those betrayed managed to escape, shooting their way through road blocks into Kenya. One group of seven was arrested and confined in the notorious State Research Bureau building at Nakasero, Kampala.

After three months of privation and torture, hours before they were due to be executed – in Amin's words – "with the self-same bazookas you intended to use against me", seven of the eight escaped from Nakasero. One of them was Major Patrick Kimumwe, who until his arrest had been second in command of the notorious Malire Mechanised Regiment. Together with another of the escapers, Silvesta Mutumba, he has written a book called *Inside Amin's Army.*

Says Kimumwe: "We have written this book because far too little is known about the real character and organisation of the military clique with which Amin now terrorises the land. Lulled by his buffoonery, rolling in laughter at his diplomatic gaffes, frankly disbelieving many of the horrific tales of torture and brutality seeping out of Uganda, the world does not seem to realise that his clowning conceals a ruthless extinction of human rights in what used to be one of the most beautiful and progressive nations in Africa."

This extract, exclusive to DRUM, covers the last two weeks of the eight's imprisonment at Nakasero and their escape from Uganda:

THE SIX WHO should have died: Top row, l-r: Chris Ssekalo, Boswal Nambale, Eddie Ssendaula, Patrick Kimumwe. Bottom: Silvesta Mutumba, Niko Kassujja.

The main interrogation centre and execution room for Amin's State Research Bureau is housed in a building sandwiched between the President's Lodge and the French ambassador's residence, less than a mile from the centre of Kampala. The facilities for holding prisoners are primitive since few of them are expected to remain in this world for long.

On September 8, 1977, the arrangements were stretched to the utmost. More than 100 captives were held in the building, including our group of eight who were involved in an abortive army/air force coup. We were packed like sardines in two cells. Cell No 1, once former President Milton Obote's emergency escape tunnel from the President's Lodge to the outside world, was more of a transit detention hole for less important captives. Ours, Cell No 2, was a windowless dungeon for those about to be condemned to death and had formerly been an underground armoury for Obote's General Service Unit.

On September 9 the accommodation position in Cell No 2 suddenly eased. A group of 12 was taken before the firing squad. After their public execution only the eight of us remained in Cell No 2:

- Major Patrick Kimumwe, from Kamuli in northern Busoga, aged 31, second-in-command of the Malire Mechanised Regiment at Bombo and 12 years in the army;
- Lieutenant Silvesta Mutumba, from Busowa in southern Busoga, aged 26, second-in-command of Amin's squadron of fighter jet trainers, with five-and-a-half years flying experience;
- Lieutenant Boswal Nambale, from northern Bugisu, aged 24, a jet pilot at Gulu Air Base;
- Pilot Officer Cadet Nicodemus Kassujja, from Bulemezi County in Buganda, aged 27, a helicopter pilot;
- Warrant Officer Eddie Ssendaula, from Masaka in south Buganda, aged 34, an air-frame technician at Entebbe Air Base;
- Warrant Officer John Okech, from Budama near Tororo, aged 35, an air-frame technician at Entebbe Air Base;
- Warrant Officer Christopher Ssekalo, from Masaka town in south Buganda, aged 31, an air-frame technician at Entebbe Air Base;
- Wycliff Kato, from Bulemezi in Buganda, aged 45 and, until he joined us in the cell, director of civil aviation in Uganda.

Kato had not been involved in our attempted coup. He had refused to sign pilot's certificates for some Egyptian airmen rushed in to replace American pilots of Uganda Airlines who had left the country after one of Amin's threats against the USA. His refusal was based on the fact that they had not even sat for, let alone passed, the necessary examination. As the order to sign had been a presidential directive and his refusal continued until Brigadier Moses Ali (Masai, Muslim, seconded from the army as minister of finance) summoned him and made him sign in his presence, Kato had, to say the least, incurred displeasure.

The taunts of our guards as they informed us we were the next for live target practice concentrated our minds wonderfully. We realised that, for that first time since our arrest in June, we were alone in a group with no outsiders, no possible spies. No-one had ever escaped before from Nakasero, but we now had nothing to lose.

One suggestion was that we seize the key of the cell from the guard, break out and fight our way past the guards. Another was that we try to fashion our own key. The first suggestion seemed too risky, the second too difficult. Then we had a long, careful look at the four ventilators at the top of the wall which opened out at ground level.

Each ventilator was nearly one metre long and 40 centimetres wide and contained four three centimetre-thick iron bars bedded deep into massive concrete walls. Behind the bars were two layers of hard wire gauze and behind the wire again were some slanting pieces of glass. If we could get rid of the gauze *and* the glass *and* thus get the space to lever away at the bars, *and* do all this without being seen *and* before the deadline of the firing squad, there was a chance. Except for the fact that we were handcuffed.

However, that was not the problem it seemed. Nicodemus Kassujja had been shot in the leg when he was arrested and it had been amputated. He was brought to the cell a few days after it was cut off before the stitches were removed and he received no further treatment. For a long time the stump gave him great pain. He would never fly again. But he was very intelligent and practically minded. Our cell was in a mess and a mass of rubbish: as it turned out, a providential mess which included some very valuable rubbish.

A few days before the execution of the 12, Kassujja had found a small piece of metal among the rubbish which he painstakingly ground against the concrete floor to a sharp point. He then used it to release the spring on his handcuffs until they opened. He tried the "key" on another one of us and opened that too. Eventually all our group was freed. Sleeping in handcuffs is surprisingly difficult and uncomfortable but from that time on, every night after lights out we got Kassujja to release us all. To speed things up he even made a duplicate key. Locking ourselves up again at first light was easier as we just snapped the ends together.

So the handcuffs were no problem. The wire gauze, however, was. We scrambled around among the rubbish until we had a treasure trove of old nails, spoons and other bits and pieces of metal. What was now needed was patience and hard work. Sergeant Major Christopher Ssekalo proved a monument of this. Slowly, terribly slowly, but effectively, he went on breaking the gauze, piece by piece, until he had forced a tiny way through to the slanting glasses.

For the first time since our arrival at Nakasero we felt a faint flicker of hope. But this was dashed when the sergeant major found that the wooden frame of the glass louvres had been securely fixed into the cement and would not come out without the glass being broken. When we tried to break the glass it made too loud a noise. It was essential to devise a way of muffling the sound.

Among the junk in the cell were a lot of dirty sacks, on which we were sleeping, and a collection of blood-stained, filthy old shirts and trousers left behind by those who had been taken before the firing squad and others who had been slaughtered in the extermination room on the ground floor. Ssekalo covered each piece of slanting glass with three of these shirts to muffle the noise when he broke it. By the evening of September 11, Sergeant Major Ssekalo had cleared away the two layers of wire gauze and the glass and we were face-to-face with the final obstacle – the iron bars. We were so near and yet, as we were to find, so very far.

We decided to tighten our security for this last stage. Whenever we were doing anything active we put one man on the gate and another at the ventilators. Neither of these two was allowed to remove their handcuffs. Our code names for Amin's thugs was rat. There were so many rats anyway in the cell that it was quite a normal word to say or hear around there. If either observer saw any of the guards, he whispered urgently this word. Also, since time was important to us, but not so important as not being heard, we decided to work only during office hours. So we started when the State Research staff arrived to work in mornings and the general hubbub was sufficient to cover our scrambling and rustling.

We had one overriding objective – to bend the iron bars sufficiently to get through them to freedom. We needed two things: an instrument to bend them and the energy to use it. Incredibly, among the junk in the cell were two old Russian-

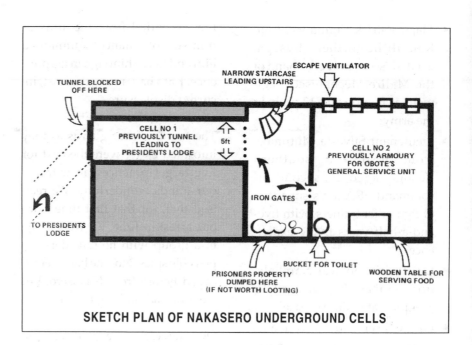

SKETCH PLAN OF NAKASERO UNDERGROUND CELLS

made film projectors on their stands. It took us a day to unscrew one of the stands from its projector, but on September 13, we were ready to start the heavy work.

At about 14:00 on that day we inserted the projector stand for the first time high above our heads between two of the bars on the ventilator nearest the door. After three days of cautious, strength-sapping, nerve-cracking labour, one of the bars began to move, not dramatically but at least a little. Shortly after, disaster struck – the first projector stand broke and we started to use the second. Two more days passed but without any noticeable progress. And always the constant need for watchfulness. One piece of foolishness, one small lapse and we would be corpses.

We needed good cover, but there had to be variations to make it more natural. One cover was a game of draughts with beer bottle tops. We always left it arranged in such a way that whoever came to check on us would find the pieces laid out on the board as if the game had been long in progress. When they found us we were always really concentrating on the game.

A week had passed and the bars still resisted our efforts. We became very worried. Our time was running out. Even the most optimistic among us began to despair. Then we thought that perhaps the bars had not been inserted very far into the walls and we tried to dig them out using spoons, nails or anything else that we found among the rubbish. As usual, the patient Sergeant Major Ssekalo was the leader in this operation.

But the deepest we could get down with the available tools was about two inches and our efforts seemed to make no difference to the rock-like stability of the bars. So we continued, hour in, hour out, with the second projector stand while Kassujja and Kimumwe experimented with a primitive, and ineffective, handmade hacksaw gleaned from the rubbish. Then the unbelievable happened. One of the bars bent, not the one we had been digging out, but the other one. Then even the first one bent a little. As the hours went by our heads began to go through.

We used to tease Kassujja that it would be impossible to take him with us as he only had one leg and he would only delay us so that we would all be recaptured. When he heard this he used prodigies of effort to show us how fit he was and how quickly he could move, despite his handicap. He was a very courageous and talented person.

As things got better we began to feel intense excitement mixed with fear. The nearer to success, the more obvious our activities became. The bend in the bar was so big by now that it could be seen by the naked eye from quite a distance. So we started hanging our sleeping sacks near the ventilator to cover it.

At last the bar was bent so far that we were sure seven of us would get through. We had experimented with leaving a gap between two old boxes on the floor. The problem was the eighth man, Sergeant Major Okech: his head could go but not his body. We continued to move heaven and earth to increase the gap. But we were now confident enough to plan our end game. We decided that very soon there must be a presidential demand for some sort of confession. If the demand came before we escaped then we would write down what they wanted in order to avoid unnecessary torture.

It was like a bad dream. Just after we had discussed it, four of us – Kimumwe, Ssekalo, Kassujja and Mutumba – were summoned by Major Faruk Minawa, the State Research Bureau operations officer. Although Lieutenant Colonel Itabuka was the official head of the Bureau, Minawa was the executive power and worked with Amin on all his activities. He was the No 1 killer in Uganda, a sadist who would think nothing of organising and enjoying the beating up of a man all night.

In his office we were ordered to sit on the carpet and were provided with small tables, paper and pens. Unlike some other sessions Minawa was accompanied by the notorious Palestinian interrogator Faizel of the Nile. The ridiculous exercise of lies began – it was really only a way of Minawa getting further into Amin's good books. He began with a lecture telling us what he wanted us to say. We did just what he asked, even embroidering it a little. He ordered us to read out what we had written, some of it obvious lies, and then sign it. He was delighted. He told us that if we had only collaborated like that before, we should not have had to suffer.

Anyway, like it or not, we had signed our own death warrants after our statements to Faruk. One of the questions had been why we wished to overthrow the government. We had listed many things, including the continued killing by the military of innocent Ugandans and the consequent total collapse of the rule of law and its replacement by military and Nubian whim. None of these home truths pleased Amin, and the result was that on September 20, three of his personal bodyguards arrived at 14:00 with some new clothes for four of us: Kimumwe, Ssekalo, Kassujja and Mutumba.

We were ordered to change into them and were taken upstairs where there were three cars. We were squeezed into the back seat of an old Datsun, and off the convoy went. Major Faruk with a lady secretary leading the pack. We drove through the city before suddenly finding ourselves at Amin's Cape Town Villa. Faruk came over to us, saying he was now going to put us in Amin's hands. If we were co-operative and lucky we could be freed there and then. If we were

unlucky, then what happened was nothing to do with Faruk.

So we waited, except for a brief break when we were taken for a tour round the peninsula on which the Villa was built. The whole place was bristling with sentries, with patrol boats zooming about on the lake and uniformed observers scanning the air. It seemed as if Amin was expecting an invasion.

Then at last we were face-to-face with the huge 280 pound bulk of this monstrous man whom we had wanted, and still desperately wanted, to kill. He started blowing at us with all the English he knew, mixed up at times with Swahili and Luganda. Like a chameleon constantly adapting its colour, he changed his mood with every sentence he uttered. At times he seemed to smile but it was no smile – it was the bitterness in his mind forcing itself out of his face. At other times he expressed anger, and this was a complete anger that seemed to take hold of his whole body as if he would stand up to fight us, or strangle us, or shoot us there and then.

It would be foolish to deny that we were frightened. But we did not give way to panic. We said nothing. We stood quietly and looked at him. Eventually the torrent of abuse lessened and he cooled a little. He looked at Kimumwe and accused him of being the one who had killed all the Acholi and Langi in Kampala. He ordered the lady from the newspaper, *The Voice of Uganda*, to make sure she stressed that in her report. He turned on Kimumwe again: "I trusted you and appointed you an adjutant of Malire Regiment after which I promoted you and appointed you the second-in-command – and shortly I was going to confirm you as the

FACE TO FACE: Four of the prisoners are brought before Idi Amin. From the left: Mutumba, Kassujja, Ssekalo, Kimumwe.

commanding officer of Malire. You had all the facilities. What else did you want?"

Kimumwe tried to reply but Amin brusquely ignored him and started on Mutumba: "You remember when we went to check the Mutukula border. You are a revolutionary man. You have been a very good pilot instructor and because we trusted you, we gave you those big responsible positions like adjutant of Gulu Base and second-in-command of a fighter squadron. Your officers and men trusted you in the base; then what did you want?"

Before he could reply Amin had already jumped over to Kassujja. "You cadet, I am the one who saved your life. You remember I promised you that you would be all right as long as you told me the whole plan and showed me where those who have the guns are: I think that your leg can be worked

on and you can continue to fly. But what did you want?" Kassujja was also not given time to answer. Amin then turned on Sergeant Major Ssekalo: "You are one of those I recruited myself from Obote's regime. Most of those I joined with are now ministers or high-ranking officers."

Amin laughed a little at this, and then Kassujja burst in with a comment that if it had not been for a traitor in our ranks, Amin would have been a dead man. This did not please Amin. Amin turned his unrelenting gaze on us and blasted out: "You will have to pay for all this and from today I have signed an instrument which I am going to hand over to Lieutenant Colonel Ali Juma who is going to be the chairman of the military tribunal which you are going to face soon. And if you are found guilty, you will have to face a firing squad in which you will be shot by the guns that you imported. You will be

fired at by bazookas so that I can see what your bodily pieces will be like after firing you!"

"But," he went on, "if you wish, you can plead to me for mercy and probably I shall forgive you because I do not want to miss you. I want you to go back to your units and serve properly as you started." Then he ordered us to be escorted outside while the attendants remained behind. Instructions were given that we were to be taken back to Nakasero. Amin ordered our driver and guards to drive us around Kampala on the way back to show us that the shops and markets were now full of essential commodities. However, by the time we left Cape Town Villa, it was already 18:00 and all the shops were closed.

As we approached the State Research Building we made the closest possible study of the surroundings to learn everything possible

but also a very shrewd person who could be expected to handle any immediate problems outside better. We pushed him through legs first but he stuck half way with his head and hands still inside. If Ssekalo could not get through, Okech certainly could not and so, after a brief and hurried discussion we decided to postpone the attempt for 48 hours.

On Friday, September 21, we sweated throughout the day at the first bar until it could bend no more and merely began to circle round itself. We managed to bend the second bar and found that now we could all get out without any trouble, except for John Okech. We slept a little waiting for the dawn. This was D Day, September 22, the day we were going to escape or die in the attempt. With the strength of desperate men, whenever we could during the morning we struggled either to bend the first bar more or somehow even remove it entirely. But we could neither move it nor remove it.

Then at noon a broad, very dark Munubi major ordered our cell to be opened, swaggered in with our guard and gave us some thudding slaps. He said nothing, though we feared at first that the odd shape of the ventilator had been noticed and these were just the pre-liminaries to something even more violent. An hour later, our guard brought in our lunch and since he did not behave in any untoward way, we felt that perhaps we were still safe. Our excitement was becoming intense, so much so that it was difficult to eat.

After lunch we played draughts or rested until around 17:00 when we began to observe the movements of the guards posted for night duties. They seemed to be checking

that might help in our choice of an escape route. But all too soon we were outside the cell door and it was already growing dark. When one of the sentries came down while we were waiting for the key, Mutumba asked him if he could use the latrine which he knew was on the ground floor at the rear of the building above the ventilators. This area was crucial to our escape and this was a heaven-sent opportunity to recce it. He was taken round at gunpoint but inside the latrine he was able to get a good look outside and most especially to see a seven-foot wall; an obstacle which would have to be surmounted.

Soon after Mutumba's return to the cell gate, the key holder arrived and opened it for us. We found those whom we had left behind miserable and anxious. They had been certain that we had been moved to Makindye Military Prison. They had decided that if

we did not come back they would have attempted to escape that night.

We told them we were going to be put in front of a military tribunal whose chairman was Lieutenant Colonel Ali Juma, and one of whose members was Captain Ssebbi. Both Ali Juma and Ssebbi were notoriously ruthless killers and, as far as we knew, no one had ever failed to be executed either as a direct result of the tribunal's sentence or, if the tribunal let them off, by an immediate secret State Research killing. Our time had run out. We decided to delay no longer, but to try the escape that very night, September 20.

We had no time for a dress rehearsal, and we were still not absolutely sure of the size of the gap between the bars. So, instead of sending the fattest man, John Okech, first, we started with Sergeant Major Ssekalo who was the second fattest on us rather a lot that evening but sometimes it was like that. At about 20:15 the warder brought us supper and took it away at about 21:00. Still nothing unusual. Between 21:00 and 24:00 the sentries who were on duty brought us various titbits like packets of cigarettes, bananas.

We had decided to move at 01:00 on the 23rd, but to our horror at about 24:00 some fresh victims were brought upstairs for torture. There was a lot of shouting and screaming and the State Research thugs came along to check on us. We had followed our normal schedule and appeared to go to bed at 22:00 but the beatings and interrogations went on right up to 01:30. We just had to wait.

We could not sleep at all. It was already getting late and we had not yet made any move at all. We listened with all our 16 ears; pushing our hearing beyond any limits we had reached before. Half of us concentrated on any sounds inside the State Research building and the rest on the grounds. All was deathly quiet inside but something was going on outside and so we switched to it. Eventually we located it at the main entrance gate. The sound was coming from the still alert quarter guard, about 15 yards from the spot at which we would depart from the ventilator.

This called for no modification in our planning as one of our surveys had shown that the trench for water drainage that ran along the building was quite deep enough to hide us from the sentries when we got out of the cell. But we now had to use extreme caution. In addition to everything else we had to make quite sure that none of the prisoners in Cell No 1 noticed or heard anything.

We were lucky to have a watch bequeathed to us by the late Galabuzi Mukasa, a former inmate, which we used for timing ourselves. It was now 02:00 on Friday, September 23. Now or never. We sat in a semicircle and prayed to God to bless our escape.

This time we began with Sergeant Major Okech, the fattest. He was lifted up to the outlet and we all pushed him as hard as we could. But it was no good. He was just too fat. There was no way he was going to get through that ventilator. None of us was under any illusions as to what this meant. The State Research thugs were not going to let the only caged bird live when seven others had flown away with his help.

Kimumwe and Mutumba had thought hard about the issues involved. Now we had to put them to him. What made it all so tragically unfair was that it was Okech who had played a large part with the efforts on the bars that had brought us where we were. Deeply disappointed and bitterly hurt, at first he was reluctant to let us try our luck without him, especially as he had no hope of concealing his involvement with us from the authorities. But Okech had the seeds of greatness in him and at last we agreed between all of us that he would not only let us go, but, would wait two hours after our departure before he raised the alarm.

Even today we do not know for sure if he is alive or dead, but we would like here to pay a tribute to this noble man to whom we all owe our lives and to say how much we wish he could be with us here to taste the freedom he fought and struggled so long and valiantly for.

It was 02:00 when we lifted Ssekalo, the second fattest, up to the bars, instructing him to do a quick recce as soon as he was out and to signal to us if all was well. The next one through was Kimumwe and then the crippled Kassujja. Fourth was Ssendaula, followed by the former director of civil aviation, then Okech and I lifted Nambale and finally Okech lifted me up. We bade Okech a sad farewell, leaving him in God's hands. "Good bye. You go. I will die for you," he said to Mutumba.

So there we were squatting outside a drainage trench but feeling as if we had just risen from our graves into some new and wonderful world. The air was fresh and cool. The sky was bright with moonlight. The night was still and silent, disturbed only rarely and distantly by a puttering motor car. The State Research quarter guards were only a few feet north of us, we could see them. We could hear them. We were a little above them as the ground of Nakasero hill slopes mainly westwards. As the guards were on the north we crawled to the south along the western wall of the building until we met the seven foot wall of the corner. This we had to get over. We quickly lifted Ssekalo on to the top of the wall and he pulled Kimumwe up. Kassujja was next but as he was lame he had to be lifted off the ground first and then pulled up. The rest of us were quickly over.

Further progress to the south was out. We were very close to the perimeter fence which was brightly lit by security lights. We had to find a darker place to get through, over or under the wire which meant moving west. As we went there was one place in a corner where two walls met and where the

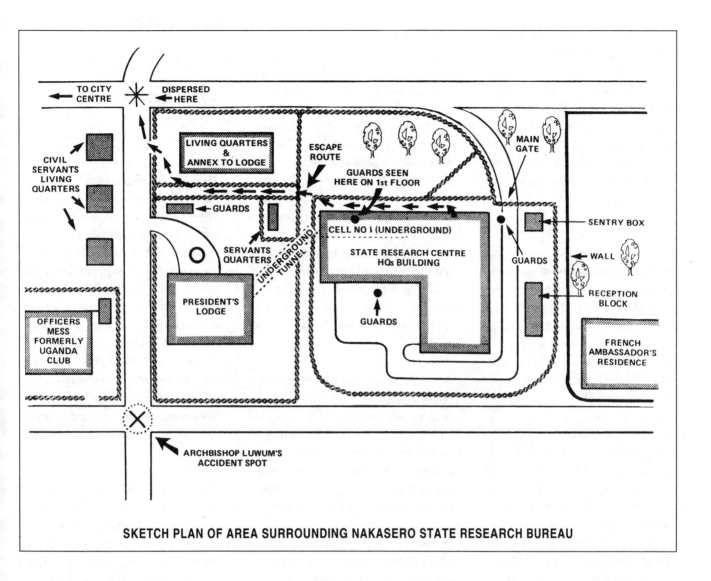

SKETCH PLAN OF AREA SURROUNDING NAKASERO STATE RESEARCH BUREAU

barbed wire was jammed tight against the wall. Even the able-bodied among us had to keep our wits about us to get through. The crippled Kassujja achieved miracles crossing this place. Meanwhile Ssekalo had already started recceing in front of us and he had found a place where the wire was not tied to the ground and we agreed to make this our route.

We found we were in an open space surrounded by more wire and the only way out appeared to be through the French ambassador's residence over to the east. There was also a corridor passing between the barbed wire surrounding Nakasero State Research Bureau and the fence surrounding the President's Lodge. But the cor-

ridor was brightly lit by security lights and led to the front courtyard of the State Research building where there were several guards. Definitely dangerous. But Kimumwe and Ssendaula decided to try it by crawling with their heads kept right down. Meanwhile Ssekalo was closely inspecting the nearby fences to see if there was any other gap we could exploit. At the same time Nambale and Mutumba went to look at the fence around the servant's quarters or the President's Lodge.

Things began to go wrong. Kimumwe and Ssendaula almost crawled into a sentry and were terrified that they had been seen. The area we were moving in was full of trees and whenever any of us

moved the noise of fallen dry leaves burst in our ears. Wherever Ssekalo went he was chased off by barking security dogs. We were all rapidly becoming convinced that only a complete fool would not investigate all these strange sounds.

We were getting really worried. There seemed no safe way out of the maze of barbed wire and it was nearly 04:00. Then suddenly one of the guards at State Research walked into a first floor room just above us and switched on the light. We could see him only too clearly as he took a bottle and gulped some liquid down his throat. He had a rifle on his shoulder. We froze. Thank God, he soon left and went downstairs. Our luck seemed to be changing.

Soon afterwards Nambale and Mutumba found what Uganda soldiers call a "panya (rat) road" into the President's Lodge. This is a path which has been surreptitiously cut as a short cut or lover's route. We signalled the others and soon we were all in the grounds of the Presidential Lodge, near the servants' quarters.

We rested there a bit while Nambale and Kato went to recce the lodge and the guards at the main entrance. These would normally be military police. Nambale and Kato came back and said all seemed quiet and then we passed through the second fence and found ourselves near a building known as the annex.

The area was again bright with security lights and the moon was full. There was still no sign of any alarm having been raised and there was just one more fence to get over. The two gates, one to the Lodge itself (which was heavily guarded) and the other to the annex, were about 20 metres from each other. By the help of God, and with the use of monkey tactics – stooping and running like monkeys – we all somehow got past the Presidential Lodge gate. We could clearly see all the guards seated in their guard room as we passed. They were either totally incompetent or dozing.

The annex gate was not a problem to get underneath, and, suddenly the ordeal was over. We were on an unfenced public road opposite some high class houses, full of barking dogs. This was our dispersal point. Each one of us from now on was on his own.

Amin was absolutely raging and wild when he heard of our escape, shooting his pistol off all over the

place. It seems he suspected our escape to be linked with another coup attempt. Within 24 hours of our escape, rumour had done its work well and even small children seemed to have heard about it. Some said we escaped with Israeli help; others said that senior military officers, involved in our attempted coup, had assisted us; yet other rumours had it that our alleged escape was part of a typical Amin cover-up; and others again said that we had been forgiven by Amin and returned to our units. No one seemed to believe the truth: we had escaped by our own efforts.

Because of our imminent execution Radio Uganda was full of us and so was the *Voice of Uganda* newspaper. Within 48 hours thousands of copies of our photographs were dispatched all over Uganda, especially to the road blocks, with a "shoot at sight" grading. Our own intelligence network, however, was by now in full operation and we knew exactly what was happening. We had little fear. We had all the sympathy, support and help we needed.

The time had come to leave Uganda. First, a bluff. We made contact overseas and asked for arrangements to be made for the BBC and other foreign stations to broadcast a statement that we had already left Uganda. As we had hoped, this threw the Ugandan authorities into confusion. Clearly the search was useless if the birds had flown.

Over the next few weeks one by one our group escaped Uganda and joined up in Kenya. The one-legged Kassujja was the last. In his usual versatile manner, he had surmounted his problems. ❐

INSIDE AMIN'S COURT OF FEAR

DRUM: February 1979

Few people have appeared before Uganda's military tribunals and lived to tell the world of their experience. To appear before the tribunal is often a sentence of death by firing squad. Early in 1975 the Uganda government laid down laws to curb serious crime in Uganda. To put more emphasis on these laws the government established a tribunal whose chairman and members were all military personnel, to try the culprits and punish them.

Following the famous economic war a decree was issued, that everyone found guilty and proved to be engaged in any of these crimes was to be publicly executed by firing squad. Despite all these measures and disregarding the fate of the offenders, people continued to defy and violate these laws – often being forced in the face of the country's deteriorating economic situation.

Ugandan money became valueless. As matters changed from bad to worse people decided that law or no law, death sentence or no death sentence, they had to live, and so they had to make money one way or the other. When it became obvious that you had to have Kenyan money to buy what you needed most people were prepared to risk their lives and join the *magendo* (smuggling).

It was at the height of this period that people were forced by circum-

Prisoner No: JR/709/75
Name: Tom Sekavila
Offence: Corruption

In November 1975 a gang of criminals stole Mr Tom Sekavila's car and used it in a robbery. Later they were tried, convicted and executed in Mubende forest.

Three months later Mr Sekavila went to a police station to collect his car. But while he was there some policemen asked him for a tip so that they could organise the release of his car quickly.

He gave them some 200 shillings to speed up the matter but because there were three officers and one of them did not get anything, he became jealous and arrested Sekavila for corruption.

When Mr Sekavila was brought to court he could not prove the intention of giving the police officers the money other than with intention of bribing them.

The court found Mr Tom Sekavila guilty of the offence of corrupting public officers in contravention of the economic war decree. He was convicted and subsequently executed on April 8, 1976.

Prisoner No: JR/917/75
Name: Issa Sembi
Offence: Corruption

Issa Sembi was a second-hand clothes dealer. In mid-December Mr Sembi was confronted by some furious military policemen. They threatened to arrest him for intending to smuggle clothes to Kenya because he was found at the bus terminus. Mr Sembi argued that he was an honest trader and he even produced his hawker's licence to support his claim. When they saw his licence the police changed their allegations and charged him with robbery.

Mr Sembi said that he could show them the receipts and cash sales for his clothes. He pulled out his wallet, but one of the officers snatched the wallet and extracted all the relevant documents and destroyed them. The policeman took some 50 shillings from the wallet and gave the money to one officer who was told to keep it. All the rest of the Sembi's money was divided among the policemen. Then Sembi was taken to Jinja Police Station and charged with corruption in giving 50 shillings. He was tried in March 1976 and executed on April 8, 1976.

Prisoner No: JR/717/75
Name: Jescah Ntafula
Offence: Hoarding

It was alleged that, between December 1–8, 1975, in Kamuli town some 14 kilometres from Jinja, Mrs Ntafula was found hoarding and overcharging on beans. She was detained until August 1976 when she was brought before the military court.

She was accused of selling a small tin of Kimbo for 12 shillings instead of 1/50, the controlled price. She was further charged with hiding two bags of beans from a warrant officer who was buying for the army barracks.

She denied all the charges and argued that in fact it was the lack of transport that forced her not to take the beans to the public market and that it was the army who misunderstood because the 12 shillings she had mentioned was for a tin of 20 kilograms and not a tin of 500 grams.

But the prosecutor produced 18 witnesses – army men – who were ready to swear that the lady was lying to the court. The court was convinced, and Ntafula was jailed for five years and her beans forfeited to the state.

stances to smuggle out of the country anything they could lay their hands on – coffee, textiles, salad oil, game skins, mercury liquid, tea, bananas, timber and oranges. Others engaged themselves in hoarding essential commodities –

cement, meat, beans and cassava. Others joined in highway robbery and embezzlement.

At this juncture the government had to intervene. Military tribunals were established all over the

country. The courts consisted of a colonel with two majors, two captains and a number of lieutenants. The following are some cases chaired by Colonel Maliyamungu in Jinja Town Hall in 1976. ❐

President Amin's Paradise Beach

WITH a powerful lunge the Presiden[t] gains possession o[f] the ball (above).

LOOKING determined the bi[g] man advances on [the] basket (right) whil[e] defenders flee.

ONE brave girl (bottom left) tries t[o] block Amin's progress but he ha[s a] huge size advanta[ge] and lines up his sh[ot]

President Idi Amin has an uncanny knack of making news and now he is courting the press at what is known as Paradise Beach, a few kilometres outside Kampala. This is where Big Daddy goes for his exercise and when he weighs more than 250 pounds that exercise is obviously good for him. During a recent visit to Uganda DRUM cameraman Abu Shaban watched the Ugandan Life President take part in a game of basketball, in which, to nobody's surprise, he scored.

AMIN shoots (bottom right) and on target for the opening score.

209

EUROPE'S LAUGHING STOCK, AFRICA'S TRAGEDY

IN HIS FIELD MARSHAL'S UNIFORM, President Amin addresses a press conference during celebrations to mark the seventh anniversary of his takeover. The celebrations were held at Amin's birthplace, Koboko, a remote village on the Sudanese border.

DRUM: April 1978

Few people have mastered the art of propaganda as well as Uganda's amiable yet ruthless dictator, Field Marshal Idi Amin Dada. During the Second World War Germany used a British traitor broadcasting under the name of Lord Haw Haw to spread their lies to the British. His stories were so outrageous that they made the beleaguered British people roar with laughter.

Now the British have been laughing at the new comic propaganda artist, Idi Amin. But to the people of Africa, he is not so funny.

Recently Amin went before the cameras of British television to answer some straight questions. These are some of his answers which had British viewers rolling with laughter:

BBC: Why do you want better relations with Kenya?
AMIN: The year 1978 is the year of love, peace and reconciliation. I want better relations not only with Kenya, but with Britain and the entire world community.

BBC: Why then do you call yourself the Conqueror of the British Empire?

AMIN: It is the members of the Defence Council and the entire people of Uganda who consider that I am the Conqueror of the British Empire.

BBC: But Britain has no empire.
AMIN: Yes, I know. But this is because the British shamefully just removed all the Union Jacks from Uganda and ran away. The next news I received was that the British envoy had left Nairobi for London and that the people were surprised. How can you shamefully run away like that? Not even leaving a *chargé d'affaires* in Kampala gave a bad impression.

BBC: Do you not think that the British would take the title Conqueror of the British Empire as an insult?

AMIN: I am very proud to be called conqueror because I am the only one in the world who conquered the British in Black Africa. Even now they are calling me "Black Power in the continent of Africa". But it is not an insult because it was official.

BBC: Can you tell us about the latest assassination attempt?

AMIN: That was not an attempt on my life. I have been driving even now. My car is just here. There is no attempt on my life. You know, I am a revolutionary leader and a strong man in the continent of Africa. The enemies of Africa do not want strong men. They want puppet leaders who can follow them, who can go and beg them.

I am expecting a lot of enemies – but not from Uganda, from outside. They might be from Britain. You might have bought some people to come and plot against me, but they are being discovered and arrested by the public themselves, not the security forces. They are taken to the security forces, and they accept that they were bribed by the British.

The British, no matter how powerful they are, will never succeed in invading Uganda I am telling you – we are small, capable and ready to smash any invader in any corner of Uganda. But today I want to invest more money in Uganda for food and beautiful houses.

BBC: What about the atrocities against the Acholi and Langi?

AMIN: These are false accusations. Even the commissioner of police today is Langi. He comes from Lango and I have some officers who are actually right in Acholi. They are Acholi and Langi and we have most of the top security people who are Acholi. These are just rumours created by exiles.

BBC: The International Commission of Jurists said in a report that between 25,000 and 250,000 people have been killed in Uganda during your regime. What is your reaction?

AMIN: It is the exiles who will never speak the truth and it is the British who speak this. There is no truth in it. They speak of several people killed in Uganda, in Kampala, each day. You will never find one body. This is a completely false accusation.

BBC: Do you expect people to believe that Archbishop Luwum and ministers Oboth Ofumbi and Oryema really died in a car crash?

AMIN: Yes, it is the *post mortem* which said that, not me. And Mr Kyemba can tell you because he is the one who brought the report to me. He was then minister of health, not me. It was completely a car accident. They were taken for interrogation and all their arms were brought to me. There were several thousand guns, mostly automatic, and several million rounds of ammunition.

Normally my country is peaceful. We co-operate very well. There is freedom of worship in Uganda. You find the Christians contributing to the building of mosques, the Muslims contributing to the building of churches. There is a good understanding in Uganda.

BBC: Why have so many prominent people disappeared in Uganda?

AMIN: The prominent people are here. Only those exiles who are in the pay of the British and who think that they must be ruled by the British have run away to Britain and to Kenya.

BBC: Did you not tell the British government that you wanted to buy Harrier jet fighters to attack South Africa?

AMIN: Yes, because you know that the enemy of all Africa is South Africa and Rhodesia. I wanted to buy them to go and attack South Africa. It is true that I asked for them and even for a destroyer and an aircraft carrier so that I could move to South Africa. This is sincere. I asked the defence secretary in my meeting with him.

BBC: What capability does your air force have now?

AMIN: I can't tell you any secrets because you might pass them on to South Africa, which I am actually aiming to destroy – Johannesburg and Cape Town. This is my aim. I am very serious about this. I am even looking to buy strategic fighter bombers which will be in a position to reinforce the freedom fighters in the southern part of Africa. I think some other countries might join me. We have got to liberate Rhodesia and South Africa.

BBC: Why did you not come to the Commonwealth Prime Ministers Conference in London last year?

AMIN: I am very happy about this. You know that I dominated the whole of the Queen's Jubilee, and the whole Commonwealth Conference was talking about me. I want you to take this message to Her Majesty the Queen, the prime minister and all the members of the government and the opposition and the people of Great Britain: I am coming to England and I will land in England. I want to see how strong you are against your conqueror. ❐

211

BOB ASTLES – AMIN'S WHITE HENCHMAN

PARTNERS IN CRIME: Idi Amin with Bob Astles, reportedly his closest and most loyal aide.

ASTLES' VICTIM: Bruce McKenzie.

DRUM: July 1979

Bob Astles has held one of the most dangerous jobs in the world for the last eight years. He has been an advisor and confidant to Ugandan dictator Idi Amin throughout his bloodthirsty and chaotic rule.

Bob Astles, a Briton by birth, is now a naturalised Ugandan. During the Obote regime of the 1960s, Astles was an intelligence officer and it was he and Akena Adoko who founded the State Research Bureau in the early 1970s, before President Obote was overthrown.

When Idi Amin took over in 1971, Bob Astles remained behind although he seemed to be a likely candidate to be killed by Amin. But he convinced Amin that he knew intelligence work. He pleased Amin by telling him that the first people to be dealt with were those who were involved in investigating Brigadier Okoya's death. He knew them all since Astles, together with the CID, was investigating the case. It was easy for him to point out to Amin the people involved. Those who were

lucky escaped, unlucky ones were killed in Mutukula Prison.

Bob Astles was buying his own safety winning popularity in the new regime. He succeeded. Amin trusted Astles very much and appointed him as a chief advisor and appointed his wife to be a minister. Astles refused the offer, made to him by Amin, to be the director of the State Research Bureau – choosing rather to be the brains behind the organisation. Lieutenant Colonel Faruk was appointed director but he never knew Bob Astles was using him. Faruk committed a lot of atrocities – many as personal missions to enrich himself – but whenever there was a state mission, it was Bob Astles who planned all its operations.

One of Astles' missions was the blowing up of the aircraft carrying

Bruce McKenzie and other important businessmen by planting a pressure bomb on board. The death in 1977 of McKenzie, a former Kenyan minister for agriculture, shocked the nation.

The question one must ask is why they killed Bruce McKenzie and his associate Keith Savage? Bob Astles, as I knew him, was a selfish man. He did not like any other European to go near the erratic leader. He feared that these Europeans might prove more influential with Amin than he himself was. He didn't feel happy when a European, coming to Uganda, did not pass through him but went straight to the field marshal.

Bruce McKenzie, Charles Njonjo and Keith Savage were business partners with Amin, together with a Mr Gaima. Astles didn't like this combination, for reasons best known to himself, and for a long time had been pondering a way to get rid of them.

He didn't get a chance until after the 1976 Israeli assault on Entebbe airport. After the incident Astles went to Amin and told him that it was McKenzie, Savage and Gaima who had collaborated with the Israelis. He said they were agents of the Mossad, the Israeli Intelligence Service. Amin had lost both soldiers and self-respect during the invasion and was very angry. He believed what Astles had told him, and it was arranged to plant a bomb in their aircraft when they next came to Uganda.

In May 1977 Bruce McKenzie went for a business trip to Uganda and phoned Amin saying that he would be coming. When he arrived in Uganda he had to wait two days before he could meet Amin. Astles had practised delay-

ASTLES TURNS THE OTHER CHEEK

TROOPING THE COLOURS, Nubian style: Bob Astles with his face scars.

DRUM: January 1979

The custom of scarification is dying among African tribes, but President Amin's chief adviser, British-born Major Bob Astles, has decided to have his face decorated in the Nubian manner with three scars on each cheek.

Colonel Bob's scarification took place in secret. He disappeared from the scene for some time, causing rumours in Uganda that he had been murdered because he was out of favour after an attempt by some of Amin's closest aides to oust him.

But the rumour-mongers were wrong because Astles came out from his hiding complete with Nubian scars with which to impress the ruling clan of Uganda. It is thought he took this extraordinary step to identify himself fully with the Nubians and to reassure Amin that he was still loyal to him. Astles has several times said that he would do anything for Amin "because he is a good man".

Although scarification is slowly dying in most African countries, it is still held sacred by the Nubian tribes. Such scars are gaining popularity in Uganda and reports have reached DRUM that people from other tribes have also gone in for this practice and are also learning the Nubian language in order to survive. ❑

ing tactics because the plot was not ready – the man who had to insert the bomb in the lion's head was too busy repairing Amin's accordion. On the third day Amin met Bruce McKenzie and after their meeting McKenzie decided to leave for Nairobi. After he and his companions had boarded the plane, Astles went on with a statue of a lion's head and told McKenzie that it was a present especially for him from the president of Uganda. As the plane reached an altitude of 20,000 feet it was blown to pieces. No one survived. ❑

I SAW AMIN'S VICTIMS KILLED – SRB OFFICER

THE SCENE IN the basement of the State Research Bureau headquarters, Nakasero, in 1979.

DRUM: June 1979

Abraham Sule joined the Uganda armed forces in April 1974, with the hope of becoming an air force officer. Before he had finished his training he was posted to the State Research Bureau headquarters where he worked first as a driver.

He was then promoted to case officer, one of the feared group who had powers to arrest and deal with anybody, anyhow.

Sule saw human heads in a freezer at Amin's Cape Town Villas. He was present at Nakasero State Research headquarters when Amin

dipped his bayonet into a pot containing human blood and then licked the bayonet. He witnessed the murder of Archbishop Luwum and was responsible for the records pertaining to the death of Kungu Karumba. Sule fled Uganda on April 9, 1979 and arrived in Nairobi the next day.

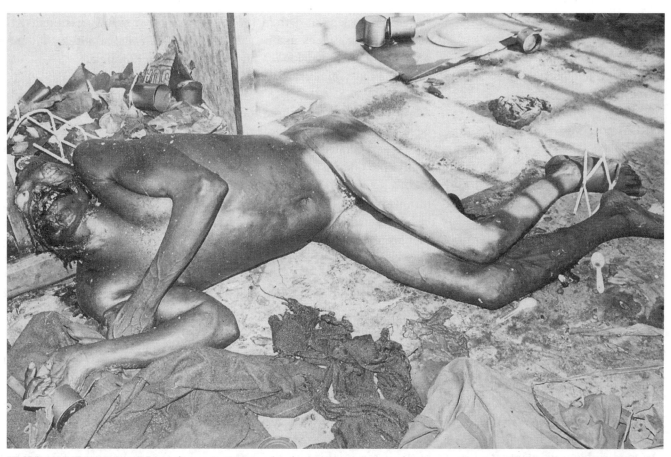

VICTIM OF THE HAMMERS: A favourite SRB mode of execution was to make prisoners beat each others' heads with hammers.

DRUM: We have heard of killings in Uganda of many people. One of the prominent personalities killed by Amin was Archbishop Luwum. Amin accused him of being a coup plotter. The archbishop is said to have been named publicly by Amin outside the Nile Mansion meeting. Were you there yourself?
SULE: Yes, I was there. Amin displayed a lot of arms which he claimed had been captured from Luwum's house. In fact, these were Amin's weapons taken from barracks. Some were actually captured, I think, from a house at Natete. There were just a few. Most of the weapons came from the barracks to enable Amin to cook up his story.

DRUM: After the Nile Mansion meeting, what happened?
SULE: Archbishop Luwum and Lieutenant Colonel Oryema and Oboth Ofumbi, both cabinet min-

isters, were arrested by Major Moses and Captain Mzee Yosa. Soon after their arrest they were driven away to Nakasero.

DRUM: What happened there?
SULE: We all left the Nile Mansion and went there. On arrival, they were taken to the underground cell

and stripped of their clothes by one of the soldiers at the State Research Headquarters, Major Mzee Kabugo. He stripped the ministers as well as the archbishop. He was tearing his robes with rage. He also plucked off the epaulettes on Colonel Oryema's shoulders. The stripping was done before they were

215

forced into the cells. Within minutes of being roughed up, beaten and kicked, Oryema and Ofumbi were taken out, and then Captain Mzee Yosa shot them both.

DRUM: Did you see him shoot them?
SULE: Yes. And we ran away. We were afraid. These men were so fierce when they killed. I had run away for a short distance. I did not really want to watch, but I saw him draw out his pistol and I heard the first shot. That must have been Oryema who was shot first. Both fell down as the shots continued. Before they were shot, inside the cell, Archbishop Luwum was praying for them.

DRUM: Then what happened?
SULE: The archbishop was in the cells by this time; he had been stripped to his underpants. Then after the shooting of the two ministers, he was dragged out of the underground cells and he saw their dead bodies at reception.

DRUM: Did the archbishop scream on seeing the bodies?
SULE: No, but he showed emotion. He was brought to the open area outside the building, that is the car park. At this time I was very shocked. I was sitting inside a car, I wanted to run away. When the archbishop was brought out to the car park, they tied his hands to his back and also tied his legs with ropes. They lay him prostrate on his back, his face looking up. They had beaten him up, but he could still walk when they dragged him to the car park.

Then Mzee Abbas, a civilian, drove his car near the archbishop. Mzee Abbas had powers because he was a Muslim. He then drove the car over the neck of Archbishop Luwum to and fro. He first drove backwards and then forwards, and then back again. The archbishop screamed loudly, and he died almost immediately.

Amin came after the three had been killed. Amin looked at the bodies and berated the dead bodies. He held his pistol in his hand and was very furious. Amin was furious because of the coup plot. He incriminated the three saying they were involved in the coup to topple him.

Amin and Lieutenant Colonel Faruk went upstairs and when they came back, Lieutenant Colonel Faruk called one of President Amin's escorts. His name was Shaban. Amin had come to the State Research headquarters in a Range Rover which had very big tyres, oversized ones. We saw one of the escorts get into the Celica car and Shaban drove the Range Rover. They went out of the headquarters, and about half a kilometre away, they placed the Celica car in an oblique position on the road leading to Nakasero State Research Bureau. The car was put near the Nakasero officer's mess. The driver came out. Shaban then drove the Range Rover at speed and crashed it into the stationary Celica car. We heard the bang. Later Amin told reporters that the three had died in a road accident while being taken to Nakasero.

DRUM: What did the members of State Research think after the killing of the three men who were respectable people in Uganda?
SULE: We were shocked, but the Nubians were rejoicing. To them killing is no problem. They were paid 1,000 shillings each for killing. They killed people at night, but they made sure that they had between 15 and 20 people to be killed in one night. This was to save transport expenses to Karuma Falls, about 200 kilometres from Kampala.

DRUM: When Palestinian hijackers forced an Air France passenger jet to divert to Entebbe airport, Amin brazenly allowed them to hold the passengers hostage. Is this really how he felt?
SULE: Amin is a mad man who poses as tough, but he gets scared easily. I remember that when the Israelis attacked Entebbe airport, I heard from the Nubians that of all people, Amin feared the Israelis most. He knew them, he knew they were tough. Amin knew when they were coming and he disappeared from Entebbe. Immediately after hearing from the ambassador to Lesotho that they were coming, Amin ordered his forces not to fire back at the Israeli planes – because he knew what the consequences would be.

We went to the airport about two hours after the assault. There were a lot of bodies around the airport. We found the dead and wounded being taken to Mulago hospital. Amin was there. He was furious, saying, "Why didn't they tell me that the Israelis were coming." He bragged that he could have taught them a lesson, but it was too late.

DRUM: We were told that Dora Bloch, one of the passengers on the hijacked plane, disappeared from the Mulago hospital where she had been admitted. What happened?
SULE: On orders from the president to Lieutenant Colonel Faruk, Dora Bloch was taken out of the Mulago hospital. Faruk ordered some guys from State Research. One of them I remember was Private Mara kwa Mara. He is a very bad man. Mara kwa Mara was sent out to get Dora Bloch and bring her

to the State Research headquarters. When he brought her, I saw her myself. She was sitting in a car. On orders, she was to be taken and eliminated at once. So they drove her to a place before Mukono on the Kampala-Jinja road. There is a small forest there, and that is where they took her.

When Mara kwa Mara came back, he told me that this woman was screaming all the way and she was telling Mara kwa Mara and his party: "Leave me alone! You are young boys, what are you going to do to me? Leave me alone! Let me go!" When they arrived at the forest, she was taken out of the car, and told: "Okay go!" and as she walked away they shot her from the back.

DRUM: The killing of Mrs Lukenya. Mrs Lukenya was expected to testify before a commission which was investigating the disappearance of a young Kenyan girl, but she never did? What happened to her?
SULE: Mrs Teresa Nasiri Lukenya was the warden of the African Hall at Makerere University. She was eight months pregnant. I saw her on the day she was brought to Nakasero. She was in the company of her brother. They were taken to Lieutenant Adams' office on the third floor of the State Research Bureau for questioning. That night she was killed. I witnessed the killing.

She was brought outside the cells to the open ground. It was dark. Simba came with a knife and stabbed the woman's stomach. He then cut the stomach open. The woman collapsed and fell down. She screamed but the screams died out almost immediately. She died. The place was full of blood. Her brother, in a state of shock, ran

about falling over several times. As he was running away, Adams shot him dead.

DRUM: In 1977 a number of air force men staged a plot to overthrow Amin. What happened to those air force men captured?
SULE: One of them was their commander, Brigadier Gwendeko. He was arrested at Wandegeya where he used to go every evening to play chess. He was brought to Nakasero and was taken to the director's office and questioned. Later he was brought out and they beat him severely. They then tied his legs and hands and hanged him upside down with ropes tied to the bars of a stair. His body was made to dangle from the rope so that he could swing when slightly pushed. In front of his head was a wall. When the body swung, the head knocked against the stone wall. They pushed him forwards and backwards and the head hit the wall many times. He died from the knocks against the wall. This was the work of the the State Research officials who were directly under Lieutenant Colonel Faruk's orders.

DRUM: Can you relate the incident where two Europeans were brought to your headquarters?
SULE: The Europeans were brought in on the Friday, three days before I fled. The two men were taken to Adams' office on the third floor. I saw them alive last when they were being taken from Adams' office down to the underground cell. The next day I found some askaris outside the cells who were inviting us to go and see. I went down to the cells. When the askaris opened the door of the cell, I saw the act of the murderers.

One of the Europeans was hanging there. A rope was tied round each wrist and then tied to the ceiling,

in a way that the body was some feet off the floor. His eyes had been gouged out and his stomach was opened from the chest all the way down. He was disemboweled. His bowels were lying on the floor.

DRUM: Have you ever seen Amin lick human blood?
SULE: At one time, yes! He put his bayonet in the pot containing human blood and licked the stuff as it ran down the bayonet. This happened at the State Research headquarters. Amin used to come there often. Amin asked for the blood, which was brought from the underground cells. It was in a pot. I think there was a big man among those who had been killed. Amin had come to speak to us and he was now demonstrating how we should be dealing with people to be killed. We were watching him. He had come to address us. Amin told us: "When you lick the blood of your victim, you will not see nightmares." He then did it.

DRUM: There have been incredible stories of human heads stored in fridges in Amin's residence. How true is this?
SULE: I have seen about five heads of people at Cape Town Villas. They were in a type of fridge. At one time we were told to go to the Cape Town Villas and remove the fridge because there was going to be a reception there for some foreign delegates. We were to move the fridge to an island which Amin used for a hideout. To be able to carry the fridge, we had to dismantle it, and this was when we saw the contents. The heads had fallen off their positions inside when the fridge was tilted so as to be carried out. Before the heads were put in the fridges, they were taken to Kawempe where they were treated with chemicals so as to be preserved. ❐

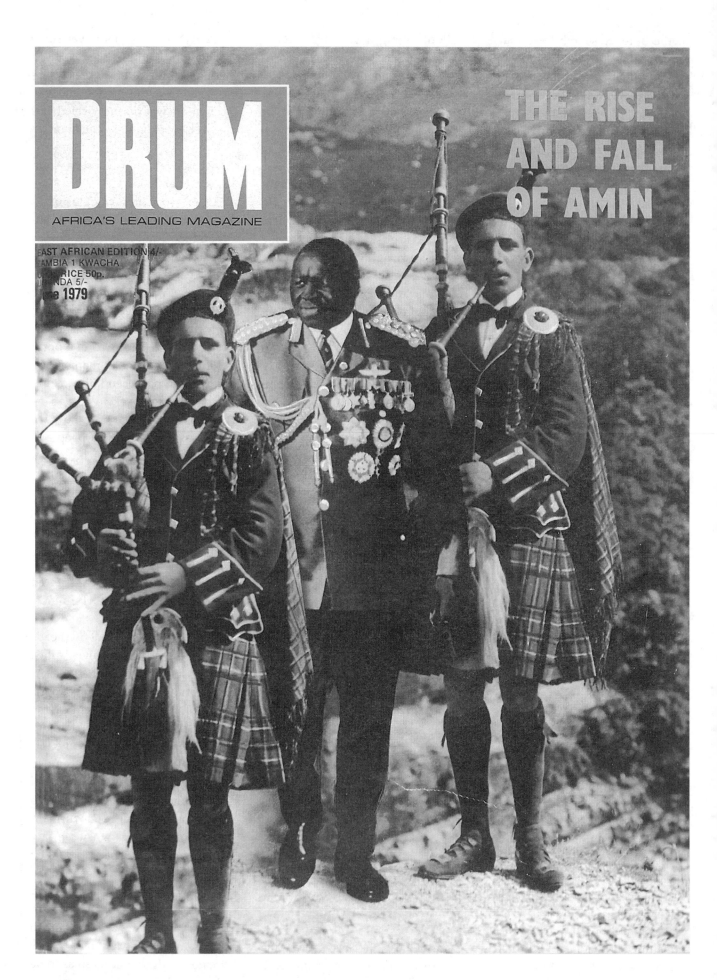

DRUM

AFRICA'S LEADING MAGAZINE

EAST AFRICAN EDITION 4/-
ZAMBIA 1 KWACHA
UK PRICE 50p.
UGANDA 5/-
June 1979

THE RISE AND FALL OF AMIN

DRUM BRINGS THE mountain to the man: This montage of Amin and the bagpipe players proved to be a very popular cover.

THE END OF AN ERA

DRUM EDITORIAL: March 1979

Amad general, with a gang of cut-throats, has raped, looted and murdered, from one corner of Uganda to the other. By this man's intransigent actions, a beautiful and sophisticated country – formerly an adornment to eastern Africa – was plunged into raging military conflict with neighbouring Tanzania. Full scale war quietened only as delegations from 49 African states gathered in Nairobi for the OAU ministerial session which will discuss this alarming situation.

Tanzanians have done their duty. When Amin invaded that peaceful country, the Tanzania army fought back bravely, pinning down a sizeable portion of the weapons and soldiery the Ugandan dictator uses.

But when there is a dangerous lunatic loose in a house, the rest of society generally steps in, captures him and locks him away in an asylum. We say that every Ugandan should be judged in future by what he does today, by the sacrifice he makes now, in the hour of Uganda's need. An end can be put – speedily, once and for all time – to Amin's manipulations of a nation which has become estranged within our continent.

If they are not guilty men, the politicians and the intellectuals who fled Uganda should be helping to put their country to rights – not living luxuriously in pretentious ivory towers in America, Nairobi or London. Ugandan monarchs, currently staying comfortably in Britain – the young Kabaka of Buganda and Patrick Olimi, Omukama of Toro, for instance – should be in there, fighting with the people. Otherwise, none of them are living up to his inheritance.

Indeed, now is the time for every responsible person in Africa to consider where his duty lies. Whilst a salient principle of the OAU charter forbids interference by others in the internal affairs of member states, nevertheless civilised men have obligations beyond the boundaries of their home countries. No nation is an island unto itself and we should remind ourselves that, if Uganda dies, the mourning bell will toll for us too.

Amin has been a boil in Africa's skin for long enough; and lancing that boil would restore this condition to better health. Every responsible African should ask himself sedulously what part he can play in corralling Uganda's madman. Write to DRUM and say what you think you can do – whether by prayers or through other considered forms of assistance – to help. The fight for Uganda's soul is on.

WAR ON THE BORDER

AT THE WAR FRONT: Ugandan troops in Tanzania examine a dead foe.

TANZANIAN TROOPS.

DRUM: March 1979

It was massive support from Tanzanians, rather than military strength, that made it possible for Nyerere to drive Ugandan invaders from Kyaka, a 1,800-square kilometre territory in southern Tanzania.

According to sources in Mwanza and Dar es Salaam, the Tanzania government received scanty intelligence reports in advance that Uganda was preparing to invade Tanzania, but nobody took the reports seriously because it was assumed that Amin's regime was so caught up in internal troubles that he would not dream of invading Tanzania.

The Tanzania government also doubted the reports because Amin had repeatedly threatened to bomb Tanzania, but had never carried out such threats. When Amin did finally invade Tanzania on October 27 – starting with bombings of Bukop, a few miles from Kyaka – the threats were tragically made real.

By October 29, the 3,000-strong Ugandan invasion force had occupied Kagera, having killed the handful of Tanzanian soldiers guarding the border post. It was a remarkable military feat, and because of poor communication, Dar es Salaam only received the full details nearly 24 hours after the invasion was completed.

Amin later announced that the occupation had set a precedent – having been successfully achieved in the supersonic speed of 25 minutes. This announcement sent shockwaves through Dar es Salaam and Nyerere swiftly summoned his top military advisors. The war took an ugly turn with the undisciplined Uganda army raping and looting the entire area under occupation.

Tanzania was clearly at a disadvantage. Transport that could quickly land the combatants on the battlefield was inadequate – most military vehicles were broken. Without the massive support given by the entire populace, Tanzania would have found things impossible. With most of their military vehicles broken down, the Tanzanian People's Defence Force turned to buses, lorries, Land Rovers – every means of transport available. There were some problems here as buses in private ownership could not be easily obtained. In Mwanza, the government had to use some force to secure the release of some of the buses.

In a 15-minute broadcast from Diamond Jubilee Hall, President Nyerere officially declared that Tanzania was at war with Uganda. Not surprisingly he put on a rare show of emotions. The Tanzanian counter-offensive was scheduled to be launched on November 6, but it was not until November 21 that Tanzania effectively outwitted Ugandan troops. In a double pronged counter-offensive, 6,000 Tanzanian soldiers faced Amin's troops from the front, while 3,000 Zanzibaris entered from the southern part of the Kagera River, and launched a massive attack which repulsed the invading troops of Amin.

A few days later the Tanzania government announced that it had captured foreign soldiers who were assisting Amin – they were Libyan radio technicians. It is not clear how many Cubans and Mozambican FRELIMO soldiers have directly helped Tanzania in her war with Amin. But when I left Mwanza there were persistent rumours that Cubans had been sighted leaving the planes at Mwanza airstrip.

This was a most vicious war. Tanzania suffered more, with whole villages being destroyed. At the beginning of the war, Amin indiscriminately bombed churches, schools and a hospital. In Mwanza, the nearest town to the battlefield, refugees poured in by the thousand. Most of them came on foot and spoke of genocide. Out of 32,000 refugees, some 10,000 were

TEARS FOR A destroyed home: A Tanzanian bears witness to Ugandan pillage.

PRESIDENT NYERERE ANNOUNCES that all invading forces have been repelled.

OAU MEDIATION: Secretary General Edem Kodjo (left) addresses a mediation meeting.

221

killed by the invading forces, according to the Tanzania government.

Tanzania's achievement in pushing out Amin's undisciplined troops did, however, show that despite Uganda's enormous military arsenal, Amin could easily be defeated by a small but disciplined army.

President Jaafar Nimeiry of Sudan tried and failed to mediate. As the two countries continued to exchange sporadic gunfire on their common border, Nimeiry, current OAU chairman, shuttled between the capitals of the three East African countries, Kampala, Dar es Salaam and Nairobi, but to little avail.

Nimeiry is one of the African presidents who has not condemned Amin, both in his capacity as the OAU boss, and as the president of Sudan. As far as Tanzania was concerned this automatically disqualified him from mediating. To make it more difficult, President Nimeiry is a member of the Arab League, an organisation which is widely believed to be financing Amin in his war.

Amin, with typical unpredictability, left the world in suspense for three days prior to President Nimeiry's visit to Kampala. On hearing that Nimeiry was coming for mediation, he stage-managed a dramatic disappearance. British-born Bob Astles, whose job included providing correspondents with the latest reports regarding the border war, even confirmed that Marshal Amin was "lost". Three days later President Amin reappeared with a story that he was not in fact lost, but was leading a task force on the southern war front.

As the war assumed a dangerous dimension in November – with frightening casualties from both sides – neighbouring Kenya offered to mediate, again with no success. In his speech formally declaring war, President Julius Nyerere told government and party leaders: "All our friends who are talking about mediation should stop doing so." Instead, Dar es Salaam told Nairobi – clearly and loudly – to cut off the supplies to Kampala and at the same time, to condemn Kampala for its aggression.

But Kenya's new president, Daniel arap Moi, while on a visit to Paris, announced that he could not meet these demands.

In an hour-long major policy statement during Tanzania's 17th anniversary celebrations President Nyerere left no doubt in the minds of Tanzanians that the war was to continue. "While we have successfully driven out the invaders," he told his people, "there are still some pockets of Ugandan soldiers in our land, ravaging and terrorising our people. Our work is to drive them out completely."

Castigating those African leaders who had not condemned Amin's invasion, and at the same time calling the Ugandan president a buffoon, Nyerere said it was a great shame for Africa to have chosen Kampala as the venue in 1975 for the OAU summit meeting.

Both countries remain on a war footing with sporadic machine-gun fire crackling across the border. And while the war has somewhat slackened, the situation in Mwanza is still tense with tired soldiers roaming the small town on the shores of Lake Victoria, guns slung on their shoulders. ❐

THE INVASION THAT WENT WRONG

DRUM: April 1979

The war between Tanzania and Uganda continues to rage on with the initiative still with the Tanzanians backed by Ugandan exiles and supporters of ex-President Obote. One marked aspect of the war has been the lack of information emerging from either side.

Here, exclusive to DRUM, is one soldier's first-hand account:

A BLOWN UP Ugandan armoured personnel carrier lies in a banana plantation on the main road from Entebbe to Kampala.

The long war with Tanzania has backfired on Amin and his followers, Kakwas, Nubians and Anyanyas and a few pure Ugandan opportunists. The war started with the mutinies in a few military units in the Chui Regiment, Gulu, where about 60 soldiers were killed with the excuse that they were robbers. The same thing happened in Mbale, Malire, Mbarara, Masindi and Tororo. These mutinies occurred because of lack of food and the delay in payment of salaries for over two months.

Amin mobilised his followers to round up the mutineers and collect them in one place for punishment. The unit chosen was Mbarara. The number of mutineers was fairly big and a company from Malire was ordered to guard them. The mutineers were from all tribes – including Amin's tribesmen. Most of them were killed. Those who remained alive had no alternative but to resort to force to save themselves. They managed to snatch guns from their guards and fought their way out. Amin's loyal guards chased these people across the border into Tanzania.

At the Tanzanian border they met a few Tanzanian guards and a three way fight ensued between the Ugandan defectors, their pursuers

TANZANIAN SOLDIERS near the border fire mortars.

managed to escape the clashes took refuge in nearby Tanzanian villages which were searched by the Ugandan troops.

It took the Tanzanian authorities some time to realise the border incursion was happening, and by the time they began reinforcing the border guards, Amin's troops had already captured several Tanzanian villages up to Kagera. The resistance they met from the Tanzanians was so small that it took them only about one hour to reach Kagera.

After taking positions on Tanzanian land, we were ordered to give strong resistance and to loot anything we found valuable and hand these to the government. Government experts were brought from Kakira Sugar Works to dismantle a whole sugar factory, the same thing happened to a sawmill. We found a number of bulldozers which were in good condition and they are now working on improving our poor roads. We got thousands of cattle, goats, chickens, sheep, iron sheets, vehicles, women and house-servants for our soldiers. Most of the captured Tanzanians are now working at

and the Tanzanians. This exchange of fire between the three groups ended in the death of most of those who were fleeing for their lives, plus the Tanzanian border guards. The Amin troops were using tanks, armoured personnel carriers and military jeeps. Those who

PRESIDENT IDI AMIN with MiG pilots: Some deserted, others cracked.

TANZANIAN TROOPS ATTACK in the

FRONTLINE TANZANIAN SOLDIERS as they advance towards the strategic town of Jinja.

Kinyala Sugar Works with no pay except food and housing. Lots of private property was also looted.

Towards the end of the second week of our stay in the captured land, Nyerere's troops began their attack on us. They came with heavy artillery but we managed to resist for some time. Experts from Kilembe Mines were flown up to Kagera to destroy the bridges. We had to use these people because our air force had tried to destroy them in the rain but kept missing their targets. Others were being shot down by the Tanzanian forces. After positioning the ex- plosives under the bridge while facing a strong Tanzanian front, we withdrew towards the border and watched the bridge blow up with hundreds of Tanzanian troops in pursuit of us on it. People from the Ministry of Information and Broadcasting were brought to take photographs of

ttle to take the eastern town of Jinja.

THE FACE OF WAR: Tanzanian soldier marches past wrecked Ugandan vehicle.

the Kagera River. From my observation, I realised that the Ugandan nationals were not happy with what they saw and this showed me that they no longer supported the present regime.

The Tanzanians managed to repair the bridge within a short time and continued running after us. The war became tense and this was when we began losing our soldiers at a rapid rate. We had a total of about 40,000 troops but so far we have lost over 20,000 soldiers in different ways.

On reaching the war zone almost 6,000 soldiers abandoned all their guns, their military equipment and their uniforms. They robbed the neighbouring civilians of their clothes, changed into them, and fled into the bush – never to be traced again. About 12,000 troops have been killed and others captured as prisoners of war.

Our Uganda army had a total of about 60 tanks and out of these, over 20 have been destroyed, five have been captured and about 15 are unusable. We had about 100 armoured personnel carriers out of which about 50 have been

TANZANIAN FIELD COMMANDER, Marwa Kambale, leads his forces into Jinja.

the dead Tanzanians. All these were later shown on the Uganda television network to show the public our success.

Civilians were very frightened when they saw crocodiles take people alive and the hundreds of dead bodies that were floating in

TANZANIAN AND REBEL Ugandan soldiers loot a blanket factory in Jinja.

A DEAD LIBYAN soldier.

destroyed, roughly 20 are totally useless, and more than ten have been captured. We had about 300 jeeps but over 100 are off the road, about 60 have been destroyed and about 20 have been captured by the Tanzanian forces. We had almost the same number of Land Rovers but they have had a similar fate. We have lost an uncountable number of bullets and we shall soon be without ammunition.

In the air we have three fighter squadrons. Unfortunately the two squadrons of MiG 15's and 17's and the L-29's are more or less grounded due to lack of spare parts. Out of the 17 MiG 21s, 12 have been shot down by the Tanzanians, and surprisingly, two timid pilots ran away with their MiG 21's leaving us with only three. Another mad pilot was ordered to go and bomb Bukoba; instead he mislocated the enemy position and dropped one of his bombs on Masajja near Lyantonde and the other bomb on a trailer which was carrying our military equipment and men to the war zone.

This incident made civilian lorry and bus drivers very worried and

CHEERING UGANDANS GREET Tanzanian troops as they enter Jinja.

now they fear to go to the frontline in order to reinforce us with troops or to carry away the dead and wounded.

The situation is so grave that if we did not have Brigadier Marela in Sudan we would be gone. Marela has done a great job of recruiting

AN AMIN SOLDIER taken prisoner.

APRIL 23: Tanzanian soldiers stride victoriously down the main street of Jinja.

227

THE LEGACY OF WAR: A bombed-out tank guards its rotting commander (above), and as anarchy seeps into Kampala, looting becomes endemic (below).

and training a good number of southern Sudanese and sending them over as reinforcements. Brigadier Maliyamungu recently recruited about 10,000 young boys from Sudan, Kibera (Kenya) and from Uganda itself. Those who were recruited in Uganda were forced whether they liked it or not, and they are between the ages of 12 and 16 years. Their main job will be on roadblocks.

We do not know whether we shall win and remain in power. Almost everybody seems to be pleased with the Tanzanian progress in the war with Uganda. Some civilians are harbouring Ugandan exiles, who seem to have already infiltrated Uganda and they are destroying things like petrol stations, railway lines and electricity supply lines.

Foreign faces are no longer being reported to the authorities as in the past. For example, those who blew up a petrol station near Kibuli were never reported to the authorities. As a result the authorities decided to massacre all the people neighbouring that petrol station.

Almost at the same time one of the main electricity supply lines to Kampala, Jinja and as far as Mbale was destroyed by unknown people.

Houses, hotels, bars and lodges are being searched every night, but no one has been found. Patrols are being made all over the country at night. Taxis, buses and lorries are being searched every day on all roads, but in vain. Consequently, the authorities have resorted to arresting people without proper documents. On their arrest they are badly tortured or killed and many have died this way.

ABANDONED ARMY ISSUES: Military uniforms and pictures of the "Life President" lie discarded under a tree.

The Tanzanian forces have got a very big machine which looks like a runway searchlight from far which we suspect to be a metal detector. Any vehicle or any armed soldier within reach of this machine's rays is immediately shot at and it never misses a target within 30 kilometres.

There is no small chance of us reaching near the enemy. When we try our long range artillery, it seems as if we do not hit the enemy at all. They just advance and continue hitting us hard. We have suffered heavy casualties. Civilians are fleeing just before time from the war zone – sometimes leaving their houses without any guard at all. This has given us easy access to food and shelter. A good number of our soldiers are looting the properties for everything they can get their hands on.

The enemy has got a threatening force on the frontline and yet inside the country too is a threatening group which is very hard to locate, just as if they are using magic, and possibly being backed by the nationals themselves.

We have done lots of grave things against the nationals and therefore they cannot be expected to spare our lives.   ❐

VICTORIOUS Tanzanian soldier.

THE END OF AN ERA

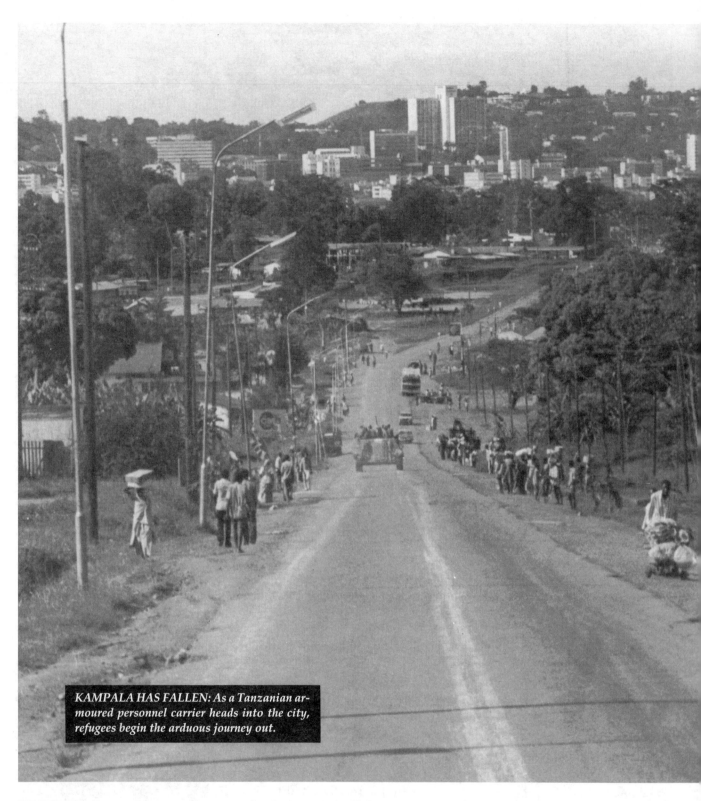

KAMPALA HAS FALLEN: As a Tanzanian armoured personnel carrier heads into the city, refugees begin the arduous journey out.

DRUM: April 1979

DRUM'S secret informant in Amin's army recounts the final moments of the despotic military regime:

This time it seems as if the Ugandans, together with the Tanzanians, the mercenaries and the Ugandan exiles are united against the Amin regime. If they continue fighting, by June, we might be totally exhausted and our regime will be toppled. So we are thinking of how to escape from Uganda without being killed.

When we think of taking the northerly direction to Sudan, the Acholi, Langi and some of the West Nile tribes are ready to slash our heads off. If we think of the easterly direction to Kenya, the Basoga, Baganda, Bagisu and other nearby tribes will not allow us to reach Busia or Tororo before our heads are slashed off. If we suggest Rwanda, there is no way out for the greatest enemies of ours are coming via that end. In

and we have retreated up to Lwera near Lukaya. Still the enemy is coming towards us.

We have a feeling that the anti-Amin group of the six soldiers headed by Major Kimumwe and seconded by Lieutenant Mutumba who escaped from Nakasero in 1977 are the ones guiding all these movements which are proving to be very complicated and very threatening to our present government position. This group of six could be fighting alongside the Tanzanian forces – for they know Uganda in and out.

One day Brigadier Taban was shot at while on his way home from Jinja. I wonder how they recognised him in the middle of the night. Colonel Gore, the recent air force commander, was shot dead at the war zone while they were travelling together with Big Daddy. This incident made the group separate and each one took his own direction. Amin luckily had a radio which he used to call for help. Brigadier Maliyamungu got lost in the bush for more than a week.

Lieutenant Colonel Kiiza was recently shot down in a MiG 21 while on his way to Bukoba and he died in it. Lieutenant Nobert Atiku's aircraft was also shot down. He managed to eject in time and he was reported captured as a prisoner of war. Our recent chief of staff, Major General Gowon has disappeared. Only hell knows where he is.

fact there is no peaceful outlet for us from Uganda.

The nationals' failure to report foreign faces to the authorities and their present attitude to us is a clear indication that they are totally tired of the Amin regime. All the president's hiding places seem to be known and he is being trailed from time to time by unknown people who have sophisticated weapons that can even destroy tanks. This time it appears we are being defeated from each and every corner for, whatever tactics we try, we do not succeed.

The enemy is just advancing. Masaka town has been captured

The situation is worsening every day and therefore our days are numbered. Whatever happens we shall die as brave men. We shall not run away from the government and when our enemies reach Kampala, we shall die fighting. ❐

DRUM

AFRICA'S LEADING M

EAST AFRICAN EDITION
KENYA 4/-
UGANDA 5/-
ZAMBIA K1
U.K. 50p

October 1979

MOI: THE
FIRST YEAR

NEW WAVE
OF TERROR
HITS UGANDA

ZIMBABWE
AT THE
CROSSROADS

THE MIRACLE THAT FAILED

On April 11, 1979, the anti-Amin forces entered Kampala and announced to great rejoicing: "The Ugandan liberation forces have captured Kampala today. The racist, fascist and illegal regime is no longer in power." Hotly pursued by his conquerors, Amin fled to Jinja, the Owen Falls Dam and then to the Kenyan border. He was next seen in Libya, on his way to an eventual exile in Saudi Arabia. Amin's successors inherited a country economically dilapidated and politically deformed. Hardly anything in the country worked: most factories had ground to a halt, agricultural production had virtually ceased and there were no foreign reserves to pay for imports. In addition to the economic disaster, Amin bequeathed to Uganda a political system in which violence had become an integral part. The attempt to separate the two was to prove one of the most difficult tasks facing succeeding administrations.

In March 1979, a conference of most of the Ugandan exile groups was convened in Moshi, Tanzania. At this meeting the Uganda National Liberation Front (UNLF) was formed to co-ordinate the battle against Amin and thereafter to govern a liberated Uganda. The UNLF was in essence a government-in-exile, and its chairman, Professor Yusuf Kironde Lule, the president-in-waiting. On April 13, 1979, two days after Kampala had fallen, Yusuf Lule was sworn in as head of state, and the UNLF's 30-member National Consultative Council (NCC) became the interim legislature. The new administration was confronted with a monumental task of reconstruction and rehabilitation. However, it soon became clear that the personal, ethnic and ideological antagonisms among the Ugandan leadership would make this impossible. The Lule administration was soon immobilised by in-fighting. When Lule demoted powerful cabinet ministers Paulo Muwanga (internal affairs) and Yoweri Museveni (defence) his end was near. Within hours of Lule's actions the NCC convened and cast a vote of no confidence in him. After 68 days in power, Lule had been deposed. Having voted Lule out of power, the NCC, at the same meeting, chose Godfrey Binaisa as his successor. Binaisa, who had been attorney general in Obote's first administration, was not a member of the NCC. The fact that he was an outsider, and thus strongly beholden to the NCC, played a large part in his appointment. Not surprisingly therefore, the Binaisa era was dominated by backroom power struggles within the NCC and the Military Commission. While Museveni, who had been reappointed defence minister, and chief of staff, Brigadier David Oyite Ojok, battled for control of the army, Binaisa was otherwise engaged – mainly in enriching himself. By August 1979 law and order had almost completely broken down. In early 1980 Binaisa did try to take control of the army, but when he moved to dismiss the already notorious Oyite Ojok, he overestimated his hold on power. The Military Commission, shocked that Binaisa had dared to act against the chief of staff, summarily announced that it had assumed the powers of the presidency.

LIBERATED UGANDA GETS A NEW PRESIDENT

THE NEW PRESIDENT of Uganda, Yusuf Lule, arrives at Entebbe airport from Dar es Salaam, Tanzania, after several years of exile. He was greeted by Tanzanian military officers and leaders of the new Ugandan army, including Brazilio Okello (left).

SWEARING-IN of the new president. The new chief justice, Justice Wambuzi, swears in Yusuf Lule as the fourth president of Uganda.

THE NEW HEAD of state with his chief of staff, Lieutenant Colonel David Oyite-Ojok. During the campaign against Amin, Oyite Ojok became a legendary figure, not only in Uganda but throughout the whole of Africa.

CELEBRATING UGANDANS greet President Lule during the swearing-in ceremony. The crowd's appreciation of the role Julius Nyerere's Tanzania played in their liberation is evident.

"WE WANT LULE BACK"

ROAR OF APPROVAL: The huge crowd in City Square, Kampala, responds to pro-Lule campaigner Mayanya Nkangi.

DRUM: August 1979

It began peacefully but ended in shooting – one of the biggest demonstrations of solidarity seen in Uganda since Amin took power.

When the news came that President Yusuf Lule had been forced out of office and replaced by Godfrey Binaisa, thousands took to the streets of Kampala. No work was done in the Ugandan capital that

day, as people began to gather, first in small groups, then in hundreds, and finally in multitudes, chanting: "We want Lule! Down with Binaisa!" Mr Mayanja Nkangi, a spokesman for the pro-Lule move-

ment told a cheering crowd packing City Square: "Why should we change leaders? Today we have Professor Lule, tomorrow Mr Binaisa, and another day we shall have a different one. Other countries are laughing at us. We have suffered enough. Didn't we learn from Amin's regime?"

But the Consultative Council would not be moved, and late that night troops opened fire, shooting mostly in the air, although at least two people were killed. The protesters fled in terror, their hopes dashed. And ex-President Lule went quietly back into exile. ❑

AMIN'S LEGACY CLAIMS NEW VICTIMS

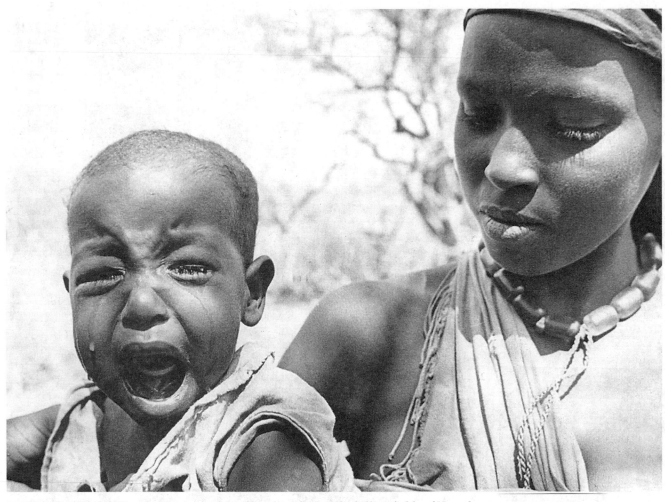

MOTHER AND CHILD at a refugee camp for Ugandans fleeing the killing fields of Uganda.

DRUM: August 1979

At least 50,000 Ugandans have fled their country into neighbouring countries in the wake of the victory of the Tanzanian-backed Uganda National Liberation Army.

Most of the refugees – about 35,000 – are in the Sudan where there is a shortage of relief supplies. At Nimule, one of the three main entry points along the border with Uganda, refugees were living on cassava given to them by the local peasants while those camping near the shore of the Nile River were depending mainly on fish.

Why did these people flee? Some of the refugees claimed that a war of revenge was going on in Uganda against people or tribes

which had a close affinity with dictator Idi Amin. Others have claimed that there was indiscriminate killing of Muslims, a claim which has been given credence by the Sudanese government in Khartoum. President Nimeri told journalists recently: "To be a Muslim in Uganda today is a crime punishable by death."

In an exclusive interview the Geneva-based deputy commissioner for refugees, Mr Kevin Lynette, said that as far as the United Nations high commissioner for refugees was concerned there were three categories of refugees from Uganda. "First, the army men and their families, then those ordinary people who ran on grounds of fear of their association with Idi Amin, tribally or religiously. These cate-

gories of people will definitely require permanent settlement here.

"Then you have another group of people who left Uganda in utter confusion as a result of the war and because they could see others fleeing in fear. We expect these will return soon because they have nothing to fear," he said. Mr Lynette also confirmed reports that refugees had little or nothing to eat. "In immediate relief supplies we need about half-a-million dollars. This will be for food and medicines as well as farm implements such as hoes so that they can start working on the land for their self-reliance."

Of all the Ugandan refugees, Amin's henchmen are the least affected by starvation and other privations. According to Sudanese authorities "they are meeting all their hotel bills themselves because they came with a lot of money." Many of these people are badly wanted in Uganda by the new government which has murder and other criminal charges waiting for them.

While more than 3,000 ordinary refugees live in guarded camps where, during my visit, there was hardly any food, the defeated soldiers live in complete peace and freedom – eating and drinking well and moving about in their luxury cars at will despite the petrol rationing. Among the prominent ones is the former vice president, General Mustafa Adrisi, who prefers to continue being called the vice president of Uganda.

He is ruminating over his past at a spacious government bungalow, only 75 kilometres from the Ugandan border. When journalists asked about his new life in exile, General Adrisi praised the Sudanese government for its hospitality, adding that he, his three wives and their 36 children were well.

I also had a chance encounter with Amin's commander of the Marine Commandos, Brigadier Taban, a very frightened man, at a military base in the Sudanese district of Yei. Brigadier Juma Bashir, Amin's last foreign minister lives with a few other officers at the Juba Hotel.

According to the president of the High Executive Council of Southern Sudan, General Joseph Lagu, the Sudanese government has refused to hand over any of the wanted men to Uganda against their will. Sudan argues that it has no extradition agreement with Uganda.   ❑

UGANDAN REFUGEE CAMP in a Kenyan sports stadium close to the border.

A GROUP OF courageous refugees agreed to brave the trip back to their homes.

AMIN'S VICE PRESIDENT, Mustafa Adrisi, in exile in the Sudan with his children.

UGANDA STORMS OUT OF OAU SUMMIT

UGANDAN PRESIDENT Godfrey Binaisa at the OAU meeting in Monrovia. Binaisa spiritedly defended Tanzania's role in ousting Amin.

DRUM: September 1979

It was the most acrimonious meeting in the history of the Organisation of African Unity, with leaders storming out of conference sessions after bitter exchanges. It was the first time that African leaders faced issues squarely instead of burying their heads in the sand or postponing decisions. For the first time in the organisation's history, they threw aside any diplomatic pretensions and levelled personal attacks at each other in clashes that led to a number of walk-outs.

The walk-outs began with the Afro-Arab delegations opposed to Egypt's peace treaty with Israel. Later that same day President Godfrey Binaisa of Uganda stormed out angrily after an argument with the Nigerian head of state, Major General Olusegun Obasanjo, who was chairing the meeting discussing whether a letter criticising the role of the Tan-zanians in overthrowing the military regime of Idi Amin should be read to delegates.

Binaisa argued that it was improper to read the letter, as he had not been given prior notice. But Obasanjo, who had joined President Nimeri of the Sudan in criticising Tanzania, tried to press the matter further, even after most delegates said the letter should not be read. Binaisa, visibly angry, then walked out. He had earlier put up a spirited defence of Tanzania, saying that the fact that Ugandan girls made love to the Tanzanian soldiers, whom he called "liberators", was indication enough of the solidarity between Tanzania and his country.

Earlier President Julius Nyerere of Tanzania had clashed with Nimeri over the Tanzanian counter-invasion of Uganda in retaliation for Amin's incursion and attempted annexation of Tanzania's Kageria Salient. Nimeri said that the removal of a government by another country had set a "sad and regrettable precedent". But Nyerere stuck to his argument that he had no choice following the OAU's failure to condemn the invasion of his country.

However, the majority of leaders, despite misgivings they may have had at the precedent set by the removal of Amin, supported Tanzania largely because of Amin's excesses. No one even questioned the credentials of the Uganda delegation, and Uganda was even chosen to be a member of the credentials committee. This says much for the sympathy the post-Amin administration enjoys in Africa. Later, although both Nigeria and Sudan still wanted the Tanzania issue decided on, the matter was dropped. ❑

BEFORE THE WALK-OUT: President Binaisa leading the Ugandan delegation.

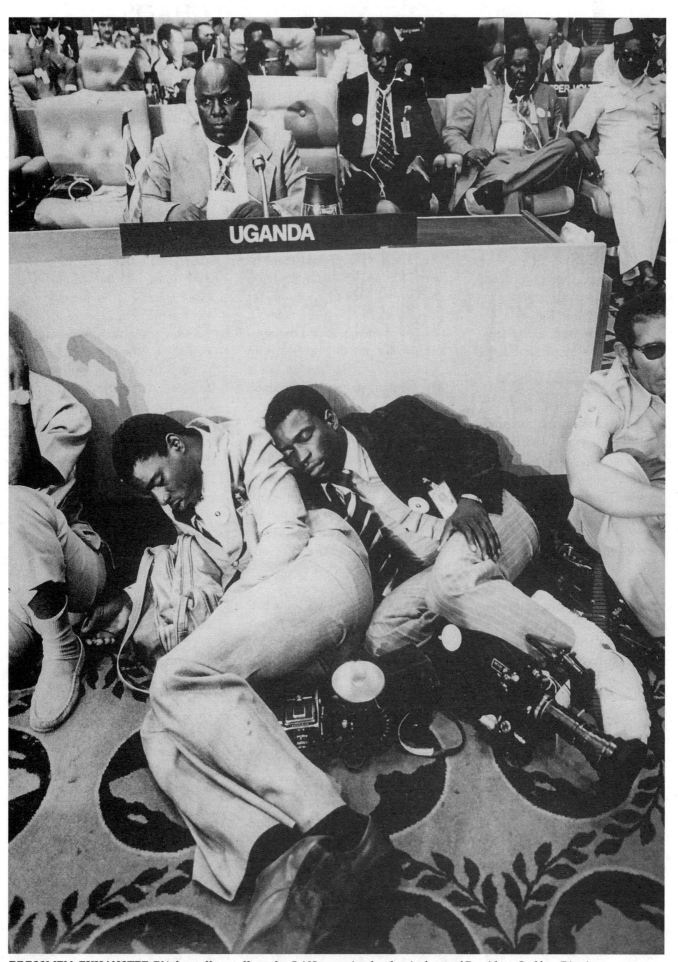

PRESSMEN, EXHAUSTED BY the endless talk at the OAU summit, slumber in front of President Godfrey Binaisa.

GUN RULE IN UGANDA

DRUM: October 1979

Once again the gun rules in Uganda. Unidentified killers, some wearing uniforms and carrying automatic rifles cast away by fleeing soldiers who served the ousted tyrant, Idi Amin, stalk the streets of Kampala and other towns by night, bent on murder. Nobody knows for sure who they are – but they are organised, they know who they want to kill, and they do so with apparent impunity. Thousands of ordinary Ugandans have been murdered since liberation in apparently random killings, but in Kampala, the target has been prominent people in positions to help rebuild the shattered country.

Who is behind the killings? Now that fugitive dictator Idi Amin, better known as *kijambiya*, or slaughterer, has gone, everyone in Uganda is wondering who is responsible for the current spate of murders.

Since Uganda's liberation there have been thousands of killings both in villages and in towns, among them, organised murders of prominent Ugandans mainly in Kampala. Many have been followed to their homes and shot in full view of their wives and children. They include:

- Tony Bagonza, Grindlays Bank manager;
- Patrick Bakuru, a senior civil servant in Lands Department;
- Kaija Katuramu, a surveyor and prominent businessman;
- Edward Karamagi, an oil boss;
- Jack Barlow, brother of the inspector general of police, a dentist and director of the dental school at Mulago hospital;
- Dr Abudon Obace, a senior physician at Mulago and a cousin of army chief of staff;
- Lieutenant Colonel John Ruhinda, the National Liberation Army's director of training.

A typical case was that of Edward Karamagi who worked for the Total Oil Company. He was in bed when he was attacked at his Ntinda home. The gunmen first arrived at his neighbour's house and asked him what his tribe was. After assuring them that he was an Itesot, they then asked him what tribe his neighbour was. He told them he was a Mutoro. One gunman burst through the kitchen door, another going round to Edward's bedroom window. When he heard the commotion he put on the bedroom light and reached to get his gown. The gunman at the window aimed and blew his brains out.

His death came just a few days after President Godfrey Binaisa had addressed the nation on television, reassuring the population about their security. He followed that by dispatching a large number of Ugandan and Tanzanian troops back to their barracks.

Although in a few cases some bad elements of both the UNLA and Tanzanian soldiers have been involved in acts of murder or robbery, these latest killings are believed to be by people making use of army uniforms and guns left by the dictator's fleeing troops. A few people in army uniforms have been arrested.

The present deterioration of security in the country is attributed to two factors. One is that Kampala's liberators opened up Luzira Prison letting out convicts and criminals. The other is that there has not been an organised method of recovering arms, ammunition and uniforms abandoned by Amin's fleeing troops. ❑

ECONOMIC CHAOS GRIPS UGANDA

DRUM: January 1980

On October 20, 1979, Uganda's new minister for finance, Mr Jack Ssentongo, announced that Amin's valueless currency was to be exchanged by the government for new notes, and the tedious exercise began the following morning. By 6 a.m. people were already queuing up outside the country's banks – not that they necessarily wanted to do away with Amin's face, but, within the period of nine days, they had much money to change.

During the reign of Big Daddy, *magendo* (smuggling) had gained momentum and many people had become rich. When the Asians left the country in 1972, for instance, the Nubians and Kakwas taking over shops were very often illiterate guys who knew something of the Koran, but businesswise were very dormant.

Big Daddy himself was a Standard Four leaver, so his knowledge was limited. He did things the way he thought best, and when he received loans from Arab countries he merely ordered that more money be printed. Then the foreign funds were used to buy munitions, luxurious goods for himself and other army officers.

The effects of the printing exercise was deterring. Money was apparently in plentiful supply, but it wouldn't buy anything, because the essentials – things which ordinary people needed – were scarce. Amin's planes left regularly from

Entebbe for Europe, loaded with coffee which was sold there, and the "whisky run", as it was called, came back with a belly full of high-priced drink but rarely the spare parts to keep factories and farms running. Big companies still operating – like Bata, Gailey and Roberts and the Uganda Transport Company (the country's sole big transport concern) – found life unbearable.

Kenya became the saviour. Coffee was smuggled out of Uganda – spare parts, essential goods like soap, salt, sugar, oils and beer went in. Individuals who took the risks in this delicate business priced their products exorbitantly. Nubians and Kakwas became absolute masters and they could spend 5,000 shillings a day. In Kampala girls fell easy prey to them, for it isn't hard to fall in love with money. Schoolgirls abandoned their studies and today illegitimate children are many in Kampala and its suburbs. The State Research boys made sure of their share of the loot and became the Croesuses of Uganda.

The nine-day money changing session of October 1979 was predictably hectic. Some people queued for three days without luck. For those who made it, banks would exchange in cash only 5,000 of the old notes. Anything above that amount must be banked, the authorities said, and this did not suit everyone.

It was very common for people to put their money into pots and then bury the pot in a safe place. Some private doctors, taxi drivers, businessmen, etc., were very good at this. But now, these pilgrims who had spurned the banks just had to lose. The note exchange caught them generally unprepared.

CROWDS QUEUE at the Bank of Uganda to exchange their "Amin" notes.

With only days to go before the deadline, taxi operators, shopkeepers, petrol station owners, even market workers, refused the old notes entirely. One man, who had not been attended to at the bank for a full two days, burned his money. "It won't buy food for my children. I can't even get a soda," he shouted, "neither can I pay my taxi fare with these notes. It's better to be without them completely."

If rumour is to be believed, there seems to have been some major abuses of the situation. A DRUM reader from Jinja voiced his "disgust and bewilderment" at the way the currency exchange was conducted. "When the cash exchange programme was announced, most people were relieved that we were at last to be saved from uncertainty, but bank officials soon dampened our enthusiasm," he said. "We became convinced that a well-organised racket was being carried out and no one will wonder if some bank officials turn up with either new cars or new houses."

The operation – so far the biggest staged by the government as it bids to salvage the faltering economy – succeeded in cutting off from circulation millions of shillings, and the Uganda government hoped that the effect would be an automatic decline in prices. But this is not likely for some time to come. Even though the circulation of worthless "Amin notes" has been killed, there are not yet enough goods and services available to meet needs.

Almost at once in Jinja the price of commodities rose by 500 per cent. Sensing a deteriorating supply of goods – and the resulting hoarding – people bought heavily and drove the prices rocket-high. Goods are not getting through the communication and transport infrastructure controlled by Kenya. Foodstuffs are now very scarce, even in the hub of Uganda, and there are many indications of hard times ahead.

The budget introduced in December, 1979, by Jack Ssentongo is therefore tough and unpopular. The economy has to be boosted by increased internal production, economists point out, and it is in this sector that hope is strongest, for overseas companies and agencies are stepping in to supply management skills and the working capital needed so urgently.   ❐

THE FACE OF FAMINE

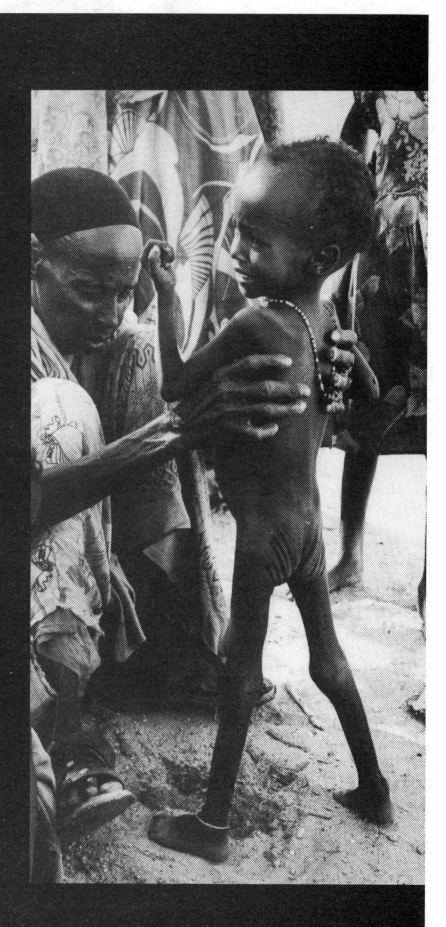

While the politicians squabble the children starve

While the politicians and soldiers in Kampala squabble over who should hold power, the children in the Karamoji area of north-east Uganda are dying like flies. Not because Uganda has no food to feed them, but because indifference, anarchy and bands of ex-soldiers turned bandits stop food getting through. The bandits, mostly remnants of Idi Amin's forces armed to the teeth with automatic weapons, ambush food convoys sent by charities and slaughter both tribespeople and their cattle alike, while Uganda's quarrelling rulers seem to have neither the will nor the means to protect them. And in the Horn of Africa, where the soldier-politicians of Ethiopia and Somalia hurl insults at each other and bullets at each other's peoples, one of the most tragic famines ever known in Africa is worsening daily — and once again it is the children who die first, after dreadful suffering. The rulers in Mogadishu seek a 'Greater Somalia'...the rulers in Addis Ababa are determined to prevent them, even if it means driving millions of ethnic Somalis from the Ogaden region by terror and starvation. They talk in the capitals of Africa, they talk in the Organisation of Africa Unity, they talk in the United Nations; the politicians talk everywhere, but still the children starve.

MEMBERS OF THE KARIMOJONG TRIBE who have fled their homes in north-east Uganda and are now housed in Oxfam refugee camps in southern Sudan – this page and following two pages.

DRUM: September 1980

What started as a mere food shortage has now become a national disaster in which an estimated 300,000 people, mostly the cattle-raising and warlike Karamojong tribesmen in north-east Uganda, have died.

In a country ravaged by disaster and death, about 300 people a day, mainly children, are dying from starvation and malnutrition. With the Uganda government in a shambles and international relief work hampered by armed thugs who ambush the food lorries heading for disaster areas, there seems little hope of preventing the deaths of several thousand more. There are many factors behind the famine, previously unheard of in a country capable of feeding three times its own population. During the liberation war which toppled Idi Amin's murderous regime, more than 20,000 automatic rifles fell into the hands of cattle raiders who had previously carried spears. The cattle raiders have also been joined by disgruntled Amin soldiers who fled into Sudan and

now come across the border to cause confusion and instability. One official said he found it hard to believe that the spear-carrying Karamojong could learn so quickly to use automatic rifles and the skills to keep the Uganda army at bay. He said: "They are either being trained by Amin's supporters or the majority of those who raid cattle are former Amin soldiers. There is evidence that Amin's soldiers have crossed the border to cause chaos."

When disaster struck in Uganda the rest of the world was preoccupied with the Russian invasion of Afghanistan with many relief organisations devoting their attention to the Afghan refugees in Pakistan, and to refugees in Somalia and South-East Asia. A relief official said: "No-one believed that there would be a drought in this part of the world. So relief came too late, after several thousand people had already died."

As a result of the armed raids, which occur every day despite thousands of troops being deployed by the Uganda government, more than 400,000 cattle have been stolen in north-east Uganda. This has affected the Karamojong tribespeople who feed on milk, blood and meat and who do not rely on food crops in an area where the rainfall is always sparse.

Now the once-proud Karamo-jong, thought to have been the healthiest, strongest and bravest tribe in the country, have re-sorted to eating grass seeds and anything else they can lay their hands on.

Official United Nations figures show that four million people in northern Uganda have been affected by drought. Of those, half a million have been scraping for food and 140,000 in Karamoja are starving to death. The World Food Programme estimates that a minimum of 1,800 tonnes of grain a month is needed to feed the starving population.

CARE officials believe that the situation will improve, but not until late September when they expect the new crop to be harvested. So far they have 25,000 tonnes of grain to feed 200,000 people. A CARE official said: "That is not good enough, but I think it is going to improve the situation tremendously. If the crop does not come out and the cattle raiding does not stop, then we are in for another disaster."

He suggested that the security question should be top priority as stability in the area would persuade other relief organisations to come to Uganda's aid. He asked: "How do you get a trader to go there when his lorry, full of essential commodities, could easily be hijacked and his goods stolen at gunpoint?"

CARE, which has already spent a staggering 60 million shillings on the famine, suggests that the government should open stores there with official prices to avoid *magendo*, supply 80 lorries to take food to the area and provide security to escort food convoys. ❐

THE COUNTRY GOD FORGOT

AFRICAN HEROES RETURN: Presidents Binaisa and Nyerere welcome 10,000 troops back to Tanzania.

DRUM: February 1980

An eerie silence envelops Kampala every night nowadays, the result of a dusk to dawn curfew imposed by the regime of Godfrey Lukongwa Binaisa. The silence is only broken by the barking of stray dogs, the coughing of weary watchmen and sometimes by intermittent gunfire. The curfew underlines the serious security problem still facing Uganda – more than nine months after the ousting of dictator Idi Amin.

Today it is clear that there will be no miracles in Uganda. The euphoria has given way to scepticism, the dreams of national unity have been subverted by personal ambition and greed. Uganda is a dispirited country teetering on the brink of new disasters.

The Tanzania army of liberation has become an army of occupation. Near anarchy reigns in parts of the countryside, and Kampala is ruled at night by bands of uniformed murderers. The economy remains a shambles, with most shops still shuttered. The government is wracked by tribal and ideological differences and manoeuvring for personal power.

"There was so much jubilation back in April, such a wonderful feeling of national co-operation," said the Anglican archbishop, Silvanus Wani. "It is hard to understand how it soured so quickly, but for now people are living in fear and suspicion and worry about what is going to come next."

While Lule was complaining in the international press about his expulsion, the National Consultative Council (NCC) – the country's miniature parliament – elected in his place Godfrey Binaisa (60). Binaisa is a man deeply hated by the majority Baganda tribe, although like Lule, he is a fellow Muganda.

It has not been plain sailing for Binaisa. After only five months in office he also clashed with the NCC when he announced a cabinet reshuffle removing the controversial Marxist Yoweri Museveni from the Ministry of Defence, and giving him the Department of Co-operation, an insignificant post carved out of the Ministry of Foreign Affairs. Binaisa said he was prepared to offer Museveni the post of minister for foreign affairs, but couldn't work with him in defence.

At the time of my visit to Kampala the "Museveni Affair" was still a boiling issue. However, Museveni and other ministers involved had agreed to swallow the changes in the interest of national unity and the need for a speedy rehabilitation of the country. Observers believe Museveni was fired because of his role in the recruitment of the new Uganda army being formed to replace the Tanzanians.

Binaisa is made from a different mould to Lule. He has set a precedent by making the cabinet changes without the approval of the NCC, and he has stood his ground. As a result, the conflict between the president and the NCC over ministerial appointments continues apace. President Binaisa wanted Mr Museveni out of defence. Mr Museveni on the other hand wanted to remain attached to defence and so he successfully applied to the NCC to be elected to the standing committee on defence and national security.

Due to a quirk of the constitution, Binaisa, who is now minister of defence, will be an ex-officio member of this committee without voting rights, and Museveni will be a full member with rights. If there was confrontation between these two men in the past with respect to defence policy, then the stage is set for further confrontation.

The NCC is the most ideologically diverse governing body in Africa and includes Marxists, monarchists and capitalists. But despite this confusion Binaisa still rules amid opposition from the Baganda. The biggest threat to the Ugandan government comes from within the government itself, because national well-being is a nebulous concept to those whose prime loyalty is to their tribe, ideology or personal ambition. ❐

By PG Okoth

BINAISA SPEAKS TO DRUM

DRUM: April 1980

Since taking over Uganda's leadership, Binaisa has weathered a number of coups engineered by pro-Obote elements within the cabinet and in the National Consultative Council, and he has already made an impact on his people. In an interview with DRUM's PG Okoth, President Binaisa pulls no punches. He speaks his mind on subjects ranging from relations with Kenya and Tanzania to ways of revamping Uganda's destroyed economy.

DRUM: What do you consider to be your achievements since taking over the leadership of Uganda from Professor Lule?
BINAISA: I think we have achieved a lot under very difficult circumstances. As you are well aware, the Uganda National Liberation Front is made up of various political groupings, each with its own ideologies and political orientation. My task has been to try to bring about a general consensus so that we can all move together in the difficult task of rehabilitating and reconstructing a country that was devastated by military dictatorship.

We have been able to reduce the incidence of insecurity and armed robberies, which were the order of the day during the military dictatorship. We have also been able to convince the international community to extend aid to us and also to interest investors and tourists to return to Uganda. There is still a lot to be done but given peace, stabil-

ity and international goodwill we will do miracles here.

DRUM: We get reports that the security situation in Uganda is still far from calm and that daily killings continue. We also have reports that thousands of people are dying of hunger in Karamoja and in the northern province. How true are these reports?
BINAISA: There have been isolated cases of murder in and around Kampala, but these have been dealt with. The security situation in the northern province and in eastern and north-eastern parts of the country has been causing us some concern. As you know there has been a long period of drought in the area, which resulted in thousands of cattle dying. The Karamojong people are pastoralists who depend on their cattle for survival. We have appealed to a number of countries for famine relief and I am glad to say that the response has been good. We have already received help from the United States and Canada and we hope to receive help from other nations.

I must take this opportunity to deny rumours spreading that there are private armies backing former presidents Obote and Amin, poised in the north, or in other parts of the country, ready to attack Uganda. These rumours have absolutely no foundation.

DRUM: Will you be a presidential candidate in the elections? If so, do you think you have support in the country?
BINAISA: I do not want to cross my bridges before I come to them. Let us wait for the elections to come. As to my support in the country, it is not for me to say.

DRUM: The task facing you and your government is that of recon-

RESTORING GOOD RELATIONS: President Binaisa's visit to President Moi is a significant advance in bilateral relations.

struction. How formidable is the task? Or, in other words, what are your priorities?

BINAISA: I am glad you asked that question. When one takes into consideration the damage caused not only by the war to get rid of the dictator but also the serious brain drain resulting from the murders and persecution of the Ugandan elite by Amin and also the depletion of the country's foreign exchange by the fleeing military looters one can best appreciate the gravity of the task that has been confronting my government.

Not a single school or hospital was built during all the eight years Amin was in power. In some areas whole infrastructures had to be built or rebuilt. Factories came to a standstill. The giant sugar works of the Madhvani and Mehta groups were left in ruins. Happily they are now being rehabilitated. Agreements have

been signed by the former owners of these factories. They have been handed back to them. Production should restart soon and former employees of the factories, who were thrown out of their jobs, will be absorbed and new employees taken on.

Indeed, the task of getting the country back on its feet is formidable. We estimate that we will need about four billion dollars, in a sort of Marshall Plan to be able to revamp the economy. Plans are under way to reactivate the Kilembe Mines and, with the abundance of the copper reserves there, the country should be able to earn some foreign exchange.

We also intend to increase agricultural production, particularly coffee and cotton, which for many years were Uganda's economic mainstay. During the military dictatorship, tons of Ugandan coffee

were exported in exchange for whisky and other non-essentials – to keep the army of the dictator happy. We intend to tighten loopholes so that Ugandan coffee will not be smuggled. The Coffee Marketing Board will be the sole marketing agency and farmers will be subsidised and paid promptly for their crops.

DRUM: Can you dwell a little on your relations with Tanzania? Is it true that the 20,000 Tanzanian troops will be pulled out soon and if so, what steps have you taken to replace them.

BINAISA: I must say that our relations with our neighbours, particularly Tanzania and Kenya, have been very cordial. We are very much grateful to Tanzania, not only for helping us in liberating the country from the military dictatorship, but also for helping us later with maintaining law and order.

THE MIRACLE THAT FAILED

However, as a country that is facing the enormous task of reconstruction, we are finding it difficult to maintain the Tanzanian troops. We have appealed to Commonwealth nations to volunteer and help us in the training of Uganda's new army, police and prison forces and also to keep law and order during the withdrawal of the Tanzanian troops. We hope this will be possible.

DRUM: The present Ugandan leadership is composed of all sorts of strange bedfellows – from Marxists, to feudalists, to those who believe in free enterprise. Does this explain why you cannot agree on legislative programmes?
BINAISA: Your guess is as good as mine.

DRUM: Elections in Uganda are scheduled for late 1980. Will you stick to the schedule? If not, when?
BINAISA: We intended to have the elections in 1981. Now they've been brought forward. The results of the last census have already been published and steps are being taken to register voters later this year. All political parties affiliated to the Uganda National Liberation Front will be free to take part in the elections.

DRUM: There were reports about Uganda's intention to set up what will be known as human rights courts to try the henchmen of Idi Amin. When will these courts be set up and will Amin be tried *in absentia*?
BINAISA: Debate on the setting up of the human rights courts is still going on in the National Consultative Council. The setting up of the courts will speed up the trial of Amin and his henchmen, numbering about 5,000, still in our jails. ❏

DRUM: May 1980

Once it was known as the "Pearl of Africa". Fertile, prosperous, its people ingenious and go-ahead, Uganda was the envy of many less well-endowed African states. Now, after eight years of barbarism and inept government followed by a devastating war, the country needs vast amounts of foreign aid and some kind of economic miracle just to get back on its feet again. And neither the aid nor the miracle have been forthcoming.

Only a Marshall Plan similar to the one launched to rebuild Europe after the Second World War can save Uganda. Its problems are vast. The root cause of the current malaise lies in the fact that inflation is up 1,000 per cent.

The Uganda National Liberation Front government inherited debts to the tune of two billion shillings and a staggering 800 million shillings in local currency was in circulation by April 1979. But while the currency ought to have been backed by substantial foreign reserves to ensure parity for the Uganda shillings against other currencies, the Lule administration found as little as 20 million shillings in foreign exchange.

The major task of the Binaisa government is to boost Uganda's foreign reserves and to encourage import substitution. This is intended to be accompanied by a major export drive to earn the country revenue from abroad.

But despite the government's efforts during the last seven months the situation has appeared to be drifting from bad to worse. Prices are escalating, production appears to be at a standstill, transport is chaotic and smuggling is rampant.

The deterioration of the economy has been aggravated by ideological differences not only among members of the National Consultative Council but also within the cabinet. A drowning nation like Uganda cannot afford to discriminate whether the rope thrown to save it is capitalist or Marxist.

Ugandans are aware that the country is bankrupt. They know that the total liabilities, both domestic and foreign, far exceed the country's present capacity to settle them. The international community is prepared to rush aid to Uganda – provided the country returns to normal and the security situation improves. But these conditions have not yet been satisfied and there is no sign that the politicians are yet prepared to face the harsh realities.

The people of Uganda are being asked by the finance minister, Jack Ssentongo, to pay up to 50 per cent more for petrol, cars, commercial vehicles, fishing boats and electricity. But the petrol increase brought heavy fire upon the minister of finance. Members of the Consultative Council and the public attacked the "belt-tightening" in the budget. In a 45-minute tirade, Kirunda Kivejinja, addressing Ssentongo directly, said: "Even though this meets the IMF standards, we have to serve the interests of our country. And whether or not you're called by your first name in the World Bank, don't forget your country is still Uganda."

When the professional murderers are on the rampage shooting everything in sight what happens when a brave fellow tries to call assistance from the police? "We cannot assist you because we have no transport. Is it possible for you to come and pick us up?" ❏

THE RISE AND FALL OF GODFREY BINAISA

THE MEN WHO ousted Binaisa: Paulo Muwanga, Tito Okello and Oyite-Ojok.

DRUM: November 1980

The 60-year-old president has had a stormy political career. In the early 1950s he was appointed advisor to the now defunct Kabaka's government but was immediately fired by the conservative Mengo rulers who would not stand the progressive young lawyer who wanted to change things abruptly.

He was compensated for his stand against Mengo by Obote when he appointed him to his cabinet as the first Ugandan attorney general after independence. An articulate barrister who was trained at the famous London's Lincoln's Inn, and who became the first African Queen's Counsel in East and Central Africa, Binaisa defied his conservative Baganda tribesmen and drafted the 1967 constitution which abolished the four kingdoms. This was the last straw for his Baganda people.

But at the same time relations between Binaisa and Obote had be-

gun to cool. According to Binaisa he could no longer stand the dictatorial tendencies which Obote was assuming and the only alternative left to him was to quit and go back to his law firm.

"There were no more intellectual discussions and things were being done without cabinet decision. Obote was very suspicious of advisors like me. He would ask me something and stare at me straight in the face to see what would be my facial reaction. He has an unbelievable inferiority complex."

When Amin took over the government, Binaisa turned down several jobs which the dictator offered him, because, he said, he did not trust Amin right from the start and was looking for a way of slipping out of the country. He finally escaped in the early 1970s and quietly lived in London where he practised at Lincoln's Inn.

At the same time he started his underground opposition to Amin and was to be seen hidden in shadow on British television screens whenever they wanted interviews on resistance to Amin. He later left for the United States where he studied for the American bar and passed it.

In America, Binaisa intensified his fight against Amin. He addressed the US Senate Foreign Affairs Committee which resulted in the cutting off of trade with Amin's regime by President Jimmy Carter. The United Nations Human Rights Committee also condemned Amin.

After Amin's departure and Lule's overthrow by the left-wing members of the interim parliament, the National Consultative Council (NCC), it was Binaisa the NCC approached to take over, and he readily agreed.

OBOTE RETURNS: After nine years in exile, ex-President Obote arrives home.

But Binaisa's takeover was the most controversial ever seen in the country. His own Baganda tribesmen, who had never forgotten the part he played in deposing their Kabaka, took to the streets of Kampala in violent demonstrations and several people were gunned down by the Tanzanian occupying army. Binaisa's opponents saw his assumption of power as just warming the presidential throne for Obote who was then waiting in the wings in Dar es Salaam.

The country was paralysed by a general strike and the people came out defiantly to oppose the NCC, a thing which had not been seen in Uganda in many years. Western countries, which had promised aid to Uganda after the overthrow of Amin, were now hesitant. The country was split right down the middle and Binaisa's ability to reunite the country was suspect.

Within the several groups which formed the Uganda National Liberation Front, each group had its own political leanings, loyalty and a private army to back it up. Binaisa was the odd-man-out who had no political group of his own and no private army to protect him. Several thousand people were killed in an organised murder plot. Blood and dead bodies were commonplace on the streets of Kampala. Uganda became ungovernable.

Besieged in the huge whitewashed colonial mansion at Entebbe under the strict protection of Tanzanian troops, Binaisa remained optimistic and unruffled by the formidable opposition which faced him. I went to interview him a few weeks after he had become president. I asked him what he would do since it was apparently clear that his peo-

ple did not like him. With his usual huge grin he said: "You don't worry about that. I know my people, I have been a politician for a long time in this country. At the end of it they are going to love me."

He was right. He started stamping the ground in the whole of Buganda appealing for understanding. Essential commodities began pouring in but the prices were still unreachable to the people. *Magendo* was still flourishing and corruption, even among Binaisa's ministers, was rampant. He could not control the army, which killed at will and terrorised the countryside.

People close to Binaisa say that he did not listen to advice. For several months before he was overthrown, friends had warned him of the impending coup which they say Obote instigated and which had the blessing of President Julius Nyerere.

Binaisa's next political crisis was to be his last. Obote announced from Dar es Salaam, where he still lived in exile, that he was ready to go back to fight elections. Binaisa had presented a bill which had been passed by the NCC about elections being fought under the umbrella of UNLF by all the political parties and groups which overthrew Amin. The UPC and the DP, two of the main political parties in the country, wanted the elections to be fought on party political platforms. But Binaisa now had the support of the "small groups" in the NCC who won the day when it became obvious that Obote and Paul Ssemogerere, the president general of the DP, had little chance of becoming president as long as the umbrella arrangement existed.

Binaisa said that after winning the vote in the NCC, a number of provocative actions were taken by Major General Oyite Ojok. Ojok ordered an army unit to attack Katwe, a suburb of Kampala, on the pretext of searching for arms, without consulting Binaisa first. Binaisa's orders to Ojok to get the army off the streets of Kampala were ignored. Binaisa had to act.

He first made sure with the Tanzanian commanders that they would support him. They agreed that, since he was the president, his orders should be followed. He then moved swiftly and fired Ojok, making him an ambassador abroad. Ojok refused to take the post and moves to get rid of Binaisa started.

Museveni, then vice chairman of the Military Commission, was the only member of the military junta who was not a friend of Obote. But Museveni had no love lost for Binaisa who had removed him from the Ministry of Defence, a mistake which cost Binaisa his presidential throne.

After the Military Commission announcement that they were taking over the reins of power, Binaisa turned to the Tanzanian commanders for their help. They looked the other way. The protesting Binaisa was removed from State House by Tanzanian troops who continued to guard him at a nearby house where he spent several months under house arrest.

Eventually he fled and as he sits in London pondering what to do next, the question for Ugandans remains: will Binaisa, a celebrated political survivor, make another comeback?   ❏

By Don Kabeba

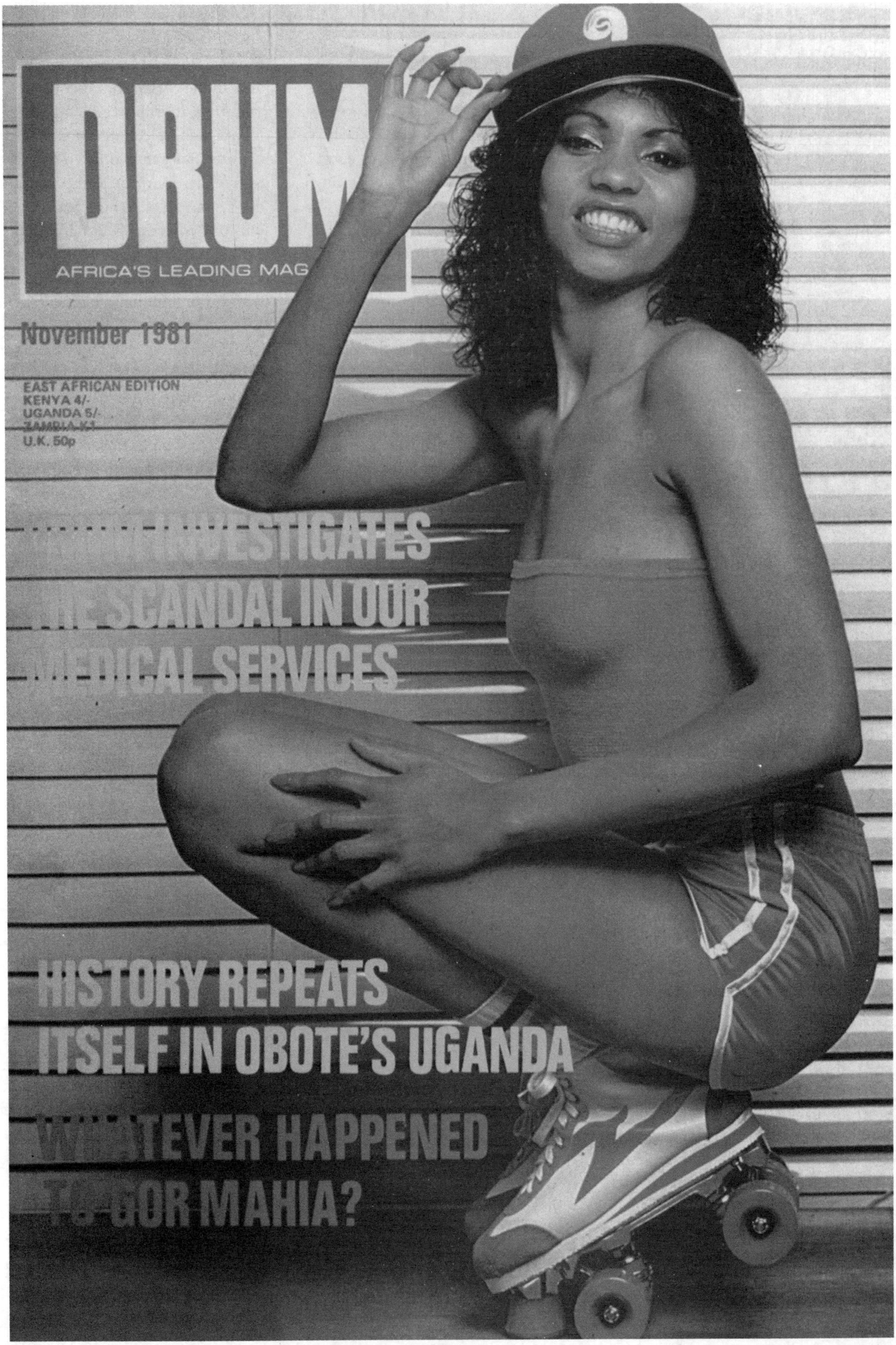

DRUM

AFRICA'S LEADING MAG

November 1981

EAST AFRICAN EDITION
KENYA 4/-
UGANDA 5/-
ZAMBIA K1
U.K. 50p

DRUM INVESTIGATES
THE SCANDAL IN OUR
MEDICAL SERVICES

HISTORY REPEATS
ITSELF IN OBOTE'S UGANDA

WHATEVER HAPPENED
TO GOR MAHIA?

THE RETURN OF OBOTE

The Military Commission which overthrew Binaisa honoured the ex-president's promise to hold a general election in December 1980. The election was contested by four parties: the Uganda Peoples Congress (UPC) led by Milton Obote, the Democratic Party (DP) led by Paul Ssemogerere, the Uganda Patriotic Movement (UPM) led by Yoweri Museveni and the Conservative Party. The UPC was by far the best organised party and won the election comfortably. Nearly 20 years after first leading the country, Milton Obote once again ruled Uganda. However the results were not accepted by the defeated parties, who claimed that there had been irregularities and intimidation during the voting. Most notable among those speaking out was Museveni, who charged that the voting had been rigged.

Unlike his two most recent predecessors, Obote understood the essential feature of political power in Uganda: the military was the ultimate arbiter of power – no civilian government could afford to underestimate its importance. Consequently the years immediately following the 1980 election saw a strong partnership develop between the government and the army. The top figures in the government and the military – President Obote, Vice President Paulo Muwanga, Prime Minister Allimandi, General Tito Okello and Major General Oyite Ojok – were all personal friends and of the same political persuasion. They were also, with the exception of Muwanga, all northerners. The hero of the anti-Amin war and army chief of staff, Oyite Ojok, played an important role in holding the different factions of the army together. However, Oyite Ojok's reputation became tarnished by repeated allegations of ethnic favouritism, corruption and brutality. His mysterious death in a plane crash in December 1983 severely unsettled the army. Before long the troops began to divide into hostile factions and the informal alliance between the army and the civilian government floundered.

After the death of Oyite Ojok, the various guerrilla forces, who had been fighting Obote since he had come to power, stepped up their activity. The largest anti-Obote force, the National Resistance Army (NRA), formed by Yoweri Museveni after the disputed general election, was particularly active in Ankole, Buganda and Toro. As the intensity of the civil war grew, Obote's army and administration unleashed a bloody reign of terror, comparable to the worst excesses of Amin. Killer squads roamed the country and imprisonment without trial became a daily event as Obote's criminal aides ran riot. Ultimately it was dissention within Obote's own army which unseated him. In July 1985 an Acholi faction of the army led by Brigadier Bazilio Okello, fearing victimisation by Opon Acak's dominant Langi faction, marched from northern Uganda to Kampala and seized power from Obote. The rebellious troops met with only token resistance during their three-day march. Obote, seemingly resigned to his fate, sent some of his ministers into exile before quietly slipping out of the country in disgrace.

UGANDAN COUNTDOWN

DRUM: July 1980

The countdown to the general election has begun with former President Apollo Milton Obote as front runner. Obote leads the powerful Uganda People's Congress (UPC) which formed the first independence government in 1962. The other major party is the Democratic Party (DP).

Both parties are torn by divisions but the UPC appears to be the most organised. It has a charismatic leader in Milton Obote. The party machinery is still intact despite Obote's nine years in exile. Obote has support in the north, in the east, in the west and to some extent in parts of Buganda.

The DP too is strong in various parts of the country, but currently its hierarchy is divided into those supporting the candidacy of Professor Lule, and those backing Paul Ssemogerere who took over the leadership of the party following the murder of Benedicto Kiwanuka in 1973.

Other factors to be taken into account include the rivalry between the Baganda politicians such as Binaisa and Lule who both want to be president, and the candidature of Yoweri Museveni, vice chairman of the Military Commission who has formed a new party. This leaves Obote as the only head of a party which will fight the elections as a united entity.

The likely lineup in the presidential race will be: Obote, UPC; Lule, DP; Paul Ssemogerere, DP; Godfrey Binaisa, no party; Yoweri Museveni, Uganda Patriotic Front (which groups his own Front for National Salvation, the Uganda Labour Party of Humphrey Luande and the Uganda National-

ist Movement). By dividing their energies the parties opposing the UPC appear to leave a clear field for Obote's comeback.

Complicating the situation is the continued presence in the country of 12,000 Tanzanian troops. President Nyerere is taking no chances with reports that Idi Amin is still harbouring thoughts of returning to Uganda. With Amin on the periphery, Nyerere cannot be expected to remain complacent. He will need guarantees that Uganda's fledgling army is capable of defending the country – a guarantee that is not likely to materialise given the present political chaos in the country. Observers believe that there can never be free and fair elections in Uganda as long as Tanzanian troops are in the country. Kenya and the Sudan have said so openly and have urged Nyerere to pull out his troops from Uganda before the September polls.

While the politicians are squabbling, the security situation is getting worse with reports that private armies are on the rampage and the famine situation in Karamoja district is getting out of control. Thousands of political detainees – most of them supporters of Idi Amin – are reported to be dying of hunger in Luzira Prison.

The tragedy of the Uganda situation lies in the fact that the country has not produced a national leader with a hold on every part of the country. When leaders derive their allegiance from their ethnic groups there is always the danger of instability and tribalism. So far the country has had five presidents since independence in 1962, and four of them – Obote, Amin, Lule, Binaisa – still harbour political ambitions. ❐

GENERAL ELECTION RACE HOTS UP

DRUM: September 1980

A new political alliance is set to challenge Dr Milton Obote in the presidential elections later this year. The new party – the Ugandan Patriotic Movement (UPM) – is a merger between different political groups formed in exile during Amin's tyranny and those who have recently left Dr Obote's Uganda People's Congress Party.

There are now three parties which will contest elections due to take place at the end of September: The Democratic Party, the Uganda People's Congress and the new Uganda Patriotic Movement.

The parties which have resolved to merge to form the UPM are the Front for National Salvation (FRONASA) led by Yoweri Museveni, vice chairman of the ruling Military Commission which toppled former President Godfrey Binaisa's government in May, the Uganda National Movement and Uganda Labour Party. Dissidents who have defected from the UPC

EX-PRESIDENT LULE

because they did not like Obote's leadership were led by local government minister Bidandi Ssali, works and transport minister Kintu Musoke and Kirunda Kivejinja, a member of the interim parliament, the Uganda National Consultative Council.

Yoweri Museveni, leader of the Uganda Patriotic Movement and vice chairman of the Military Commission and the second most powerful man in the country, has a hero's record after successfully leading his guerrilla army to capture the town of Mbarara in western Uganda during the liberation war which ousted Idi Amin.

Dr Obote, who ended his nine year exile early this month, says he will pursue policies more moderate than his former Marxist policies. He was the first to declare that he would not nationalise any foreign business, he would not make Uganda a one-party state and he would allow a free press.

"Uganda of today is very different from Uganda of 1970. That time we were talking of development and right now we are talking in terms of rehabilitation. Uganda is not in a position to start any development projects. We have the

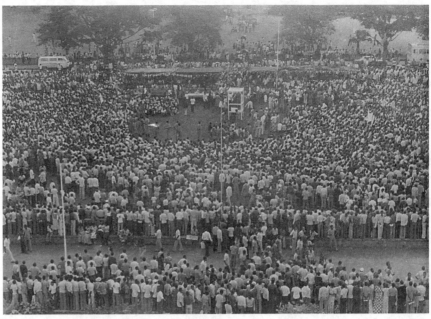

THE FIRST DP RALLY in Uganda since Obote banned political parties in the 1960s.

enormous task of rehabilitation. We cannot rehabilitate Uganda with policies we were following in 1970. Those policies could only work in a state of development," Dr Obote has said.

But many of his followers have not been convinced by his new policies and have decided to desert him. Amongst those who declared their allegiance to the Democratic Party include his cousin and former minister of economic development in his government, Adoko Nekyon, who has declared that he could not agree with someone – Dr Obote – who thinks that Uganda could not be led by someone else.

But UPC officials are quick to point out that all those who have deserted the party have left because of personal differences with Dr Obote rather than political reasons, and feel confident that the people are behind Dr Obote. "We are not at all worried about people leaving us and joining the other two parties. It shows beyond doubt they have no political principles. If they do not like Milton Obote's leadership, they should fight within the party to vote him out of the leadership."

By any standards Dr Obote's rallies since he came back from exile have been very small compared to the crowds he attracted before he

PAULO MUWANGA

FRONASA LEADER MUSEVENI

EX-PRESIDENT OBOTE

was toppled from the presidency in 1971. It is said by many political observers that Obote's chances of recapturing the job are very slim.

Many of his opponents and especially senior members of his party who have joined the other two parties, blame him for the current political misfortunes in the country. They say it was Obote's mistake to promote Idi Amin, who they say was given the running of the government since the crisis of 1966 when Obote suspended the constitution, introduced a one-party state and Draconian detention laws.

But Dr Obote has argued that he promoted Amin purely on merit, like any other person who was in government at the time. "I did not create Amin. It is God who created Amin. Those people who say I created Amin are the very people who after the coup sided with Amin, and who created the situation which enabled him to consolidate his position."

Although another former president, Professor Yusuf Lule, has been stopped from coming back from a year's exile by the ruling Military Commission, their decision might affect the Democratic Party, the party which has been tipped to win the elections with a large majority.

The Commission's announcement was designed to put the blame for Lule's failure to return on the DP. The Commission has exploited the power struggle within the DP between Lule and Mr Paul Ssemogerere, the interim chairman of the DP.

Lule, who is a member of the DP, was coming to Uganda to contest the DP leadership which would

have automatically made him the presidential candidate. But that would have brought a split in the party between the northern Uganda tribes and the Baganda where both Lule and Ssemogerere belong.

Lule would have been an asset to the party in Buganda where it was predicted that he would have carried all 46 seats in a parliament of 135 seats. But he would not have been able to do well for the party outside Buganda. While Ssemogerere is expected to do badly in Buganda, because of his progressive ideas which are not liked by the conservative Baganda. He would do well outside Buganda, including the northern areas, simply because he has been secretary general of the party and is liked throughout the country.

Now the DP is finding itself in a dilemma. They cannot issue statements denying involvement in the decision to bar Lule from returning because that would annoy the Military Commission. No party at the moment in Uganda would like to antagonise the Commission because any clash with the Commission might render that party being banned from the elections.

In a country accustomed to disaster and death, several deaths and serious injuries have been reported during the campaign. DP and UPM delegations complained to Presidents Julius Nyerere of Tanzania and Samora Machel of Mozambique that supporters of Dr Obote were involved in the acts of violence. But reports which have come to the police have indicated that all the parties which are contesting elections have been affected and therefore it is very difficult to pin down one or two parties. ❐

OBOTE WINS RIGGED GENERAL ELECTION

DRUM: January 1981

The Ugandan elections are now over and a new government has been sworn in. But the results will always be hotly contested.

On the day following the polling, as the results started coming in, it was obvious that the Democratic Party was winning. Their figure in fact passed the half-way point needed for outright victory. It was then that the Military Commission chairman Paul Muwanga took a step which shocked all but his UPC supporters.

He announced that only he, not the Electoral Commission, would pass the figures, and that he had the right to nullify them with impunity. It was only a matter of time before the results were being upturned in most parts of the country, and a DP victory, as if by a magic wand, became a UPC one.

For Ugandans it would be impossible, as well as foolish, to forget the sequence of events, not only following the casting of votes, but of all that went on from the day the Tanzanian forces started their counter-attack against Idi Amin. Many people see the day in April 1979 when Kampala fell as the moment when Obote's return as Ugandan leader was assured, principally by his great friend and protector, President Nyerere, with his thousands of troops.

It is argued that under no circumstances, whatever happened,

OBOTE RETURNS TO THE PRESIDENCY: On December 15, 1980, Milton Obote was sworn in as president of Uganda.

would the DP have been allowed to take office. Going back, Professor Lule had tried to play the part of an independent leader and had paid the price. His detention in Dar es Salaam after his removal showed clearly where the decision had been made. President Binaisa went the same way, although his detention was in Uganda. A line begins to emerge: Lule to Binaisa, Binaisa to Military Commission, Military Commission to Obote – by accident?

Lule had allegedly been overthrown for abrogation of powers – the Commission made him look a beginner in this art but they stayed. Binaisa, it was said, was removed for corruption, after the Commission took over even the trickle of foreign exchange dried up, but Tanzania stayed faithful to the Commission. What a powerful combination: Tanzania, Military Commission, Tanzanian forces in Uganda, leadership of the Uganda army!

Ranged against this compact were people with only the strength of the ballot box, but conservative estimates would put their numbers at not less than 75 per cent of the population. But it has to be admitted that, through weak leadership at the top, they too often played into the hands of their opponents.

If the DP had fought harder, and in detail, in opposing such positions as wrong demarcation of boundaries, registration of voters and candidates, and the unfairness of the multi-ballot boxes – to say nothing of the unfairness in the election of returning officers – and had refused to yield, it is most conceivable that pressure would have been applied to gain them these concessions, that Obote would have lost, and that Nyerere's fairness would have been acknowledged and his standing as a world leader applauded. Africa would have been a gainer.

What now? Uganda is in a terrible mess. The majority of her people have been crudely brought to a point of despair after years of suffering. Its north and north-west boundaries will be in a ferment for a generation. The army is divided. The economy has collapsed. ❐

"LET'S UNITE" – PRESIDENT OBOTE

DRUM: January 1981

Idi Amin was responsible for Obote's ousting and he was also responsible for his return. Had Amin made a good job of government perhaps Obote would have died in exile. Yet history has now repeated itself.

With the re-inauguration of Obote as president on December 15, 1980, and with his Uganda People's Congress Party winning a clear majority in parliament – despite the reported irregularities which are now a matter for the courts – Obote has made history as the first civilian president in Africa to have regained power through the ballot box after being overthrown in a military coup.

Indeed by 1971 Obote had been too scared to call for a general election not knowing whether he could win. Now his popularity has been vindicated through the polls. There is not any other politician of his stature in Uganda today.

As Obote said during his inauguration, the time for recrimination in Uganda is now over. The major task is to reconstruct the economy, revitalise essential services, reactivate industries, and regenerate Ugandans morally and psychologically.

The major task, however, is law and order. Thousands of guns are in private hands. The country must be disarmed and law and order handed back to the police force. The army must return to the barracks.

Obote pledged to follow Kenya's *harambee* policy of pulling together, he also pledged to borrow something from Tanzania's self-reliance and Zambia's humanism.

Uganda is perhaps one of the world's most gifted countries. It has abundant manpower, it has natural resources, it has enough food, if only people can work on their *shambas* and forget smuggling. It has copper and other minerals. With strong government and a return to law and order, food production can be improved, thus leading to a drop in prices, and Uganda's currency, whose value has plummeted, can be resurrected. ❐

POLITICAL DIVISIONS STILL RIFE

A CHIEF INSTRUCTOR of the National Resistance Army of Yoweri Museveni inspects recruits at the Kabale training ground.

DRUM: May 1981

Many Ugandans have still not accepted the results of the general election last December that saw former President Milton Obote's Uganda People's Congress win an overall majority of 74 of the 126 contested parliamentary seats.

The opposition Democratic Party of Paul Ssemogerere won 51 and a lone seat went to the Uganda Patriotic Movement of former defence minister and vice chairman of the now defunct Military Commission, Yoweri Museveni.

The truce following the general election lasted less than two months before the vicious circle of opposition, leading to violence and repression resumed. Eight police stations, a military training camp and the Luzira Maximum Security Prison in Kampala were attacked on February 8, 1981 with the aim of securing large quantities of arms.

In January President Obote lifted the curfew and began to withdraw the army from the streets and from the many roadblocks. This work he promised would be handed over to police trained by Canadian and British advisers under United Nations auspices. However, the February 8 attacks halted these tension-relaxing processes with the army returning with renewed

force and amid reports of renewed brutality.

Responsibility for the February 8 attacks has been claimed by three groups which have hitherto been unknown. One of them, the Uganda Freedom Movement, is said to involve ex-President Yusuf Lule. The attack on the military training camp in western Uganda

SOLDIERS OF MUSEVENI'S guerrilla army survey a bombed-out building.

is believed to have been the work of former defence minister Yoweri Museveni, the UPM leader who has been underground since the February attacks. His aides in Nairobi have since claimed that Mr Museveni has raised a 5,000-man armed guerrilla force in western Uganda under the banner of the Movement for the Struggle for Political Rights, with which he has declared war against the current regime of President Obote.

It is believed that, following the attacks, Museveni, who trained in guerrilla warfare in Mozambique, had involved Mozambican forces in the country in the abortive uprising. This has prompted Ugandan authorities to demand their withdrawal and replacement by Tanzanian forces.

A third group, the recently formed Uganda Liberation Movement, threatened to kidnap or kill United Nations aid personnel in the country if the world body's assistance did not stop. The UN, as a result, has now decided to stop the Police Training Programme and its advisors are set to leave the trouble-torn East African nation.

Compounding these internal divisions is the problem of Idi Amin's former soldiers who still roam the ex-dictator's birth place in the north-west of the country, reportedly under heavy arms. The brutality and massacres reportedly perpetrated by the Uganda army and the People's Militia in these areas and elsewhere in the country are causing mass exoduses into Sudan, Zaire and Kenya.

Many Baganda in the south, who have remained hostile to President Obote since his first term in office, are reported to have reacted drastically to his return to power following last December's controversial general election. Many are said to have cut down their coffee trees to reduce Uganda's main export crop.

The shops have remained empty in the capital following the government's decision to unilaterally slash retail prices, a move which critics say only hurt the small traders at street level but bypassed the big fish at the top who actually were responsible for the smuggling and black marketeering. The difficult situation has been further aggravated by the current drought in East Africa.

Opposition leader Paul Ssemogerere warned that unless the government took urgent measures to end the insecure situation in the country, a civil uprising could not be ruled out. President Obote himself has acknowledged the difficulties confronting his country when he told the nation that "we had never experienced the type of poverty we are now going through. We have nothing to give to our children in schools, parts of the country have been hit by droughts and famine, our hospitals are malfunctioning, the industries are not working, and our agriculture has turned into subsistence farming."

One aspect that has operated in President Obote's favour is the concerted support he has received from his immediate neighbours – Kenya, Tanzania and the Sudan – following the general election last December. The opposition leadership, which had been mainly based in Kenya, has been forced to go underground following President Daniel arap Moi's warning that Nairobi would no longer tolerate their political activities against the Uganda government. ❐

AMIN SURFACES, BUT NO SIGN OF HIS ARMY

DRUM: July 1981

Ex-President Idi Amin wants to make friends with the British again. He phoned the *Guardian* newspaper of London from Saudi Arabia to say that

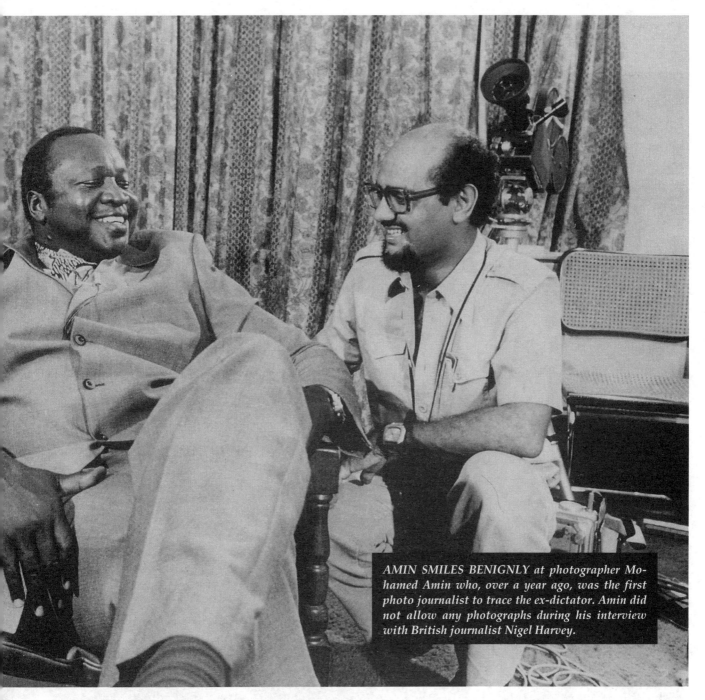

AMIN SMILES BENIGNLY at photographer Mohamed Amin who, over a year ago, was the first photo journalist to trace the ex-dictator. Amin did not allow any photographs during his interview with British journalist Nigel Harvey.

troops loyal to him were a short distance from the Ugandan capital. The ex-president described himself as "young, strong and brave".

Nigel Harvey, a British journalist, then arranged to meet Amin at a hotel in Jeddah. Amin turned up 15 minutes late. He was wearing a long white Saudi robe and was accompanied by two of his children. Amin looked slightly nervous, and immediately sought to leave saying that he had merely wanted to establish that he was alive and well and that his phone call was not a hoax.

Amin was in a rush but under prompting said that four West Nile groups opposed to the government that he claimed to be leading, only disclaimed him as their leader because he told them to do so. He then proceeded to tell the hotel receptionist what great things in agriculture and industry he had intended for Uganda.

At several points in Amin's rambling conversation he stressed that he was now pro-West: "I am now very friendly to all British and American old friends, and I want to assure you that I will make Uganda in the future very produc-

tive and a very good friend of the people."

He was anxious that no photographs should be taken as he left the hotel and it became apparent as he drove himself off in a green limousine that he was being followed by three Saudi security men. General Amin is in Saudi Arabia as a Muslim guest. He would be expected to be discreet so as not to embarrass his host.

Observers in Uganda described his claims to military success as preposterous, and said that there was no political future for him. ❐

CAN IT BE STOPPED FROM BLEEDING TO DEATH

MASSACRE IN OBOTE'S UGANDA: A woman and her two children killed for no apparent reason.

DRUM: November 1981

For the whole night of April 11, 1979, I did not sleep a wink. Idi Amin, the bloody dictator who drove me out of my country into eight-and-a-half years of exile in cold Britain, was on his way out. Invading Tanzanian troops accompanied by Ugandan exiles had him surrounded, and it was a matter of time before Kampala fell into the hands of the invading forces. The BBC kept the world abreast with the progress of the war, and I had

the radio announced that Kampala had fallen, the people were simply ecstatic. For me too, it was the time to prepare for my long journey back home, the home which I never thought I would see again as long as Amin remained in power.

When I arrived in Kampala in May, my eyes would not believe what I saw. From the Kenyan border to Kampala, it looked as if the entire population had fled and left the country to dilapidate. Bushes were skyhigh, roads full of potholes, buildings half ruined. To find a kilogram of sugar one would drive more than four miles.

The havoc which Amin had wreaked on the country was simply unbelievable, but what I shared with other exiles, and indeed the people who stayed on in Uganda, was a feeling of optimism.

But that optimism was wrecked when suddenly the first government, which had hardly settled in after 68 days, was overthrown and its leader, Professor Lule, flown to Tanzania for detention. Uganda was back in chaos. Organised murders increased, both Ugandan and Tanzanian soldiers went on a rampage killing innocent citizens at will, prices shot up and pledges promised by foreign governments were withheld.

The reaction of the people to the removal of Professor Lule was unbelievably spontaneous. It was hard to believe that the people who had been kept under the thick thumb of dictator Amin would be so politically aware. They were demanding to be heard although the demonstration and the general strike which paralysed Kampala were suppressed by all military

might. Several people were killed in the demonstrations because they were demanding to know why Professor Lule had been removed and Godfrey Binaisa was being imposed on them.

Brigadier David Oyite Ojok, the army chief of staff, a Langi, and Paul Muwanga, Obote's proxy, were to convince Binaisa that he was in danger of being overthrown if he did not remove Museveni from the Ministry of Defence. Museveni was removed and what was then left was Binaisa himself. When the Military Commission, all composed of Obote's supporters besides Museveni, who was then vice chairman, made their coup against Binaisa, Museveni had no love lost for Binaisa.

But what Museveni overlooked was that the men he had ganged up with were moving to make Obote's return to politics as smooth as possible. They dismantled the Uganda National Liberation Front (UNLF), a coalition of all fighting forces which overthrew Amin. All parties would have contested elections under the famous umbrella of UNLF. UPC and Obote did not like it because it would have made it difficult to come to power.

Now the rulers of the Military Commission who had fixed the December 1980 date for the elections had the government machinery in their hands, which made it easy for them to rig the elections.

In the ensuing period of the reign of the Military Commission, the insecurity was appalling. Dead bodies on the roadside, by the lakeside and in forests were a common sight. A commission of inquiry promised by chairman

no doubt that this time the monster was going, which would mean that the nightmare that Uganda had lived with for over eight years was soon to end. When

Muwanga, after several dead bodies were found on Entebbe Road and at Kaazi near Lake Victoria, did not materialise.

As the election campaign loomed, there was still hope that the government which was to come to power would restore peace in the country and embark on the road to economic recovery. That dream again became a nightmare. The UPC government which came to power after the elections was accused of rigging the elections. Peace is as distant as ever.

It was at the nomination of candidates that the rigging became obvious. The Democratic Party and the Uganda Patriotic Movement (UPM) candidates were disqualified on trivial, sometimes absurd reasons. In the strife-torn West Nile region, where registration of voters was interrupted by renewed fighting, all DP candidates were disqualified, which

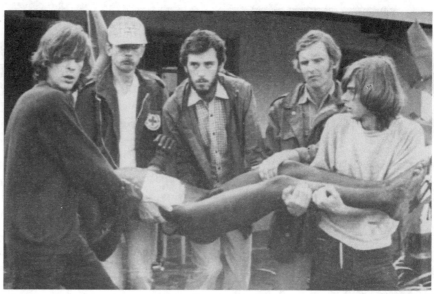

MASSACRE IN A mission hospital: Red Cross men care for one of the wounded.

allowed UPC candidates to run unopposed.

In the east of the country, the Rev Yona Okot, now under detention, and Chango Macho, both UPM candidates, were disqualified because they could not prove their English aptitude. Okot was a member of NCC prior to his candi-

dature. He had attended a seminary in Tanzania before he was ordained as a priest and worked there. Macho was a senior lecturer of Makerere University and an author of books and papers in international literary journals. Their exclusion to stand for parliament because they could not prove that they knew English was absurd.

I WAS KICKED AND PUNCHED

DRUM: November 1981

My detention for three weeks was a result of my writing about the horror, anarchy and disregard of human life – the very things which I attacked Idi Amin for all my eight-and-a-half years exile in Britain.

I was detained because one of the reports I filed to Associated Press and Africa News Service was about 14 dead bodies which I had discovered in Namanve Forest after a tip from a policeman. In the pile of bodies there included two girls which I believe were about 12 to 14 years old and still clad in their

school uniforms from Old Kampala Primary School. The bodies were bullet-ridden and had been there three days, according to my police source.

Police chief, Sam Baker, came for me at dawn in my hotel room and turned the room upside down. After taking a number of documents, including several copies of the stories I had filed, he led me to Nile Mansion. Besides being a refuge for ministers who fear to live in their homes, Nile Mansion is also a torture chamber for detainees.

Rooms 211 and 233 are where the

notorious Military Intelligence and the newly created National Security Services agents hang about. Atrocities have been committed there. I was taken to room 211, and much later people told me that I was lucky to have come out of it in one piece. Some of the detainees have come out with broken ribs and jaws and others have lost their lives.

I was not all that lucky. I had my share of the violence which the Ugandan regime has chosen to solve their problems with. I was kicked and punched. I had two rifle butt hits on my forehead. The method of interrogation there is that you are ordered to confirm that you are a guerrilla, and any denial brings punches and kicks. "You are lucky, you know," one

Then came Muwanga's bomb-shell. He decreed on the day when the results were being announced that no one, not even the Electoral Commission, should announce the results unless such results had been approved by him. Anybody who did not comply with the order would have to pay a fine equivalent to US$ 70,000.

Uganda is politically divided along tribal lines like never before. A number of politicians in the present government have used tribalism to win votes. Soldiers have been given orders to kill at a nod because a certain group of people were of a different tribe or may be of the same tribe but did not support them during the last elections.

The cheapest commodity in Uganda is still life, a thing which forced four religious leaders in the country to tell President Obote at a recent meeting that his country is bleeding to death and that the security situation is worse than it was under Amin.

In anarchy and confusion, the guerrillas opposing the government have taken advantage of the situation. Their small successes since they started their campaign to overthrow Dr Obote are due to the local population which gives them food and shelter. They are supported simply because of the hatred the local population has for the government forces.

After clashes with guerrillas in a given area, the security forces would come back and take their revenge on the local population who are accused of harbouring the guerrillas. Tens of thousands of the rural population whose relatives have been killed, their women raped and their homes looted, have fled their homes seeking refuge in distant villages.

What is quite clear from the sad story of Uganda is that Milton Obote, who once called himself the most experienced driver in the country, has lost control of his vehicle.

That old magic of calculation has waned. The Ugandan leader, it seems clear, is no longer in grip of the country. When he preaches reconciliation, what one hears the next day are massacres in West Nile and Mukono.

Even Obote's own cabinet ministers do not agree with his policy of reconciliation. David Anyoti, the minister of information, shocked journalists when he said: "I do not know about this reconciliation. I really do not mind if Kampala was down just like Ajumani" [a town in West Nile which was demolished by the government as revenge during fighting in the area]. "I am absolutely serious."   ❐

By Don Kabeba

---

soldier said calmly. "If you had been brought here at night I do not know how you would have looked the next day. You will see what I mean tonight."

A middle-aged man sat huddled in one corner of the room and had blood all over his face and complained of a broken jaw. A little girl whispered to me that she had been beaten and raped by several soldiers. Both of them had been picked up just before dark while walking home. No charges had been made against them.

I sat there without knowing what was going to happen to me. Was I going to end up in the notorious Makindye Prison, or be taken to Nakasero, the headquarters of the NSS, just a stone's throw from the former headquarters of the dreaded State Research Bureau – which would mean death.

I considered myself lucky when, to my surprise, special branch men picked me up for questioning but with orders to bring me back later to Nile Mansion – probably, I thought, for torture. The special branch officer suggested he would see me again the next day and that I would be taken back to Nile Mansion to spend a night there. I told him that he would not be able to see me the next day if he took me back to Nile Mansion because I would be dead by then. After consulting his boss, he decided to put me in a police cell instead.

Barefooted, I was pushed into a cell seven metres square which ac-commodated 16 people. In three cells which were supposed to accommodate 60 people, I counted 170 people one night. Some were sleeping in the toilet which did not flush. I was allowed to get food from home although political prisoners are not allowed any provisions from outside. The food offered to us was half-cooked maize meal and boiled cabbage without salt.

For several weeks I was forgotten, until international pressure started to build up. I was finally released, I think because Amnesty International had said it was going to take up my case unless I was released immediately and also because the regime was trying to mend its despotic image abroad.   ❐

By Don Kabeba

BINAISA PLOT FAILS

DRUM: November 1982

Former Uganda President Godfrey Binaisa, undaunted by the exposure of his attempted invasion of Uganda using the despised soldiers of fortune, has promised that he will again try to topple the beleaguered government of President Obote.

Binaisa, whose mercenary invasion plan fell flat on its face when he failed to raise two million pounds for its execution, said he was not ashamed to use White mercenaries to overthrow an African government. He told an interviewer: "I am not the only one who is trying to overthrow the UPC mafia in Kampala. I have no qualms using black, white, yellow or brown mercenaries. Obote's days are finished. We have our boys inside Uganda but have to supply them with weapons. We shall try again next year." Binaisa said that Obote himself was using mercenaries to keep him in power.

Binaisa, who was overthrown by the military under Paul Muwanga which supported President Obote, has vowed to topple Obote's government in return. He was jointly appointed head of the Uganda Popular Front (UPF) with another former president, Yusuf Lule, whom he replaced when Lule was also overthrown.

The UPF is an umbrella organisation which brings together all the fighting forces bent on getting rid of Obote. These forces include the National Resistance Movement (NRM) led by Lule, the Uganda Freedom Movement (UFM) whose leader Balaki Kirya is under detention in Uganda, the Uganda National Rescue Front (UNRF) led by Moses Ali, Amin's former minister of finance, and the Nile Regiment

(NR) led by Felix Onama, one time Obote's minister of defence and former secretary general of the ruling Uganda People's Congress.

Binaisa's mercenary plan was first hatched at his west London flat with the mercenary recruiter Raymond Ingram, a burly ex-British army sergeant. Ingram recruits mercenaries openly under his International Security Agency. Talks between the two started early this year and D-day was set for the end of August.

A group of Ingram's crack men would have launched a two-pronged attack on Uganda from neighbouring Zaire, using helicopter gunships and C-130 troop-carrying aircraft. The invaders were expected to be supported by troops on the ground in Zaire, possibly the ex-soldiers of Amin who Binaisa says are still loyal to him. Several thousand of them are based in eastern Zaire and launch attacks on Obote's forces from there. Binaisa would also have had support from his own men inside the country.

According to a tape which was secretly recorded by Ingram during the meeting and which was given to a British weekly newspaper, Binaisa is heard to say that he had contact with ex-Amin soldiers and named several high-ranking officers, who he said would support the invasion and would be called to London for the final preparations.

But the invasion fell flat because the financiers who Binaisa thought would provide two million pounds would not part even with a penny. Binaisa says that the financiers who let him down are from the "southern states of America". ❐

MUSEVENI – THE MAN BEHIND THE LINGERING REBELLION

DRUM: April 1983

The scholar-turned-guerrilla, Yoweri K Museveni, who has been declared "wanted dead or alive" by the government of Uganda, is a mysterious man. He is said to be moving with impunity in Uganda without being apprehended by the forces loyal to the Obote government.

A former staunch ally of Obote, Museveni went into hiding after the December 12, 1980, general election which returned Obote to power. He vowed to topple the government claiming that the elections were rigged. Three years later Obote is still firmly in power and Museveni is still on the run.

His movement, known as the National Resistance Movement (NRM), is based in Uganda, mainly around the country's capital, Kampala. It has claimed a force of 8,000 men but this claim – like Museveni himself – is shrouded in mystery.

Museveni is 38, married with four children, and does not drink or smoke. He studied at the prestigious Ntare school and graduated in political science from the University of Dar es Salaam in Tanzania. While at university he was a dynamic student leader. When he returned to Uganda he worked as an administrator in the president's office. The president was then

THE SCHOLAR-TURNED-GUERRILLA, Yoweri Museveni, who has been declared "wanted dead or alive" by the government.

Obote. During that time he championed Obote's message of the Common Man's Charter.

Following the military takeover by Amin, Museveni went into exile in Tanzania. Later he studied guerrilla warfare in Mozambique learning the techniques from FRELIMO. During his exile in Tanzania, Museveni was among the top men who planned Amin's downfall. He took part in the 1972 attack on Uganda by guerrillas based in Tanzania which totally failed. In that attempt, which lacked the people's support, many guerrillas were killed. Back in Dar es Salaam, Museveni criticised the structure of the exile movement, and launched his own, the Front for National Salvation (FRONASA).

According to someone who shared military experiences with Museveni, he has a broad mind about wars, and has made real research into protracted armed struggles. Museveni advocated armed struggle during the 1980 elections. The elections came and Obote won.

Museveni set himself to struggle. I met Museveni shortly after the election. He was with only one bodyguard. I asked him whether he was planning to go into exile to team up with anti-Obote forces, and he said: "I am going to start something here." The following week he was declared "wanted dead or alive".

Whether Yoweri Museveni is a misguided patriot or a traitor only time will tell. One thing, however, is clear – he is a man nobody in Uganda can ignore. ❐

ESCAPE FROM THE JAWS OF DEATH

DRUM: September 1984

In June 1981 Daniel Ogutu left Nairobi for Rwanda as a turn-boy on a petrol tanker. He never reached Rwanda and it was nearly two years before he could return home – years in which he was arrested, tortured, forced to eat human flesh and nearly killed. Here he tells DRUM his terrible story:

We left Nairobi in June 1981 to start our long journey to Rwanda. There were two of us – the driver, Muhammed, and myself. We entered Uganda without trouble and successfully passed two road blocks manned by Tanzanian and Ugandan soldiers.

In the forest, only three kilometres from Kampala, we met Ugandan soldiers occupying both sides of the road with three Land Rovers hidden in the nearby bushes. They ordered us to stop and come out of our tanker, which we did. They started inspecting our tanker. They found nothing wrong. Then they ordered us to remove whatever we had in our pockets and put it down. They then collected all the items we had, including clothes and blankets, and put them in their Land Rovers, together with our documents. The driver was ordered to give the tanker keys to one of the soldiers and we were then ordered to lie on our stomachs in one of the Land Rovers.

The soldiers were very hostile. One of the soldiers told my driver, Muhammed, to explain where Amin was since he was a Muslim and Amin was a Muslim. This soldier insisted that Muhammed was one of Amin's soldiers and must know where he was.

Muhammed was a Kenyan and knew nothing about Amin. He was only a driver doing his duty and knew nothing about Uganda and Amin. But the soldiers started stabbing bayonets at us telling us that we must tell them where Professor Lule was in Kenya. They said they knew that some Ugandans were being trained in Kenya, near Nyahururu, to overthrow the Obote regime which was about to have elections.

We were taken inside the Makindye Military Barracks and there the Ugandan soldiers started beating us saying that we were their enemies from Kenya who were helping Professor Lule. The soldiers who brought us to the barracks did not report our claim that we were just Kenyan drivers taking petrol to Rwanda. Instead they told their comrades we were enemies taking oil to Professor Lule's men in the forest.

When they heard this the soldiers in the barracks started whipping us so mercilessly that we cried out. I cried loudly, pleading with them in Luo. One of the soldiers, Lieutenant Colonel Basileo Okelo, could understand my language. He pleaded with the soldiers and told them that I was one of his brothers, a Kenyan Luo, and that we should be spared. They stopped torturing us although my friend was already unconscious through loss of blood.

Lieutenant Colonel Okelo ordered the soldiers to put us with the others in the cells and said he would see us the following day. But inside the cells the criminals with whom we were placed started beating us. They were Ugandan soldiers who were put in for various crimes such as murder and robbery. Inside were six corpses of Amin soldiers who had been killed inside the cells and left there by Ugandan soldiers.

The other prisoners insisted that we were the ones keeping Lule and his group in Kenya.

They ordered us to eat the corpses which were now decaying. We pleaded with them and with the soldiers guarding us but they wouldn't listen. I was the first person to be forced to eat human flesh. I knelt down and took a bite of the nearest body. I chewed the flesh and forced it down. My friend did the same. We were then ordered to lick the blood of another corpse, which we obediently did.

The soldiers said: "This is Uganda and not Kenya. You must understand that this is not the Uganda of Amin when you Kenyans used to act the way you wanted. This is Uganda of the Military Commission and you have to obey orders properly."

The following morning a Lieutenant Mkwana and a Second Lieutenant Mbeshira ordered their soldiers to give me and my friend ten strokes to force us to tell where Lule and his group were hiding in Kenya. We were ordered to strip naked and painfully received the ten strokes. We prayed loudly to God, saying that we were Kenyans who did not know anything about Lule or Amin.

We stayed for two days and nights without food. In the next cell were other prisoners from Uganda whose cells were never opened. We learned later that the Ugandans had been arrested near the Kenya-Uganda border, allegedly trying to join the Lule group. When their cells were eventually opened they were on the point of death. About 30 of them were terribly beaten and later thrown in the lake.

A BATTLE-HARDENED CHILD carries the skull of a victim of Obote's regime.

UGANDAN BEAUTY PAGEANT: Victims of Ugandan-style greed and lawlessness.

The soldiers opened our cell and told us that my friend and I had to die and be thrown into the lake like others. After many hours in the cell we were moved to the *godown* where people were being killed. We found many people and joined them, awaiting our turn to be killed.

It was terrible to see people getting killed like animals. There were three soldiers waiting for each victim. One soldier held a hammer and hit the victim's head. The next soldier held a long, thick, sharp iron bar to stab the victim. The third soldier held a sharp knife to finish the victim if he was still

alive. The soldiers used to stab the victim even after he was dead.

By the time our turn came, the executioners were so tired that they had to rest. The dead included old and young – even school boys and girls were executed.

The soldiers told us that we were lucky for a time but they would come to finish us after lunch, at 2 p.m. Only six of us escaped execution that morning: one Ugandan woman, three Ugandan men and two Kenyans. We were locked in the *godown*, left on top of the corpses.

But at 2 p.m. the soldiers failed to turn up. Three long hours passed before they came back and then, miraculously, they said they did not have time to kill us as they had to throw the corpses in Lake Victoria. They told us to kneel down and pray to our God. After praying for a few minutes the soldiers ordered us to stand up and said it was our duty to put the corpses in their lorries. We were whipped to work faster. By the time we finished packing the corpses, it was about 10 p.m.

We were ordered to get in the two big lorries which we had already filled with the dead. When we reached the lake we were ordered to throw the corpses from the two lorries and we fully expected to be thrown in afterwards. But the soldiers said we were lucky that God had helped us. They told us to get back in the lorries and we were taken back to Makindye Military Barracks but to a different section.

But inside the barracks my friend Muhammed was ordered to remain in the lorry as they claimed he was Amin's brother in religion. The woman who was with us was

TWO ORPHANS POSE almost oblivious to the spectre of death before them.

UGANDA'S LEGACY OF RELIGIOUS STRIFE

DRUM: September 1984

The army of the deposed Idi Amin was almost 100 per cent Muslim and the new UNLA is three quarters Christian. The Amin army was accused of excesses against Uganda's Christian population and the same accusations are now being levelled against the UNLA but in reverse: it is committing excesses against the Muslims in the country.

Today Uganda is led by Christian rulers and the army likewise is dominated by Christian officers and men. Yet there are allegations that the army now is more brutal than Amin's army. Several irreligious acts have been committed by the UNLA.

In February 1982, after the rebel group UFM carried out a raid on the Lubiri Barracks in the centre of Kampala, the UNLA men retaliated by invading the Rubaga Cathedral on Sunday morning when the church had opened for morning mass. They overturned the Holy table, drank all the altar wine, looted the Holy communion cups, killed and raped nuns inside the cathedral, and took away 30 people including priests who were never seen again.

In August 1983 the UNLA massacred 30 people in a village near Kampala, and four clergymen who dared come out in their robes to try to talk to the men were greeted with bullets. Later an officer told parliament that he and his men killed the people by mistake. No disciplinary action was taken.

In Arua, West Nile, at the Ombace Catholic church headquarters, 62 people were killed by men under the command of Lieutenant Aguma. Details were published world-wide by the Red Cross. On that same day a total of 12 clergymen were killed in various churches in West Nile. There seems to be a feeling that the people of West Nile are regarded as ripe for slaughter due to the mistakes of Idi Amin.

As recently as May 1984 UNLA men killed 90 people in Namugongo Catholic Seminary and the Church of Uganda's Bishop Tucker College at Mukono. Some 16 clergymen plus the principal of the college were among the dead. It is unfortunately significant that no Acholi or Langi clergy have been killed since the formation of the UNLA. The UNLA men say a genuine priest is only an Acholi or Langi.   ❐

By Rev Isaac Bakka

---

also left behind. To this day I do not know what happened to my fellow driver, Muhammed, or the woman.

Now the four of us were put in a very big building where corpses lay on top of one another. These, we came to learn, were hunger victims. The smell in that building was horrible with all types of human waste.

At around 12 noon the following day the late Brigadier Oyite Ojok of the Uganda army came with military and police officers to enquire about missing people, especially Kenyans whose trailers had been confiscated by Ugandan military men.

When the Ugandan soldiers realised that the matter of the missing people had reached the headquarters of the Red Cross in Geneva and the Kenya government was demanding action, they started to treat us slightly better. Food was given to us once a day. We were told that if Obote lost during the elections which were about to start, we would be killed, and if he won, then we would live. We stayed there for months.

I was starting to have hope but after a few days things started to deteriorate as so many prisoners were brought in. Most of these were political prisoners and there was a conflict between the Ugandan and Tanzanian soldiers, to the extent that the Tanzanians were deciding to move to Entebbe ready to go home. When we were left behind with the Ugandan soldiers things became even worse as we were now being denied food. People started to die due to hunger and sickness. I fell sick and almost died.

The prison commissioner ordered that I should be given proper treatment because they did not want me to die in Uganda since matters had gone so far as to reach the Red Cross. I stayed in hospital for four months and then I was taken back to Luzira Military Barracks.

A Kenyan senior army officer was told of my arrival and was allowed to greet me. After one week, President Milton Obote ordered all prisoners kept in military barracks without charge to be set free. On January 22, 1983, we were all released.   ❐

By Daniel Ogutu

POWER STRUGGLE – BAZILIO VERSUS OJOK

AN ALMOST LONE figure fighting for civil liberties, Brigadier Bazilio Okello.

DRUM: November 1985

Brigadier Bazilio Okello has long been waging an unseen war against the cruelties and corruption of David Oyite Ojok and the military establishment at the notorious Makindye Barracks. On many occasions Okello has set free prisoners brought to Makindye to be murdered. His actions often brought him into conflict with the powerful Ojok, and even put his life and reputation in danger.

Immediately after Uganda's liberation war of 1979, Okello was appointed commanding officer of 15 Battalion, with his headquarters at Makindye. His rank was lieutenant colonel but although he was the battalion's commanding officer he had no powers to stop the killing going on every day. The barracks were being used by David Ojok and his close friends as their butcher houses to slaughter human beings for political reasons, for personal reasons, and for the accumulation of wealth.

Frequently Bazilio Olara Okello would have terrible arguments with Ojok and his friends. He didn't like the way these people were behaving but they had bought his soldiers by giving them power to arrest anybody and kill without complaint. Makindye Barracks was allocated more army trucks than any other unit, and it came to be known as the Red Army Unit.

Two Tanzanian intelligence officers, Seapara and Charles, were attached to the unit. Both were on Ojok's payroll. These two officers, and two UNLA officers, Stephen Mbazira and Edward Mukwana, were Ojok's executioners at Makindye.

These four officers did not even realise that Bazilio Olara Okello was the boss of the unit, because they had direct contact with Ojok as chairman of the Military Commission, and latterly, the minister of defence. Whenever Ojok came to the unit he would first see these junior officers, instead of Okello, the senior officer in the UNLA.

On many occasions Okello would set free prisoners who had been brought in to be killed. Whenever Ojok learned of this through his agents, he would accuse Bazilio Okello of being a Democratic Party supporter, describing him as the last Acholi. During senior army officers' meetings Ojok would say openly that Okello was not with them, that he was a Democratic

BRIGADIER DAVID OYITE OJOK and Major General Tito Okello.

OJOK'S STRANGE DEATH

Party supporter. Ojok would even say this openly when addressing militia and soldiers.

He was especially rude when the UPC won the 1980 general election. On this occasion the soldiers of 15 Battalion looted and killed many civilians in and around Kampala. The following day Okello told the looted civilians to come and identify their property at Makindye. Although his intelligence officer, Lieutenant Mukwana and his adjutant captain were Ojok's agents, Okello forced them to go into the residence of every soldier and search for looted property.

Every barracks in Kampala was searched. The soldiers were very annoyed with their commanding officer, and they told him openly that he was anti-government. Ojok summoned Bazilio Olara Okello to his office in Nile Mansions, abused him as a cowardly Acholi, and ordered him to be detained for three days at Nile Mansions. Meanwhile the slaughter of prisoners continued at Makindye. General Tito Okello intervened and Bazilio was released, and sent back to his battalion, with a heavy warning from Ojok. But this cool, critical Acholi officer from Kitgum District did not scare easily.

Having seen that Bazilio Okello was becoming a hindrance to their plans, the junior officers at Makindye advised Ojok to transfer him to another battalion. He was sent to Bombo, as brigade commander, Southern Axis, where guerrillas of the NRA were fighting with the government troops.

On arriving at Bombo in the middle of 1981, Bazilio Okello found that the situation there was even worse. Soldiers could loot, arrest, rob and kill under the pretext that

OBOTE WAS WIDELY SEEN as being behind Oyite Ojok's (above) death.

their victims were guerrillas. Brigadier Okello started releasing many civilians from Bombo – the ones he was convinced were not guerrillas at all.

Before he left Makindye, Bazilio Okello had convinced Tito Okello that the soldiers there were undisciplined and that they should be transferred far away from Kampala. Tito Okello waited until Ojok was on a trip abroad, then he sent military police to Makindye very early in the morning before the soldiers left the barracks for town, and arrested all of them, transferring them to Bombo and Arua, where there was fighting going on.

The situation in Kampala returned to normal for some time, but later Captain Ageta did terrible things as Ojok's chief executioner. ❒

By Timothy Okello

DRUM: April 1985

David Oyite Ojok, or as he was commonly known, the Lion of Uganda, fled to Tanzania in 1971 after the coup of Field Marshal Idi Amin. He was then a lieutenant colonel. From exile he waged a constant guerrilla war against Amin and his mercenaries until the liberation of Uganda in 1979 by a combined force of Tanzanian troops and Oyite's exile forces.

During his campaign against Amin, Oyite Ojok was a legendary figure not only in Uganda but throughout Africa. He was reputed to have sneaked into nightspots in Kampala, and after eating and drinking, would ask that the bills be sent to Amin. At one time Amin became so infuriated with his soldiers over the presence in Uganda of Ojok that he offered $70,000 to anyone who could bring Ojok to him "dead or alive".

Ojok played a commanding role when the joint Tanzanian-UNLA task force attacked Idi Amin's forces and put Amin and the senior members of his regime to flight. A renowned tactician and senior commander, he learned guerrilla warfare and military theories in Britain which he put to good use during his eight year campaign against Amin.

After the 1979 liberation war many people were so busy accumulating wealth after years in exile, that nobody cared about anything else. They were busy dividing the spoils left behind by Amin's soldiers who had run off. The victorious officers enjoyed the fruits of Uganda – money, cars and women in plenty. And David Oyite Ojok accumulated as much as any.

He took over a large company and became responsible for exporting Ugandan coffee as the new chairman of the Coffee Marketing Board. In the chaos after liberation the first thing Ojok did was to form his own killing squad under the command of Captain Patrick Ageta. The captain used to drive around Kampala with two jeeps mounted with machine guns and about 30 soldiers. He was Ojok's most trusted man, and was used to kill most of his opponents.

Ojok carried on building his position. He had already won supporters within the army by allowing soldiers to accumulate wealth, and leaving them to rob and loot. By 1983 Ojok had recruited various military units, like the People's Militia of Langi, Acholi and Teso

and other tribes who were loyal to him. He had also formed the National Youth Army (NYA).

The People's Militia had greater power during Ojok's time than the Uganda National Liberation Army itself. They were very fierce soldiers and fought in West Nile when Amin's men invaded Arua and Koboko. In 1982, they fought against the Ugandan Freedom Movement at Mpigi and scattered them. They were assisted by Korean troops who are presently in Uganda. They have also fought Museveni's troops in Luwero District. They were loyal to Ojok and nobody else.

By November 1983, Ojok's henchman, Captain Patrick Ageta, was becoming a public nuisance to the government. The captain was feared by all his fellow officers. Nobody could be sent to arrest him because he was always moving with his jeeps full of soldiers, called the Wreck Platoon. So Lieutenant General Tito Okello, the commander of the UNLA, summoned all his officers, including Ageta, to attend a meeting in the Nile Mansions and secretly ordered all the other officers to enter the meeting armed. In the conference room, when every officer was seated, Lieutenant General Okello ordered the arrest of Captain Ageta.

Ojok could do nothing while Ageta was put under arrest and driven under heavy escort to Luzira Military Police Prison. Afterwards Ojok planned to send some boys to rescue him, but information leaked through to Okello via his loyal officers who hated Ageta. In prison, word was sent to Ageta not to worry since a coup was planned and all the Acholi, Langi, Teso and Badama soldiers and officers in jail would be released.

But on December 1, 1983, news arrived that Ojok had died in a plane crash at Kasoozi military camp. He died with 13 other officers, including the directors of the air force, military intelligence, political education, and personnel and administration.

Sources close to President Obote talk of tension between him and Ojok. One day Ojok reportedly told Obote that he was the one who had put him in power, so he was the boss. Ojok was selling Uganda's coffee and most of the money was banked in his own account in America. Obote planned to replace him as chairman of the Coffee Marketing Board. Ojok responded by sending Ageta to the home of the man Obote wanted to appoint as the new chairman of the coffee board. He was eliminated along with his family.

The day Ojok died, President Obote was in India. It was one-and-a-half days after Ojok's death before it was announced. At first no Ugandan could believe that the super power of Uganda was dead – the hero, the man who had defeated Amin.

The day it was announced, Uganda was quiet everywhere. Many Ugandans expected trouble from the army. Ojok's loyal troops, the People's Militia and the NYA killed a lot of people as revenge because they were convinced that he had been killed by the guerrillas.

The guerrillas claimed responsibility, but after one week some soldiers were told by their officers that it was an inside operation. Sources suggested that a Ugandan air force officer planted a bomb in the aircraft that killed Ojok.   ❐

By Timothy Okello

OBOTE TOPPLED BY ACHOLI OFFICERS

A BELEAGUERED PRESIDENT OBOTE, *guarded by heavily armed soldiers, puts on a brave face for the media.*

DRUM: September 1985

A new leader has stepped up to tackle the job of ruling the battered and torn nation, Uganda. And the ordinary people of Uganda once again look into a future clouded by doubt. Once again they wait to see if their hopes will be fulfilled, if promises made will be kept, if tribalism will be curbed and most eagerly awaited, if peace can be returned

277

THE NEW HEAD OF STATE: General Tito Lutwa Okello, a veteran soldier who has new battles to fight against socio-economic chaos, and Museveni's army.

to this beautiful land of potential prosperity.

The rule of Dr Milton Obote is over. In the last few days before he was ousted, the pressures on his regime mounted. The NRA forces claimed more victories and took control over a greater part of the country's territory, creeping ever nearer Kampala. Rumours grew of splits and tribal battles in the ranks of the army and even Dr Obote had to publicly acknowledge the difficulties. The NRA took advantage of the chaos in the army and took control of the western town of Fort Portal.

The end came in the all too familiar manner on June 27, 1985. The broadcasts of Radio Uganda were interrupted by an army spokes-

man announcing the coup. The first name to be given as one of the men behind the action was Brigadier Bazilio Okello, an Acholi, and leader of the crack Tenth Brigade. But later in the day it became clear that the most senior figure in the army take-over was General Tito Okello, chief of the defence forces.

The coup was described as bloodless although later Brigadier Bazilio Okello said that commandos loyal to Dr Obote had killed some civilians in the Presidential Palace in Kampala. But the lack of resistance to the troops left them free to indulge in the orgy of looting that Kampala has seen on many occasions in the past. Shops were wrecked and drunken soldiers wandered the streets firing into the air. What remained of the Obote

supporters appears to have fled in the direction of their power base.

Generally calm was restored quickly and one missionary commented: "Compared with 1979, casualties have been very light and the soldiers have been behaving very well." But the physical calm is belied by the political tension as the new administration tries to create a platform for stable government. The underlying problems remain unresolved. The besetting curse of tribalism had contributed greatly to the army splits which caused the collapse. The Acholi soldiers, like Bazilio and Tito Okello, are believed to have resented the rapid promotion of Obote's own Langi tribesmen.

Like all incoming leaders, General Okello has called for an end to tribalism and now his government has to deliver. One of the first acts of the new army council which promised elections within a year, was to bring in as prime minister Mr Paul Muwanga, who is expected to try to woo his fellow Baganda and, as a veteran political operator, to try to reach some form of conciliation with other civilian politicians. But Mr Muwanga is also identified with the success of Dr Obote in the 1980 elections which have been widely criticised as rigged.

Early efforts appeared to fail to win over Dr Paul Ssemogerere, leader of the Democratic Party which claims it was cheated of victory in 1980. In the first hours of the coup it was reported that troops in Kampala were chanting DP slogans. But eventually Dr Ssemogerere accepted a portfolio as interior minister although his party still seems unhappy about the role of Mr Muwanga.

HOW THE STORM CLOUDS GATHERED

The biggest question mark hangs over the role of the NRA. With his forces intact and apparently still in charge of west and central areas including Fort Portal, Yoweri Museveni still has enormous leverage. His initial demands were for the replacement of half the Military Council with his own men, a demand which was resisted. Only time will tell if an offer can be made which will persuade Museveni and his lieutenants to take a full part in the new government.

Mr Ssemogerere, who often denounced the abuses of liberty under Obote, has immediately set out trying to undo some of the damage. He announced that one of the new government's priorities was the release of political detainees, who numbered 1,000 at Luzira Prison alone. Members of the secret police force under Obote – who spread a reign of terror and suspicion, were in their turn thrown into maximum security prisons.

Mr Ssemogerere is from Buganda and further evidence that the Acholi military men were trying to spread the power came with the appointment of Colonel Wilson Toko, from West Nile.

Perhaps the biggest difficulty is that Uganda is still under the shadow of the gun. The country has become used to violence and killings. The senior army officers who now run the whole country have to close the ranks of their own notoriously undisciplined army. If a political settlement is reached with the guerrilla leaders their forces have either to be assimilated into the already splintered army, or be disarmed and provided with rewards which will satisfy them. ❐

DRUM: December 1985

When David Ojok died in a mysterious plane crash in late 1983, Bazilio Olara Okello was still brigade commander, Northern Axis. After Ojok's death, many Ugandans believed that Obote would appoint someone from another tribe to become his new chief of staff. But what made them suspicious was Obote's decision to bring in an acting chief of staff from the Tanzania army. Subsequently he appointed a fellow Langi to be chief of staff of the Uganda National Liberation Army.

Smith Opon Acak, according to the history of the Uganda army, was too junior to be appointed chief of staff. The reason Obote appointed Brigadier Acak was that he wanted the position to be taken by a Langi, not by an Acholi, and by a man whom he could trust. Obote believed Brigadier Bazilio Okello to be a Democratic Party supporter.

Obote risked his regime by electing Smith Opon Acak. This proved to the Acholis and to the other senior officers from other tribes in the army to be too tribalistic for them to stomach.

So from August 1984, when Smith Acak was appointed, Bazilio Okello and other officers started planning how to overthrow Obote.

The Acholi officers started inciting their soldiers in the army. First, they saw the weakness of the Uganda army. Many Acholi officers saw that the guerrillas of Yoweri Museveni were likely to take over the government. They also knew Obote was ever alert and likely to run away when he saw that the situation was dangerous and leave them behind to suffer the consequences.

On many occasions Tito Okello and Bazilio Okello had advised Obote to compromise with the guerrillas since they were stronger than the army and might easily overthrow the government in the future. Obote had always answered that he could not strike a compromise with bandits.

In July, Museveni's troops had already taken over Fort Portal and most parts of the Western Province of Uganda. Many Acholi officers were now growing uneasy about the military situation. They tried to get in touch with Museveni, but he was in Sweden.

The superiority of the NRA guerrillas prompted the army to topple Obote just to save their own skins. They sought a compromise with the guerrillas because they knew that their UNLA troops and the NSA had committed numerous atrocities. If the guerrillas were to take over, they would be in very big trouble as the Uganda army had then more licence than under Amin. So toppling Obote was the only possible decision.

On July 25, when Bazilio Olara Okello and his troops were leaving Gulu and Kitgum for Kampala, the NRA guerrillas were only 48 kilometres from Kampala. It took Bazilio Okello three days to arrive in Kampala.

On July 26, a very senior officer in the army tipped off Obote about the approach of troops from the Northern Province, Obote's home region. This gave Obote, and Chief of Staff Brigadier Smith Acak time to loot the Bank of Uganda of its foreign currency before they made their exit to Kenya. By the time the troops of Bazilio Olara Okello were entering Kampala, Obote was on his way into exile. ❐

DRUM

AFRICA'S LEADING MAGAZINE

REGISTERED AT THE GPO AS A NEWSPAPER

E.A. EDITION.
OCTOBER 1987.

9/-

KARANJA: THE LOST CORPSE

Museveni best for Uganda—Obote

KIKUYU GIRLS DEFENDED

Uganda Asians' hopes dashed

GOLD FOR KIPKOECH

MUSEVENI
MAN OF THE PEOPLE

The leaders of the July 27, 1985 coup had acted to prevent further bloodshed, rather than with any grand ambition to hold power. The new regime had no political programme and was not prepared for government. This lack of a vision for the future meant that the Okello administration got off to a poor start – a handicap it never managed to shrug off. After taking power the primary concern of head of state General Tito Okello and chief of the defence forces Lieutenant General Bazilio Okello was to form a government of national unity. By the end of August it had succeeded in gaining the co-operation of all the political parties and fighting forces in the country, with the exception of Museveni's NRA. A two-tier governmental system was formed with a civilian cabinet overseen by the Military Council. However, the new regime was inept and ineffectual. The government was sharply divided ideologically and personally and there was no single strong leader capable of welding the various strands together. The Military Council focused most of its energy on making peace with the NRA, to the exclusion of virtually everything else.

When the Okellos took control of Kampala, Museveni took effective command of western Uganda: Hoima, Masindi, Fort Portal, Mbarara, Kabale and eventually Masaka fell to the NRA. Before the coup, the NRA had been effectively restricted to the Luwero triangle by Obote's army. Making full use of the new-found room to manoeuvre, Museveni quickly established a civilian administration in the areas he controlled. Throughout their five-year-long guerrilla struggle, the NRA fighters had maintained a good relationship with the ordinary people, and as a result, their new administration enjoyed a high degree of popular support.

In December 1985, it seemed as though Tito Okello's preoccupation with making peace with Museveni had payed off. After four months of tortuous negotiations in Nairobi, a peace agreement between the Military Council and the NRA was signed. The Military Council made sweeping concessions to Museveni, who was to become vice chairman of the Supreme Military Council, second only to Tito Okello who would be chairman. However, the Nairobi agreement never got off the ground. Okello's inability to curb the atrocities committed by his troops allowed Museveni to accuse him of violating the agreement. As the charges and counter-charges mounted, Museveni's forces closed in on Kampala. On January 25, 1986, the NRA moved into Kampala and overthrew the Military Council.

In contrast to the Military Council, the NRA exhibited extraordinary political astuteness. While in the bush Museveni produced a very sophisticated political manifesto. It was a realistic and practical guide to achieving national reconciliation, security and economic development. His miraculous successes to date were born of this commitment.

SIGN! OR GO BACK AND FIGHT

PEACE AT LAST: Yoweri Museveni and Tito Okello shake on their agreement as mediator, Kenya's President Moi, looks on.

DRUM: February 1986

There could be no happier news for the people of Uganda and, indeed, the whole of East Africa, than the announcement that the long-awaited Ugandan peace pact had at last been signed. The Ugandan peace talks which had dragged on in Nairobi for four long months had finally yielded the desired result.

For the people of Uganda, who for most of the past 15 years had known virtually nothing but vio-lence, death and terror, the outcome of the talks was greeted with a sigh of relief.

The road towards signing the peace agreement had been a long and difficult one for the parties involved: the Ugandan Military Council led by the head of state, General Tito Okello, and the National Resistance Movement (NRM) led by Mr Yoweri Museveni. Because of the armed clashes and the war of words between the two parties during the peace talks, many people had

given up hope that the Okello and Museveni forces would ever reach an agreement.

The prospects looked bleak from the time Okello toppled former President Milton Obote in July last year. The NRM declared that the new regime was no more than a changing of the guard of the Obote regime which they had been fighting in the bush war for over four years – and they vowed to fight on.

Okello set up a military council and began forming a cabinet,

cord could be reached. The hostilities and distrust were still running very deep, such that both Okello's Military Council and the NRM, while making efforts towards a negotiated peace, also prepared for war.

While the talks in Nairobi under President Moi's chairmanship were underway the world was, for over four months, treated to a situation where the peace talks continued against a backdrop of heavy fighting in Uganda, accompanied by typical war rhetoric from both sides.

The most important thing now is that both Okello and Museveni have bound themselves to the peace agreement in the belief that it will be their common formula for the restoration of peace in Uganda.

The two main protagonists called it a victory for the people of Uganda. And the man who brought about the victory was Kenya's President Daniel arap Moi. Moi's fear was that if there were further delays, the escalation of fighting in Uganda could reach a point where a peace accord would be impossible to negotiate. But each time one side agreed to a suggestion, the other side would come out with a new argument as to why it was impossible.

These procrastinations began to irritate the Kenyan president, who became publicly critical of their commitment to a quick return to peace. Early in December 1985, Moi gave the Ugandans an ultimatum: sign the agreement or go back home and fight! Moi's terse pronouncement sounded like intimidation to some, but it was also understandable. The peace talks had taxed the president's emotional and physical resources, and it ap-

peared as if Okello and Museveni were not serious about the peace process.

By the time of the agreement the peace talks had been going on for 51 days. For every one of those days, Moi chaired the talks personally, while the leaders of the two delegations varied. Often, Moi would be at his office in Harambee House, the venue of the talks, as early as 8 a.m. and would remain there until late into the night. There were days when only one delegation was in town and Moi would spend the whole day waiting in vain for the other side to appear so that the talks could continue.

Some Kenyans resented the impression that Ugandans sometimes gave that they were not as committed to the quest for peace as Kenyans believed they should be. There was a day when Museveni addressed a press conference in Nairobi and was asked his delegation's reaction to President Moi's ultimatum. "We have 93,000 square miles in Uganda. We can go and talk there," he retorted. Many Kenyans saw such conduct as an affront to Moi. But if the president thought so, he did not let on. Instead he dedicated himself even more to the task of reaching a negotiated solution.

The final day of the talks was probably the longest and toughest for all involved. On that day, Moi arrived at his office early in the morning and remained there until after 9 p.m. – without even a lunch break. At 9:10 a beaming President Moi emerged, accompanied by the leaders of the two delegations, and announced that agreement had been reached and the accord would be signed the following morning. ❐

By BG Bundeh

much to the chagrin of the NRM, which wanted to be consulted and involved in the formation of the new government. Then there were the numerous guerrilla groups which also wanted to be heard and when a fragile cease-fire broke, hardly two weeks after Obote's overthrow, it appeared that Uganda was no nearer to peace than it had been before the coup.

Still, both sides made clear indications that they were prepared to sit and talk. But it was also clear that neither side was certain that an ac-

THE BOY WHO CAPTURED KAMPALA

CHRISTOPHER LUBEGA: "I'd like to train to become a professional soldier."

DRUM: August 1986

He posed as a beautiful girl so as to penetrate enemy territory. Sounds like the stuff of war novels, but this is the true story of one of Museveni's child soldiers. Here is Christopher Lubega's own account, as told by DRUM's Dick Namadoa:

One day in mid-February 1981 at around 3:30 a.m. UNLA soldiers arrived at my house after being tipped off by our neighbour who disliked us because my father was a DP supporter. I was woken by my mother's weeping. I saw a soldier with a sub-machine gun standing over her and her head was bleeding. My father lay groaning in pain from bayonet wounds on his thighs. I started crying and one of the soldiers hit me on the head with the butt of a gun and I passed out.

When I regained consciousness the soldiers were gone. My father and mother lay dead on the floor and my sister was nowhere to be seen. Up to this day I do not know whether she is dead or alive.

A few days later I packed what clothes had survived the UNLA looting and set out for the National Resistance Army (NRA) base. I arrived there three days later and I immediately volunteered to be recruited. At the age of eleven I started my training with bitterness and patriotism. I was in a different world where there were no more killings and rapings.

After nine months training I was allowed to go on field operations. Over the years I got seriously involved in intelligence gathering and urban guerrilla warfare. I was among the troops who captured Mbarara and Masaka. I have lost count of the number of UNLA soldiers I have killed.

My toughest operation was during our advancing on Kampala to overthrow Tito Okello. When we arrived at Nsanji township – about 16 kilometres from Kampala – we were met by UNLA's heavy artillery defence. Though we exchanged fire with them for two days, we couldn't advance.

After a brief security meeting, the senior NRA officers decided that one soldier was to volunteer to penetrate the UNLA defence and bring back intelligence information. Nobody was ready to perform such a task so I stepped forward. I was dressed like a young Muganda girl and told to pretend to have lost my parents to NRA soldiers. I was barefooted and had a water container in my hand. Inside my dress were two pistols and six grenades – my favourite weapons.

NOW ITS MUSEVENI'S TURN

NRA FIGHTERS SING "solidarity songs" at their Mbarara training camp.

The distance between the NRA and UNLA positions was four kilometres. I had a radio transmitter with me to keep my colleagues up to date. As I approached the UNLA, I started crying bitterly and begged for water. To make the act more impressive I sometimes fell down and staggered. I was stopped about 500 metres away by a crew manning the heavy Katusha gun. I gave them my story while crying and sobbing bitterly. I could see the doubt on their faces and at the same time my feminine appeal getting the better of them. The major ordered them to allow me in and give me water.

I felt frightened. My life was in the balance. Should they discover that I was a boy and not a girl before I did anything I would be finished. When I was about 20 metres from the Katusha I saw them relax and eye me hungrily. At last I was in their compound and the major ordered one of them to take my container and fill it with water. Meanwhile he held my hand and uttered consoling words, but in his eyes I could see naked desire.

I knew that if I waited for the container to be filled, my mission would be foiled, so I acted swiftly. I removed my pistol from under the dress and shot the major before he knew what was happening. The other soldiers were caught unawares, and I took advantage. I pulled the pins from two grenades and threw them one by one at the surprised soldiers. There were screams of pain, and three of them died. I threw another grenade and it killed one of the remaining soldiers immediately and seriously injured a second. I pulled out the second gun and ordered the remaining soldier to surrender, which he did without resistance.

I then radioed my base and told them I had one soldier alive, six dead, a Katusha heavy artillery gun, six sub-machine guns, two light machine guns, several grenades and food. Within minutes my comrades had arrived. From there we marched on to Kampala. In Kampala we found that the UNLA troops had run away and that only a few who wanted to surrender still remained. ❐

DRUM: March 1986

Yoweri Museveni has taken over Uganda. We on DRUM wish him well. Perhaps no country in Africa has so failed to live up to its real and true character since independence. Uganda is a country of great beauty with a people as beautiful as the country.

For 15 years DRUM has carried stories of Ugandan savagery – of bloodletting which Museveni himself estimates has claimed one million Ugandan lives. The figures of the dead do not describe the manner in which the people, mostly little, simple people, died – the hideous cruelty they practised upon each other. DRUM will be with you to help you realise your true character.

The ruin set in under Dr Milton Obote. The horror was expanded, even caricatured, under Idi Amin. And when Obote came back, the savagery continued unabated.

Ugandans must realise that, in the eyes of the world, the whole of Africa is like their country. Their disaster is our disaster, their humiliation is our humiliation. The responsibility that lies before Yoweri Museveni is not just for Uganda, but for the good name of all Africans.

For all these reasons, readers and staffers, all of us, wish Museveni well. Go in peace. At long last, be true to yourselves Ugandan brothers and sisters! For the sake of all of us. ❐

Mr DRUM

MUSEVENI TRIES TO END CYCLE OF SHAME

DRUM: April 1986

President Yoweri Museveni, whose NRA became the first guerrilla force in Africa to unseat an established government, is still scoring marks on the diplomatic front.

Many diplomats have since been so mesmerised by Museveni's style that they now speak glowingly of his apparent grasp of Uganda's needs and problems. Even the Washington establishment, usually suspicious of radical-sounding leaders, are now willing and keen to do business with Museveni's administration.

The Americans have already offered to assist the wrecked economy and to provide other forms of aid. The West Germans, for their part, have lifted an aid embargo they imposed on Uganda in 1984 because of human rights violations.

In his determination to unearth the atrocities committed by the Obote regime, President Museveni showed diplomats and journalists 237 neatly arranged skulls at Kiboga in Uganda which were exhumed from a mass grave north of Kampala.

He told the pressmen that the grave was one of the many from atrocities committed under former two-time president, Milton Obote. ❑

DRUM: April 1987

In a recent address to the army, President Yoweri Museveni, spoke on the state of the nation, a year after coming to power. President Museveni, who has spent almost 20 years actively involved in guerrilla activities, assured the NRA soldiers and the nation at large that the rebels in the country were not a threat. He referred to them as mere "criminal bandits".

"We are totally determined to wipe out insecurity. West Nile is calm. In the southern and western areas there is complete security and relaxation. Strategically speaking the situation is excellent," he said.

EXPOSING ATROCITIES: New Ugandan President Yoweri Museveni leads representatives of the international media to a mass grave north of Kampala.

The president continued to tell the nation that as the war in the north had reached a decisive stage, the economy was now a primary concern. "We need people who are not corrupt, people who are not working for ten per cent or who embezzle their enterprises. These people are not doing what they are supposed to do. Either by commission or omission they do a lot of damage.

"The real problem is to get reliable people. Cadres of a technocratic type. This seems to be much more of a problem. The biggest problem now is cadreship. We lack cadres. We do not have fellows who know what they are doing. This is our major problem, especially in the economic sector. The fellows we found there are simply not equal to the job.

"We earn US$ 400 million from coffee as our major and sole export earner. We inherited a debt left by Obote where we have to pay US$ 200 million per annum, in addition to the US$ 80 million for petroleum and US$ 50 million for sugar. So within one year we cannot have done much. In two years time, we shall have reversed the situation.

"The airline has been restored with our own money. The Mulago hospital has been partially rehabilitated with our money. Barter trade has been very successful. So far, we have concluded deals with Cuba and Tanzania, and we are about to conclude deals with Zimbabwe, Yugoslavia, Egypt, Italy and General Motors of America. So strategically speaking, the situation is not very bad for our economy."

Turning to tribalism, the president said that Ugandans should "forget tribalism and build a prosperous

Uganda. Tribalism is not going to work with the NRA. The problem with Africa is that Africans are still backward. The foreigners came to Africa and started to encourage us to think in our tribes and then later on sold us arms to kill one another in order for them to exploit us. These foreigners do not want to see us united. But, as for the NRA, they can go to hell.

"Because Africa has been so weakened by these so-called tribes, they are a weapon in the hands of those who want to keep us weak. And, we in the NRA have known this for a long time, and we have waged a conscious struggle against it. We waged it right from the grassroots."

GUERRILLA TURNED STATESMAN: *Museveni urged Ugandans to "forget tribalism and build a prosperous Uganda".*

Talking about the children who are in the NRA, the president emphasised that the young combatants or *kadogos* are being catered for. "We have army schools. During the fighting, there used to be schools in the barracks. They are still there. The *kadogos* are our children of the

army. They will be doing school curriculum, also continuing their military training. All these children would feel very deprived if they were removed from the army. They would be very destabilised because they are very proud of the army."

The president admitted that there are many soldiers in the towns, and that they are armed 24 hours a day. "The NRA soldiers are beginning to misbehave when they are drunk. We are trying to stop them from drinking in public places. We have given severe punishments. We have dismissed some, imprisoned others, but still they can't give up drinking."

He said to the soldiers: "I order you to abstain from all sorts of vices. Stop accepting bribes. Stop moving with women here and there. You should continue to observe the discipline which contributed to our success. Justice must be maintained among all NRA soldiers." ❐

POSTSCRIPT

REMORSELESS: *When recently asked at his Saudi Arabian home (above) whether he had any regrets, Amin seemed puzzled and then began to talk of the Tanzanian invasion and his own downfall. When pressed, he admitted to the runaway power of his security apparatus. "Intelligence made the most mistakes," he says. "The State Research Bureau. Even they were trying to kill me."*

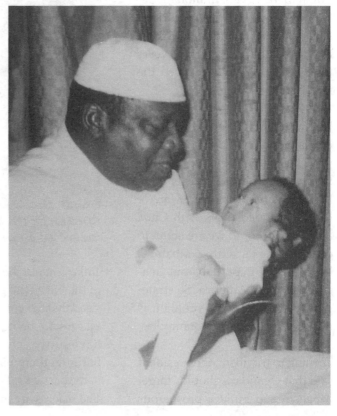

IDYLLIC EXILE: *Idi Amin lives in a roomy villa with the last nine of his children and Mama'a Cumaru, mother of the youngest four. Iman, pictured left, is his 43rd acknowledged child.*

TABLE OF DRUM STORIES

THE DRUM LEGACY

Photograph by David Goldblatt for Leadership Magazine

JIM BAILEY – Proprietor of DRUM and Editor-in-Chief.

DRUM magazine, which proudly called itself "Africa's leading magazine" was in its heyday a recorder of a continent in transition through its outstanding photographs and inspired reporting.

One of DRUM's enduring legacies is the role it played in initiating photo-journalism in Africa, and in nurturing a generation of African journalists.

THE ARCHIVES

Bailey's African Photo Archives holds 40 years of material from all the editions of DRUM magazine and its various sister publications – Golden City Post, Trust, True Love and City Press. The Archives contains a wealth of information on the politics, cultures and complexities of the vast African nations.

At the Archives a team of archivists, researchers and book editors are documenting the major African events, trends and personalities of the past four decades.

Bailey's African Photo Archives is a major library of visual knowledge, embracing as it does all the major English-speaking regions of Africa. The files, with top-class magazine and newspaper photography, record the day-to-day life of a continent: it is a record of beauty, optimism, frustration, defiance and courage.

Publications by Bailey's African Photo Archives

Bailey's African Photo Archives holds 40 years of material from all the editions of DRUM magazine. The Archives contains a wealth of information on the complexities, politics and cultures of the vast African nations… from Cape Town to the boundaries of the Sudan on the east coast of Africa, across central Africa to Nigeria and Ghana on the west coast. Under proprietor and executive-editor, Jim Bailey,

Zimbabwe: The Search for Common Ground
The Pioneer Column, the dramatic years of the early 1960s, the crushing UDI, the tragic liberation war and the difficult first few years of freedom are covered with flavour of the time.
(Available from: Munn Pubs, Box UA460 Harare)

Kenya: The National Epic
Beginning with the bloody Mau Mau rebellion, this book presents the figures – notably Jomo Kenyatta – and policies which guided modern Kenya to its unique African successes.
(Kenway Publications, Box 45314 Nairobi, 1993)

Tanzania: The Story of Julius Nyerere
Granted independence without so much as a fuss, the real drama of Tanzania as told by this book revolves around Julius Nyerere and his unique brand of political vigour.

Uganda: The Bloodstained Pearl of Africa
This account of the descent into murderous anarchy of one of Africa's jewels under the despotic rule of Idi Amin and Milton Obote, ends with the tale of Uganda's rescue by Yoweri Museveni.

Ghana: The Birth of the Nation
The energy and enthusiasm of Africa's pioneering nation led by the mercurial, charismatic Kwame Nkrumah as captured at the time by DRUM comes alive again in this book.

Nigeria: The Birth of the Nation
This colourful history chronicles the build-up to independence. It is a story of highly-spirited people caught between sophistication and fetish, morality and corruption, unity and tribalism, led by men of great stature and character.

Nelson Mandela and the Rise of the ANC
The emergence of the South African ANC in the tumultuous decade of the 1950s.   (1990)

The Fifties People of South Africa
Vignettes on some 95 personalities who shone in the 1950s. Over 300 photographs.   (1987)

The Finest Photos from the Old Drum
A superb collection of photos by the DRUM photographers capturing the humour and innocence of the 1950s.   (1987)

Profiles of Africa
A portrait gallery in words and pictures of those African personalities who shaped the modern continent.   (1983)

The Rise of Africa
A chronicle of a continent in transition as told by DRUM in words and historic pictures.   (1982)

Foundations of the Future
Original writing by Africa's greats.   (1983)

The Bedside Book
A lighthearted anthology of a continent, packed with a myriad of vignettes of African life. (1984)

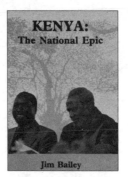

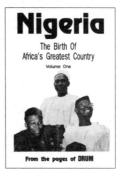

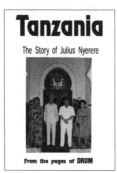

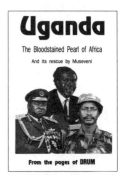

Enquiries: Bailey's African Photo Archives   P.O. Box 37 Lanseria South Africa
Telephone +27 11 659-2615   Fax +27 11 659-1470.